Perkins Act of 2006:
The Official Guide

The authoritative guide to federal legislation for career and technical education

The Carl D. Perkins Career and Technical Education Act of 2006

from
the Association for Career and Technical Education

with
Michael Brustein

ISBN-10: 0-89514-012-8
ISBN-13: 978-0-89514-012-8

Published by the Association for Career and Technical Education, 1410 King Street, Alexandria, Virginia 22314

INTRODUCTION
ACKNOWLEDGEMENTS

We at the Association for Career and Technical Education (ACTE) would like to take a little space out of this important publication to express our thanks to the many people who spent countless hours in the development of *Perkins Act of 2006: The Official Guide.*

The ultimate thanks and appreciation goes to ACTE members and career and technical educators from around the country. Without their passion, we might not be writing this publication. The passage of the Carl D. Perkins Career and Technical Education Improvement Act of 2006 is a testament to the dedication career and technical educators have to their profession and to their willingness to voice that passion to local, state and federal legislators.

Not far behind, ACTE would thank the members of the U.S. Congress for their overwhelming support of career and technical education. In their states and districts, they know the important role that career and technical education plays in building a strong, well-educated and prepared workforce. The passage of this legislation helps ensure that education dedicated to those outcomes continues.

We would also like to thank the staff of all the Members of the House Education and the Workforce Committee and the Senate Health, Education, Labor and Pensions Committee for the hard work they put into this critical legislation. In particular, committee staff Whitney Rhoades, Scott Fleming, Denise Forte, J.D. LaRock, Beth Buehlman, Stephanie Milburn, Lloyd Horwich and Carmel Martin worked long hours and were extremely dedicated to the advancement of career and technical education throughout the legislation process. Without their efforts, and the efforts of many others behind the legislative scenes, this new law would not have become a reality.

ACTE is also grateful to the Office of Vocational and Adult Education in the U.S. Department of Education; to its state associations for their active involvement and support; to the Career and Technical Student Organizations for their grassroots efforts in this campaign; and to the other education-related associations who helped further the campaign by sharing, gathering and disseminating information.

While the people who helped in the capacities referenced above are too numerous to name individually, there are a few people worthy of additional praise. The person at the top of that list is Alisha Dixon Hyslop, ACTE's Assistant Director of Public Policy. Her tireless efforts were instrumental in the success ACTE and career and technical educators had in the passage of this legislation. Those efforts have continued as ACTE has developed resources and disseminated information focused on helping career and technical educators understand and incorporate the law.

Also on the list are Janet Bray, ACTE's Executive Director, whose passion, dedication and vision continue to benefit the career and technical education field; Matthew Gardner, ACTE's Graphic Designer, whose eye for design and attention to detail make the materials you read, including this publication, simple to understand and easy to read; and Michael Brustein, long-time CTE advocate, who provided his expertise to assist with the development of this guide.

ABOUT THE OFFICIAL GUIDE

The Association for Career and Technical Education (ACTE), in coordination with Michael Brustein, is pleased to present this comprehensive guide to the Perkins Act of 2006. We are confident you will find this new Guide to be informative, information packed and most importantly, user friendly.

The key to ensuring that your use of Perkins funds over the next six years complies with the federal law is a full understanding of the content and context of the new legislation. With new requirements for local accountability and programs of study, it is more important than ever that all CTE professionals, at all levels, understand the priorities set forth for the nation's CTE programs. In this Guide, ACTE provides all the knowledge you need to understand the new 2006 Perkins Act in this one, easy-to-use reference.

In this guide, you can:

- *Review selections from the congressional record that provide insights into congressional intent and priorities in the legislation.*
- *See how the 2006 Perkins Act evolved throughout the legislative process and the key themes that emerged.*
- *Examine a side-by-side comparison of the 1998 Perkins Act and the 2006 Act to note new provisions and similarities.*
- *Reference a section-by-section summary summarizing each provision in the new law.*

- *Read the entire text of the 2006 Perkins Act.*
- *Gain insights into the coordination of the 2006 Perkins Act, the No Child Left Behind Act, and the Workforce Investment Act.*
- *Check references to other federal legislation.*
- *Look up key terms in a comprehensive index.*

These sections will enable you to understand the new legislation, apply its principles, and maintain program quality and fiscal integrity. Use the information as you develop your new Perkins plans and continue to update and expand your CTE programs.

While this Guide provides comprehensive information about the federal Perkins Act, be sure to also consult with your state CTE leaders on policies specific to your state and local area. While the federal Perkins Act provides a strong foundation, there will numerous detailed decisions made by states during the law's implementation.

The 2006 Perkins Act provides the direction and the funding to support continuous improvement in career and technical education. It is up to the community of educators around the country to ensure this continuous improvement happens, and that CTE is seen as integral to secondary and postsecondary reform efforts underway in communities like yours. We hope this Guide will provide all the information you need on the new Perkins Act to be successful.

INTRODUCTION
WORDS OF WISDOM
COMMENTS FROM KEY POLICYMAKERS ON THE CHANGES IN THE 2006 PERKINS ACT

By completing the reauthorization of the 2006 Perkins Act, Congress showed its overwhelming support for career and technical education. Throughout the legislative process, Members of Congress emphasized the importance of high quality CTE programs that prepared students to be successful in further education and careers. Congress intended for the new Perkins Act to be a sign of its support, and for the new Act to go further than ever before to improve CTE programs and provide for new innovation at the state and local level. Below you will find excerpts from speeches made by Members of Congress during the vote on the final version of the 2006 Perkins Act. You will see that they were extremely proud of the new law, and have high expectations for its implementation around the country. Their comments will provide you with insights into critical areas of the legislation, and to the new provisions and themes that will be explored throughout this Guide. We hope the words of policymakers will inspire you to look beyond the minimum requirements of the 2006 Perkins Act and begin to think about how you can use this new legislation to continue to move CTE programs forward to meet the needs of students in the 21st century.

PILLARS OF THE LEGISLATION

"The conference report before us will help states better utilize federal funds for secondary and postsecondary career education programs, increase accountability, and emphasize student achievement and strengthen opportunities for coordination between secondary and postsecondary career and technical education.

"In 1998, reforms made to the Perkins Act were aimed at increasing the focus on both technical skills and rigorous academic knowledge and helped us move further away from the school-to-work model. Our goal in this Congress was to build on that success.

"Our principles at the outset of this reauthorization effort were straightforward, and I am proud to say that more than a year later, they are unchanged. The pillars of this conference report are: we're maintaining a focus on rigorous student academic and technical achievement; we're protecting the role of states and local communities and asking for results in exchange for the money we are already spending at the federal level; and we are seeking more opportunities for coordination between secondary and postsecondary career and technical education."

Education and the Workforce Committee Chairman
Howard "Buck" McKeon (R-CA)
Congressional Record, page H5974
July 27, 2006

IMPORTANCE OF KEY CHANGES

"This legislation is important for three reasons. The first reason is the added emphasis on academic achievement . . . . The second reason this legislation is important is because it will help ensure we are preparing students for tomorrow's work-force . . . . The final reason that this legislation is important is because it provides a foundation for the redesign of federal education policy. We need to structure federal education policies that provide students and adult learners access to lifelong education opportunities. In this 21st century economy, learning never ends, and school is never out."

Health, Education, Labor and Pensions
Committee Chairman Michael Enzi (R-WY)
Congressional Record, pages S8322 & S8323
July 26, 2006

"This reauthorization does a number of important things. First and foremost, it emphasizes accountability and improved results. Second, it improves monitoring and enforcement. Third, it disaggregates performance goals and report information by special populations so no one will fall through the cracks. And fourth, it strengthens the ties between industry, high schools, and higher education by ensuring that teachers are well-trained, students are academically ready for college, and high schools are training students for the actual needs of their communities.

"The premise of this legislation is that high schools, industry, and higher education institutions need to work together to provide our workforce with the skills they need in order to achieve and compete in the 21st century. This bill works to ensure that American students are not just getting a world class education, but the best education in the world."

Sen. Christopher Dodd (D-CT)
Congressional Record, page S8325
July 26, 2006

NAME CHANGE

"Since the passage of the Smith-Hughes Act in 1917, the federal government has recognized the important role of career and technical education in the life of the nation. As the needs of American business and industry have evolved, the revisions made to the Act over the years have reflected those changes. It is clear that vocational education is no longer the 1950s version. It has evolved from shop classes into courses that use cutting-edge technology and focus on emerging and growing fields that will become the jobs of the future. That is why we now call it career and technical education, and I am pleased to see that change reflected in the new title of this bill."

Sen. Edward Kennedy (D-MA)
Congressional Record,
pages S8323 & S8324
July 26, 2006

CTE AND REDUCING THE DROPOUT RATE

"This legislation will help to reduce the dropout rate. If the schools across this country will work out the programs that are envisioned in this report, I think our schools will make giant strides in reducing dropouts, because it will allow students at the high school to get a vision of what can be achieved, what they can do in technical education and what they can do in employment opportunities and what a better future they can have. This should be billed as a hope bill, it is a future bill."

Rep. Ralph Regula
Congressional Record, page H5976
July 27, 2006

SERVING SPECIAL POPULATIONS

"Particularly pleasing is that this bill not only has expanded math, science and technical programs, it also has continued and strengthened the Perkins Act commitment to preparing women and men for occupations that are nontraditional to them, to ensuring access to career and technical education for special populations who face unique challenges, and to preparing those students for careers that will lead them to self-sufficiency.

"In this competitive global economy, Mr. Speaker, we can't afford to waste the potential of any of our people, so these provisions will help to ensure that this does not happen."

Rep. Lynn Woolsey (D-CA)
Congressional Record, page H5974
July 27, 2006

PREPARING STUDENTS FOR NONTRADITIONAL OCCUPATIONS

"The Carl D. Perkins Career and Technical Education Improvement Act takes the next step in strengthening career and technical education for the 21st century. I am particularly pleased that this bill improves programs and services for women and girls pursuing nontraditional occupations. Families, industries and our economy as a whole benefit when women and girls pursue nontraditional, traditionally "male" careers—in technology, math, science, and the construction and building trades . . . .

"This bill requires states to measure students' participation and completion in career and technical programs in nontraditional fields and to disaggregate the data on performance by gender and race. In addition, programs will be required to prepare special populations for high-skill, high-wage occupations that will lead to self-sufficiency. These important provisions will go a long way toward helping more women achieve economic security for their families."

Sen. Hillary Clinton (D-NY)
Congressional Record, page S8327
July 26, 2006

NEW ACCOUNTABILITY PROVISIONS

"This conference agreement contains new measures of accountability for career and technical education systems. I do not doubt that some programs may have difficulties in meeting this new system. However, there have been too many programs that have chosen the status quo, to the detriment of our workforce competitiveness. Successful career and technical education programs produce students that outperform their counterparts and make higher wages. We must demand that all programs work toward this same goal. The accountability systems move us in that direction."

Rep. George Miller (D-CA)
Congressional Record, page H5975
July 27, 2006

PROGRAMS OF STUDY

"One of the unique attributes of vocational and technical education programs is their ability to show students a path that could end in a certificate, credential, employment, military or postsecondary education . . . . Along this same track, we include a new requirement for state development of career and technical programs of study for career and technical program areas. These sequences of courses will incorporate a nonduplicative progression of both secondary and postsecondary elements which will include both academic and vocational and technical content. Local recipients at both the secondary and postsecondary level would adopt at least one model sequence of courses as developed by the state. I believe this will also help drive program improvements by ensuring that states clarify the progression of academic and vocational technical courses needed for the postsecondary education, training or employment of a student's choice."

Rep. Michael Castle (R-DE)
Floor Speech
July 27, 2006

PROFESSIONAL DEVELOPMENT

"As a co-sponsor of the Senate version of this bill, I am pleased that many of its comprehensive provisions on the recruitment, preparation, support and professional development of career and technical education teachers, which I authored, have been included in the final version of the bill before us today. I believe having a well-trained, qualified and effective teacher in every classroom is the key for ensuring that students participating in career and technical education programs will achieve their fullest academic and career goals and aspirations."

Sen. Jack Reed (D-RI)
Congressional Record, page S 8327
July 26, 2006

"We made important strides in the area of professional development. This conference agreement strengthens the instructional connection between academic and career technical programs. We heard from numerous teachers that successful career tech programs allow academic and vocational teachers to develop curriculums together to teach together so that students can apply the academic content to the real world context."

Rep. George Miller (D-CA)
Congressional Record, page H5975
July 27, 2006

IMPORTANCE TO RURAL AMERICA

"In rural America, if you do not have vocational technical education you have real problems. So this has been critical.

"Also, we currently lack the skilled workforce in our country to maintain our economy; and a big key to this, of course, is vocational training."

Rep. Tom Osborne (R-NE)
Congressional Record, page H5977
July 27, 2006

CONNECTIONS WITH BUSINESS AND INDUSTRY

"One of the most critical improvements we have made to the Perkins program in this bill is to strengthen the connection of career and technical education programs to the needs of businesses. If we are going to help fill the growing need for skilled workers, we need to ensure Perkins programs are coordinating their instruction with current practices in industry and the needs of the local workforce."

**Health, Education, Labor and Pensions
Committee Chairman Michael Enzi (R-WY)**
Congressional Record, page S8323
July 26, 2006

TECH PREP

"Tech Prep creates seamless pathways for secondary students to transition into post-secondary education programs in the high-skill, high-wage technical fields. These academically and technically prepared graduates are critical to the economic growth, productivity and internal competitiveness of the United States. Knowing how critical this funding is to our local communities, I am pleased funding for the Tech Prep program has been kept separate from the Perkins block grant."

Rep. Ron Kind (D-WI)
Congressional Record, page H5978
July 27, 2006

VALID AND RELIABLE ASSESSMENTS

"It is essential to develop valid and reliable assessments of technical and career competencies that are aligned with national industry standards and integrate industry certification assessments, if available and appropriate. To address this need for high-quality technical assessments, this bill permits state leadership funds to be used to develop valid and reliable assessments of technical skills that are integrated with industry certification assessments where available.

"In addition, the bill includes several new provisions for data collection, utilization and analysis, including provisions which allow the state allocation to be used to support and develop state data systems, and state leadership funds to be used to develop and enhance data systems to collect and analyze data on postsecondary and employment outcomes."

Sen. Jeff Bingaman (D-NM)
Congressional Record, page S8326
July 26, 2006

CONNECTION BETWEEN ACADEMICS AND CAREERS

"In today's world, career and technical education is an important component of most any student's education as it helps prepare high school students for either a transition to the workforce or a postsecondary degree. The programs help students begin thinking about different careers of interest, provide opportunities for exploring those career options, and start students down a path toward accomplishing their career goals. Moreover, the program helps students see a connection between the academic subjects in the classroom and the application of that knowledge in the working world. For many students, this connection is critical to their decision to stay in high school and graduate with a diploma."

Rep. Mark Souder (R-IN)
Congressional Record, pages H5976 & H5977
July 27, 2006

HISTORY AND SYNOPSIS OF THE 2006 PERKINS ACT

HISTORY OF THE LEGISLATION

The Administration released its initial blueprint for reauthorization of the 1998 Carl D. Perkins Vocational and Technical Education Act in February 2003, months before its scheduled expiration. The Administration requested significant changes to the program along with a drastic cut in funding. The complete program overhaul would have included the possible transfer of Perkins funds to No Child Left Behind Act activities, competitive funding, and a shift away from a focus on career and technical skill achievement. The CTE community responded swiftly to oppose the proposed changes, and Congress did not indicate a willingness to go down this path.

Instead, in the spring of 2004, Congress began to hold its own hearings on the reauthorization of the Perkins Act, showing bi-partisan support for CTE. While the Administration released a slightly revised plan in May of 2004, Congress continued working on its own legislation in bi-partisan fashion.

In June 2004, the House of Representatives introduced the first piece of reauthorization legislation, H.R. 4496, the "Vocational and Technical Education for the Future Act." When the House bill was introduced, it maintained many elements of current law and made some positive changes. The bill included enhancements to local accountability systems; provisions for targeted technical assistance and program improvement to ensure the operation of quality programs; and the separation of performance indicators for secondary and postsecondary programs.

However, there were four significant concerns with the bill as it was originally introduced, including the proposed combining of the Tech Prep and Basic State Grant funding streams, a cut in funding available for state and local administration, changes to the maintenance of effort provision (which requires states to expend, from state sources, as least as much as they spent in the prior year on career and technical education), and language in the law continuing to refer to "vocational" education. The Education and the Workforce Committee's Education Reform Subcommittee held its "mark-up" to amend and approve the bill on July 14, 2004, and at this time the maintenance of effort provision was restored to current law. On July 21, 2004, the full Education and the Workforce

Committee marked up and passed H.R. 4496, and in the new version of the bill passed by the full committee, local administrative funds were restored to the currently allowed 5 percent. State level administrative funds remained cut to 2 percent.

The Senate also began its reauthorization action during the summer of 2004. After holding one hearing, on July 19, 2004, the Senate Health, Education, Labor, and Pensions (HELP) Committee introduced S. 2686, the "Carl D. Perkins Career and Technical Education Improvement Act of 2004." The Senate bill made many of the same positive changes as the House bill. Unlike the House bill, however, the Senate bill maintained Tech Prep as a separate program, reserved 15 percent of the Basic Grant for state administration and state leadership, and updated the language throughout the law from "vocational and technical" to "career and technical." The Senate bill also increased the focus on career guidance and academic counseling, and included new provisions allowing for more attention on the recruitment and retention of CTE professionals.

The Senate HELP Committee approved S. 2686 on September 22, 2004, by a unanimous vote. However, as Congress moved toward adjournment, efforts to reauthorize the Perkins Act came to a halt. The House and Senate were unable to schedule floor votes on their legislation before the 108th Congress came to a close.

Activity began again promptly when the 109th Congress convened in 2005. On January 26, 2005, House Education and the Workforce Committee leaders introduced H.R. 366, the "Vocational and Technical Education for the Future Act." The Senate followed quickly with the introduction of S. 250, the "Carl D. Perkins Career and Technical Education Improvement Act of 2005," on February 1, 2005. These bills were almost identical to the bills (H.R. 4496 and S. 2686) that had been moving through Congress the previous year.

Both bills were approved by their respective committees on March 9, 2005. The Senate bill went quickly to the floor the next day and was approved by the full Senate by a 99-0 vote on March 10, 2005. The House bill was approved by a 416-9 vote on May 4, 2005. After these floor votes, staff spent more than a year working to negotiate differences between the two bills before a formal conference committee was named.

This conference committee was finally appointed

in July 2006, and approved a compromise bill on July 20, 2006. The final bill, the "Carl D. Perkins Career and Technical Education Improvement Act of 2006," was then approved by the Senate by unanimous consent on July 26, 2006, and the House by a 399-1 vote on July 29, 2006. President Bush signed the bill on August 12, 2006 as Public Law 109–270.

 ## SYNOPSIS OF THE NEW LAW

The new Act would authorize the legislation through Fiscal Year 2012, for a total of six years instead of the current five. While the bulk of the law is very similar to the 1998 Perkins Act, there are some significant changes in content and focus. Several themes are evident throughout—accountability for results and program improvement at all levels, increased coordination within the CTE system, stronger academic and technical integration, connections between secondary and postsecondary education, and links to business and industry.

The new Act also uses the term "career and technical education" instead of "vocational education" throughout, maintains the Tech Prep program as a separate federal funding stream within the legislation, and maintains state administrative funding at 5 percent of a state's allocation. These are huge victories for CTE and were ACTE's top three priorities for the Perkins reauthorization conference. Positive outcomes on these issues show the respect Congress has for CTE programs and advocates.

Accountability

While accountability was already a strong component of the 1998 Perkins Act, the 2006 Act adds a new section on local accountability that will require local programs to set specific performance targets on each performance indicator and be responsible for meeting these targets. Locals may choose to accept the state performance targets or work with the state to negotiate levels more applicable to their specific circumstances.

Sanctions for local programs and states have become more specific. If local programs or states fail to meet at least 90 percent of an agreed upon target, they will have to develop and implement an improvement plan. If no improvement is made, or the program fails to meet at least 90 percent of a performance level for 3 years in a row, then a portion of Perkins funding could be withheld. The new local requirements and sanction specificity will require each program to think much more strategically about the use of Perkins funds, and to focus activities on efforts that help to meet performance targets.

Several changes were also made to the specific performance indicators that states and local programs will have to report on under the 2006 Perkins Act. At the secondary level, academic attainment will now have to be measured by the academic assessments a state has approved under No Child Left Behind (NCLB). Graduation rates will also have to be reported as defined in NCLB, and technical proficiency should include student achievement on technical assessments that are aligned with industry-recognized standards when possible.

At the postsecondary level, academic attainment will no longer have to be reported as a separate measure, but, like at the secondary level, technical skill proficiency should include student achievement on technical assessments that are aligned with industry-recognized standards when possible. Also at the postsecondary level, student placement in high-wage, high-skill or high-demand occupations or professions must be measured.

Coordination within the CTE Community

While the new law maintains the Tech Prep program as a separate Title within the law with its own federal funding stream, there are several changes made to Tech Prep and throughout the law to increase coordination between the different programs within CTE. States will have the flexibility to combine either all, or a portion, of their Tech Prep grant with funds received under the Basic State Grant. If a state chooses to utilize this option, the combined funds must be distributed to local programs using the same formula as is used for Basic State Grant funds, and must be used for the same activities as those funds.

If a state does not choose to combine Tech Prep funds with funds under the Basic State Grant, there are new accountability requirements that will be applied to Tech Prep consortia. In addition, there is a new requirement for a single state plan that covers Basic State Grant activities and Tech Prep activities, linking the two programs more closely together.

There is also additional coordination evident in increased integration of language related to occupational and employment information throughout the law. While Section 118 of the law maintains the Occupational and Employment Information program authorization with a few minor changes, additional references are included in areas such as state leadership funds. This language would allow states to use leadership funds to support occupational and employment information resources, and links those resources to other information required in the law. Congress has not funded Section 118 since June 30, 2006, and thus many states are currently using leadership funds to support occupational and employment information activities.

Academic and Technical Integration

This is another theme that has existed in prior Perkins laws, but continues to be expanded upon. With additional links to NCLB (described in *Appendix A*), the 2006 Perkins Act goes much further toward integrating the academic and CTE accountability systems at the secondary level.

One of the biggest concerns expressed in the hearings leading up to Perkins reauthorization was that academic integration was often not occurring with as much frequency as may be possible, and that there was often a divide between academic and CTE teachers when working toward this goal. To address this, the new law puts a specific emphasis on professional development that addresses the integration of academic and technical skills, and that involves academic and CTE teachers working together whenever possible.

Connections between Secondary and Postsecondary Education

Connections between secondary and postsecondary education are again addressed through the Tech Prep program, but they are also emphasized in a new Basic State Grant requirement. The new law requires the development and implementation of "programs of study." These programs of study must:

- Incorporate secondary education and postsecondary education elements;
- Include academic and career and technical content in a coordinated, nonduplicative progression of courses; and
- Lead to an industry-recognized credential or certificate at the postsecondary level, or an associate or bachelor's degree.

States must develop the programs of study in consultation with local programs, and each local recipient receiving funds under the Act will be required to offer the relevant courses of at least one. Programs of study are very similar to, and build on, positive initiatives already underway in CTE programs around the country, such as Tech Prep, career pathways, career academies, and career clusters. In many states, the foundational elements of programs of study may already be in place.

While Section 203(c)(2) of the Act relating to Tech Prep also uses the term "program of study," the term is defined there in the more traditional Tech Prep framework of "two plus two." Tech Prep programs should, however, use "programs of study" as described above to the extent practicable.

Links to Business and Industry

A much stronger theme within the 2006 Perkins Act is increased coordination with business and industry. In fact, two new purposes of the law allude to this theme—"supporting partnerships among secondary schools, postsecondary institutions, baccalaureate degree granting institutions, area career and technical education schools, local workforce investment boards, business and industry, and intermediaries;" and "providing individuals with opportunities throughout their lifetimes to develop, in conjunction with other education and training programs, the knowledge and skills needed to keep the United States competitive."

Additional focus is also placed on "high-demand" occupations, in addition to those that are high skill and high wage. References to entrepreneurship, small business, and the involvement of workforce investment boards are also added. These changes emphasize the role that employment availability and local economies should play in CTE programs.

Overview Chart:
the Perkins Act of 2006

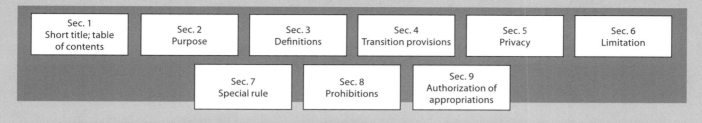

Sec. 1 Short title; table of contents	Sec. 2 Purpose	Sec. 3 Definitions	Sec. 4 Transition provisions	Sec. 5 Privacy	Sec. 6 Limitation

Sec. 7 Special rule	Sec. 8 Prohibitions	Sec. 9 Authorization of appropriations

Title I—Career and Technical Education Assistance to the States

Part A—Allotment and Allocation

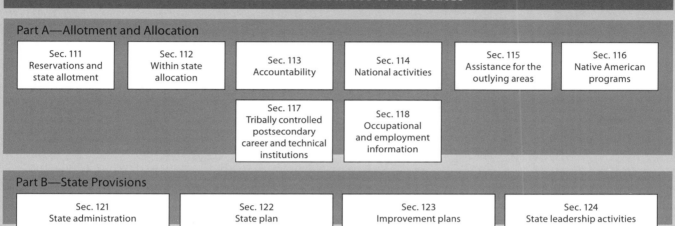

Sec. 111 Reservations and state allotment	Sec. 112 Within state allocation	Sec. 113 Accountability	Sec. 114 National activities	Sec. 115 Assistance for the outlying areas	Sec. 116 Native American programs

Sec. 117 Tribally controlled postsecondary career and technical institutions	Sec. 118 Occupational and employment information

Part B—State Provisions

Sec. 121 State administration	Sec. 122 State plan	Sec. 123 Improvement plans	Sec. 124 State leadership activities

Part C—Local Provisions

Sec. 131 Distribution of funds to secondary education programs	Sec. 132 Distribution of funds for postsecondary education programs	Sec. 133 Special rules for career and technical education	Sec. 134 Local plan for career and technical education programs	Sec. 135 Local uses of funds

Title II—Tech Prep Education

Sec. 201 State allotment and application	Sec. 202 Consolidation of funds	Sec. 203 Tech Prep program	Sec. 204 Consortium applications	Sec. 205 Report	Sec. 206 Authorization of Appropriations

Title III—General Provisions

Part A—Federal Administrative Provisions

Sec. 311 Fiscal requirements	Sec. 312 Authority to make payments	Sec. 313 Construction	Sec. 314 Voluntary selection and participation	Sec. 315 Limitation for certain students	Sec. 316 Federal laws guaranteeing civil rights

Sec. 317 Participation of private school personnel and children	Sec. 318 Limitation on federal regulations

Part B—State Administrative Provisions

Sec. 321 Joint funding	Sec. 322 Prohibition on use of funds to induce out-of-state relocation of businesses	Sec. 323 State administrative costs	Sec. 324 Student assistance and other federal programs

ANALYSIS
SIDE BY SIDE COMPARISON OF 1998 PERKINS ACT AND 2006 PERKINS ACT

Topics	1998 Perkins Act	2006 Perkins Act
Title	Carl D. Perkins Vocational and Technical Education Act of 1998 *[Section 1]*	Carl D. Perkins Career and Technical Education Act of 2006 *[Section 1]*
		Throughout the Act, references to "vocational and technical" education are replaced with "career and technical education." If this is the only change in a section, it will be referenced below with "Same as previous law."
Purpose	The purpose is to develop more fully the academic, vocational and technical skills of secondary and postsecondary students who elect to enroll in vocational and technical education programs by—	Same as previous law.
	• Building on the efforts of states and localities to develop challenging academic standards.	• Building on the efforts of states and localities to develop challenging academic and technical standards, and to assist students in meeting the standards, including preparation for high-skill, high-wage or high-demand occupations in current or emerging professions.
	• Promoting the development of services and activities that integrate academic, vocational and technical instruction, and that link secondary and postsecondary education for participating students.	• Promoting the development of services and activities that integrate rigorous and challenging academic and career and technical instruction, and that link secondary and postsecondary education for participating CTE students.
	• Increasing state and local flexibility in providing services and activities designed to develop, implement and improve vocational and technical education, including Tech Prep education.	• Same as previous law.
	• Disseminating national research, and providing professional development and technical assistance, that will improve vocational and technical education programs, services and activities. *[Section 2]*	• Conducting and disseminating national research and disseminating information on best practices that improve CTE programs, services and activities.
		• Providing technical assistance that—

» Promotes leadership, initial preparation, and professional development at the state and local levels; and

» Improves the quality of CTE teachers, faculty, administrators and counselors.

- Supporting partnerships among secondary schools, postsecondary institutions, baccalaureate degree granting institutions, area CTE schools, local workforce investment boards, business and industry, and intermediaries.

- Providing individuals with opportunities throughout their lifetimes to develop, in conjunction with other education and training programs, the knowledge and skills needed to keep the U.S. competitive. *[Section 2]*

"All aspects of industry" is expanded to include information as described in Section 118, which is occupational and employment information. *[Section 3(2)]*

The definition of an "articulation agreement" is moved from Section 202 to Section 3. "Articulation agreement" means a written commitment that is agreed upon at the state level or approved annually by the lead administrators of a secondary institution and a postsecondary institution, or a subbaccalaureate degree granting postsecondary institution and a baccalaureate degree granting institution; to a program that is designed to provide students with a nonduplicative sequence of progressive achievement leading to technical skill proficiency, a credential, a certificate or a degree and is linked through credit transfer agreements between the two institutions. *[Section 3(4)]*

Definitions

Thirty words and phrases used in the Act are defined. Definitions are listed below for comparison with changes made in the 2006 Act, where applicable. All definitions not listed remain essentially the same, and can be found in the text of the Act. *[Section 3]*

"All aspects of an industry" means strong experience in, and comprehensive understanding of, the industry that the individual is preparing to enter. *[Section 3(2)]*

"Articulation agreement" means a written commitment to a program designed to provide students with a nonduplicative sequence of progressive achievement leading to degrees or certificates in a Tech Prep program. *[Section 202(a)(1)]*

Topics	1998 Perkins Act	2006 Perkins Act
Definitions, (cont'd)	"Career guidance and academic counseling" means providing access to information regarding career awareness and planning with respect to an individual's occupational and academic future that shall involve guidance and counseling with respect to career options, financial aid, and postsecondary options. *[Section 3(4)]*	Career guidance and academic counseling now specifies that students, and parents when appropriate, should be the recipients of information, and specifies baccalaureate degree programs as an option about which students are counseled. *[Section 3(7)]*
	"Eligible institution" means an institution of higher education, a local educational agency providing education at the postsecondary level, an area vocational and technical education school providing education at the postsecondary level, a postsecondary educational institution controlled by the Bureau of Indian Affairs (BIA) or operated by or on behalf of any Indian tribe that is eligible to contract with the Secretary of the Interior for the administration of programs under the Indian Self-Determination Act or the Act of April 16, 1934, an educational service agency, or a consortium of 2 or more of the above. *[Section 3(10)]*	Institutions of higher education must be public or non-profit private to qualify as "eligible institutions," and offer CTE courses that lead to technical skill proficiency, an industry-recognized credential, a certificate or a degree. *[Section 3 (13)(A)]*
	"Eligible recipient" means a local educational agency, an area vocational and technical education school, an educational service agency, or a consortium, eligible to receive assistance under Section 131; or an eligible institution or consortium of eligible institutions eligible to receive assistance under Section 132. *[Section 3(11)]*	The definition of an "eligible recipient" specifies that public charter schools operated as local educational agencies are included. *[Section 3(14)]*
	"Nontraditional training and employment" means occupations of fields of work, including careers in computer science, technology, and other emerging high-skill occupations, for which individuals from one gender comprise less than 25 percent of the individuals employed in each such occupation or field of work. *[Section 3(17)]*	The term "training and employment" is replaced with "fields" in the term and definition, and in all future references to the term. *[Section 3(20), et. al.]*
	"Outlying area" means the United States Virgin Islands, Guam, American Samoa, the Commonwealth of the Northern Mariana Islands, the Republic of the Marshall Islands, the Federated States of Micronesia, and the Republic of Palau. *[Section 3(18)]*	The Republic of the Marshall Islands and the Federated States of Micronesia are eliminated from the definition of "outlying area." *[Section 3(21)]*
	"Special populations" means— • Individuals with disabilities;	"Individuals with other barriers to educational achievement" are eliminated from this definition. *[Section 3(29)]*

The specific definition of a Tech Prep program is eliminated, and instead, a "Tech Prep program" means a Tech Prep program described in Section 203(c). The content of the definition is incorporated into that section. [Section 3(32)]

- Individuals from economically disadvantaged families, including foster children;

- Individuals preparing for nontraditional training and employment;

- Single parents, including single pregnant women;

- Displaced homemakers; and

- Individuals with other barriers to educational achievement, including individuals with limited English proficiency.

[Section 3(23)]

A "Tech Prep program" is a program of study that—

- Combines at a minimum 2 years of secondary education (as determined under state law) with a minimum of 2 years of postsecondary education in a nonduplicative, sequential course of study

- Integrates academic, and vocational and technical, instruction, and utilizes work-based and worksite learning where appropriate and available

- Provides technical preparation in a career field such as engineering technology, applied science, a mechanical, industrial, or practical art or trade, agriculture, health occupations, business, or applied economics

- Builds student competence in mathematics, science, reading, writing, communications, economics and workplace skills through applied, contextual academics, and integrated instruction, in a coherent sequence of courses

- Leads to an associate or a baccalaureate degree or a postsecondary certificate in a specific career field

- Leads to placement in appropriate employment or to further education

[Section 202(a)(3)]

Topics	1998 Perkins Act	2006 Perkins Act
Definitions, (cont'd)	"Vocational and technical education" means organized educational activities that offer a sequence of courses that provides individuals with the academic and technical knowledge and skills they need to prepare for further education and for careers (other than careers requiring a baccalaureate, master's, or doctoral degree) in current or emerging employment sectors; and include competency-based applied learning that contributes to the academic knowledge, higher-order reasoning and problem-solving skills, work attitudes, general employability skills, technical skills, and occupation-specific skills, of an individual. *[Section 3(29)]*	"Career and technical education" means organized educational activities that offer a sequence of courses that provides individuals with coherent and rigorous content aligned with challenging academic standards and relevant technical knowledge and skills needed to prepare for further education and careers in current or emerging professions, provides technical skill proficiency, an industry-recognized credential, a certificate, or an associate degree, may include prerequisite courses (other than a remedial course) that meet other requirements; and include competency-based applied learning that contributes to the academic knowledge, higher-order reasoning and problem-solving skills, work attitudes, general employability skills, technical skills, occupation-specific skills, and knowledge of all aspects of an industry, including entrepreneurship, of an individual. *[Section 3(5)]* NEW DEFINITIONS: "Postsecondary education Tech Prep student" means a student who has completed the secondary education component of a Tech Prep program, and has enrolled in the postsecondary education component of a Tech Prep program at an institution of higher education. *[Section 3(23)]* "Scientifically based research" means research that is carried out using scientifically based research standards, as defined in Section 102 of the Education Sciences Reform Act of 2002 (see *Appendix C*). *[Section 3(25)]* "Secondary education Tech Prep student" means a secondary education student who has enrolled in two courses in the secondary component of a Tech Prep program. *[Section 3(26)]*
Transition Provisions	The Secretary shall take steps to provide for the orderly transition from the previous version of the Perkins Act to the new one. *[Section 4]*	Same as previous law, but also includes the provision that state eligible agencies will have the opportunity to submit a transition plan for the first fiscal year following the enactment of the 2006 Perkins Act. *[Section 4]*

Limitation	All of the funds made available under Perkins shall be used in accordance with the requirements of this Act. No funds may be used to provide funding under the School-to-Work Opportunities Act of 1994 or to carry out, through programs funded under the Perkins Act, activities that were funded under the School-to-Work Opportunities Act of 1994, unless the programs funded under Perkins serve only those participants eligible to participate in programs under the Perkins Act. *[Section 6]*	All of the funds made available under this Act shall be used in accordance with the requirements of this Act. *[Section 6]*
Prohibitions	Not included in 1998 Perkins Act.	Nothing in the Act shall authorize an officer or employee of the federal government to mandate, direct or control a state, local educational agency, or school's curriculum, program of instruction, or allocation of state or local resources, or mandate a state or any subdivision thereof to spend any funds or incur any costs not paid for under the Act (except matching and maintenance of effort funds). *[Section 8(a)]* Any state that declines to submit an application to the Secretary for assistance under this Act shall not be precluded from applying for assistance under any other program administered by the Secretary. *[Section 8(b)]* Notwithstanding any other provision of federal law, no state shall be required to have academic and career and technical content or student academic and career and technical achievement standards approved or certified by the federal government in order to receive assistance. *[Section 8(c)]* Prohibitions shall not affect the Act's accountability requirements in Section 113. *[Section 8(d)]* "Coherent and rigorous content" shall be determined by the state consistent with the Elementary and Secondary Education Act (see *Appendix A*). *[Section 8(e)]*
Basic State Grant Authorizations and Reservation	Such sums are authorized for Fiscal Year 1999 through Fiscal Year 2003 for the Basic State Grant. *[Section 8]* 1.25% is reserved for Native American programs.	"Such sums as may be necessary" for each of fiscal years 2007 through 2012 is authorized for the Basic State Grant. *[Section 9]* Same as previous law.

Topics	1998 Perkins Act	2006 Perkins Act
Basic State Grant Authorizations and Reservation, (cont'd)	0.25% is reserved for Native Hawaiian programs.	Same as previous law.
	0.2% is reserved for the outlying areas.	0.13% is reserved for the outlying areas.
	In FYs 2000 – 2003, 0.54% of the appropriation is reserved for incentive grants.	Incentive grant reservation and program are eliminated.
	[Section 111(a)(1)]	*[Section 111(a)(1)]*
State Allotment	50%—population aged 15 to 19	Same as previous law.
	20%—population aged 20 to 24	
	15%—population aged 25 to 65	
	15%—population aged 15 to 65	
	[Section 111(a)(2)]	
	No state shall receive, less than ½ of 1 percent of the amount appropriated but not reserved by the Secretary. Amounts necessary for increasing such payments to states to comply with this allotment shall be obtained by ratably reducing the amounts paid to other states. No state shall receive more than 150 percent of the amount the state received for the preceding fiscal year, or more than 150 percent of the national per pupil payment of Perkins funds multiplied by the number of individuals counted in the state's Perkins formula. *[Section 111(a)(3)]*	This paragraph applies for years with no additional funding (above FY 2006). *[Section 111(a)(3)]*
		For years with additional federal funds, of any new money that is appropriated over the FY 2006 funding levels, small states would receive 1/3 of the new money until they reach the small state minimum (going first to those states that are farthest away from getting their ½ a percent). The remaining 2/3 of new money would be allotted by the formula. *[Section 111(a)(4)]*

Same as previous law.

Same as previous law.

"Areas negatively impacted by changes in within-state formulas" is deleted as an option for reserve funds (because there were no changes in the formula during this reauthorization). Likewise, the requirement to spend reserve funds on at least two of the specified categories is deleted. [Section 112(c)]

Same as previous law.

One new allowable activity, "Supporting and developing state data systems relevant to the provisions of this Act" is added to state administrative activities. [Section 112(a)(3)(F)]

Same as previous law.

No state shall receive an allotment for a fiscal year that is less than the allotment the state received under part A of Title I of the 1990 Carl D. Perkins Vocational and Applied Technology Education Act for fiscal year 1998. If for any fiscal year the amount appropriated for allotments is insufficient to satisfy the hold harmless requirement, the payments to all states shall be ratably reduced. [Section 111(a)(4)]

Within-State Allotment

Not less than 85 percent distributed to local programs, of which:

States may reserve not more than 10 percent for distribution to local programs in rural areas, areas with high numbers or percentages of vocational students, and areas negatively impacted by changes in within-state formulas. Each state utilizing the reserve fund shall use the grant to serve at least two of the categories of recipients listed above. [Section 112(a)(1), (c)]

Not more than 10 percent may be reserved for state leadership activities, of which:

• An amount equal to not more than 1 percent of the state allotment shall be available to serve individuals in state institutions

• Not less than $60,000 and not more than $150,000 of state leadership funds shall be available for services that prepare individuals for nontraditional employment

[Section 112(a)(2)]

Not more than 5 percent (or $250,000, whichever is greater) may be reserved for state administration, which may be used for developing the state plan, reviewing local plans, monitoring and evaluating program effectiveness, assuring compliance with federal laws, and providing technical assistance. [Section 112(a)(3)]

States must match, from non-federal sources, funds spent on administrative activities. [Section 112(b)]

ANALYSIS

Topics	1998 Perkins Act	2006 Perkins Act
Accountability— Core Indicators of Performance	States, with input from local recipients, shall establish and identify in the state plan core indicators of performance that include, at a minimum, measures of the following: • Student attainment of challenging state established academic and vocational/technical skill proficiencies. • Student attainment of secondary diploma or its recognized equivalent, proficiency credential in conjunction with a secondary diploma, or a postsecondary degree or credential. • Placement in, retention in, and completion of postsecondary education or advanced training, placement in military service, or placement or retention in employment. • Student participation in and completion of vocational and technical education programs that lead to nontraditional training and employment. *[Section 113(b)(2)(A), (D)]*	States, with input from local recipients, shall establish and identify in the state plan core indicators of performance for secondary and postsecondary CTE students, that are valid and reliable, and that include, at a minimum, measures of the following: Core indicators for secondary students shall include: • Student attainment of challenging academic content and achievement standards, as adopted by the state under ESEA and measured by the state determined proficient levels on the academic assessments under ESEA. • Student attainment of CTE skill proficiencies, including student achievement on technical assessments, that are aligned with industry-recognized standards, if available and appropriate. • Student rates of attainment of each of the following: » a secondary school diploma, » a GED, or other state-recognized equivalent (including recognized alternate standards for individuals with disabilities), » a proficiency credential in conjunction with a secondary diploma (if such credential is offered by the state). • Student graduation rates as described in ESEA. • Student placement in postsecondary education or advanced training, in military service, or in employment. • Student participation in and completion of CTE programs that lead to nontraditional fields. *[Section 113(b)(2)(A)]* Core indicators of performance for postsecondary students shall include:

- Student attainment of challenging career and technical skill proficiencies, including student achievement on technical assessments, that are aligned with industry-recognized standards, if available and appropriate.

- Student attainment of an industry-recognized credential, a certificate, or a degree.

- Student retention in postsecondary education or transfer to a baccalaureate degree program.

- Student placement in military service or apprenticeship programs or placement or retention in employment, including placement in high-skill, high-wage or high-demand occupations or professions.

- Student participation in and completion of CTE programs in nontraditional fields.

[Section 113(b)(2)(B)]

Same as previous law, except the "attainment of self-sufficiency" is offered as an example. [Section 113(b)(2)(C)]

Same as previous law.

In developing core indicators of performance, a state shall, to the greatest extent possible, align the indicators with other federal and state programs so that similar information can be gathered. [Section 113(b)(2)(F)]

Same as previous law.

A state may identify additional performance indicators in its state plan. [Section 113(b)(2)(B)]

Currently identified state performance measures that meet the requirements of the Act may be used. [Section 113(b)(2)(C)]

States, with input from local recipients, shall identify levels of performance for each of the core indicators. Levels of performance shall be expressed in a percentage or numerical form so as to be objective, quantifiable and measurable, and require the state to continually make progress toward improving the performance of vocational and technical education students. [Section 113(b)(3)(A)(i)]

**Accountability—
Levels of Performance**

Topics	1998 Perkins Act	2006 Perkins Act
Accountability— Levels of Performance, (cont'd)	The Secretary and the state shall reach agreement on the final levels of performance that shall be incorporated in the state plan for the first two program years. The agreement shall take into account how the levels of performance identified by the state compare with other states, characteristics of participants, services and instruction provided, and the extent to which the levels of performance promote continuous improvement. *[Section 113(b)(3)(A)(iii),(vii)]*	Same as previous law.
	Prior to the third program year, the state and the Secretary shall reach agreement on performance levels for the third, fourth, and fifth program years covered by the state plan. *[Section 113(b)(3)(A)(vi)]*	Prior to the third program year, performance levels must be agreed upon for the third and fourth years, and prior to the fifth program year, performance levels must be agreed upon for the fifth and sixth years. *[Section 113(b)(3)(A)(iv)]*
	State may request changes in agreed upon performance levels due to "unanticipated circumstances." Secretary shall issue objective criteria and methods for making revisions. *[Section 113(b)(3)(A)(vii)]*	Same as previous law.
	The role of the Secretary is limited to reaching agreement on the percentage or number of students who attain the adjusted level of performance. The Secretary may disapprove a state plan if he/she determines that the state's levels of performance are not sufficiently rigorous to meet the purposes of the Act. *[Section 113(b)(3)(A)(iv), Section 122(e)(1)(B)]*	Same as previous law.
		Local accountability of eligible recipients is required in addition to state-level accountability. *[Section 113(a)]*
		Each local program must agree to accept the state adjusted levels of performance or negotiate their own unique levels of performance for the appropriate set of core indicators. Local levels of performance are negotiated in a substantively identical manner to state levels of performance, with the eligible agency taking the supervisory role of the Secretary and the eligible recipient the role of the eligible agency. *[Section 113(b)(4)]*

Accountability—Reporting

A state shall report annually to the Secretary regarding its progress in meeting the agreed upon levels of performance. The report shall include a quantifiable description of the progress of special populations in meeting the state performance levels. *[Section 113(c)]*

The Secretary shall make state reports available to the public and Congress and shall disseminate state-by-state comparisons of information. *[Section 113(c)(3)]*

Same as previous law, but the state report shall also include data disaggregated for each of the indicators of performance by the categories of students identified in ESEA and the categories of students defined as "special populations" that are served, and shall identify and quantify any gaps or disparities in performance between any such category and all students served by the state. A quantifiable description of the progress each category of students served has made in meeting the levels of performance must be included. This disaggregation should avoid duplication in the categories of students and need not be done where the number of students in a category is insufficient to yield statistically reliable information or where the results would reveal personally identifiable information about an individual student. *[Section 113(c)]*

Same as previous law, except that reports must be made available in a variety of formats, including electronically through the Internet. *[Section 113(c)(5)]*

Local programs are now required to submit annual reports as well, in essentially the same manner as state reports are submitted. Each eligible recipient shall publicly report, on an annual basis, its progress in achieving its levels of performance on the core indicators of performance. *[Section 113(b)(4)(C)(i)]*

Each eligible recipient shall disaggregate data for each of the performance indicators by the categories of students identified in ESEA and the categories of students defined as "special populations" that are served (consistent with state disaggregation to avoid duplication), and quantify any gaps or disparities in performance between any categories of students and all students served by the local program under Perkins. *[Section 113(b)(4)(C)(ii), (iii)]*

Disaggregation need not be done where the number of students in a category is insufficient to yield statistically reliable information or where the results would reveal personally identifiable information about an individual student. *[Section 113(b)(4)(C)(iv)]*

The local report must be made publicly available in a variety of formats, including electronically or through the Internet. *[Section 113(b)(4)(C)(v)]*

Topics	1998 Perkins Act	2006 Perkins Act
National Activities—General	The Secretary shall collect performance information about and report on the condition of CTE and its effectiveness in aggregate annually to Congress. *[Section 114(a)(1)]*	Same as previous law.
	The National Center for Education Statistics (NCES) shall collect and report information on vocational and technical education for a nationally representative sample of students as a regular part of its assessments. *[Section 114(a)(3)]*	Same as previous law.
	The Secretary may, directly or through grants, contracts, or cooperative agreements, carry out research, development, dissemination, evaluation and assessment, capacity building, and technical assistance. The Secretary shall develop a single plan that shall identify the specific activities to this regard that the Secretary will carry out and describe how the Secretary will evaluate such activities. *[Section 114(c)(1)]*	Same as previous law.
	The Secretary may collect and disseminate information from the states regarding state efforts to meet adjusted levels of performance and submit a report to the Committee on Education and the Workforce of the House of Representatives and the Committee on Labor and Human Resources of the Senate. *[Section 114(c)(4)]*	Same as previous law, except Committee language is updated.
	The Secretary may carry out demonstration vocational and technical education programs to replicate model programs, to disseminate best practices information, and to provide technical assistance upon request of a state. *[Section 114(c)(6)(A)]*	Same as previous law.

This provision is eliminated.

The independent advisory panel shall be appointed by the Secretary and shall advise on the implementation of the national assessment, including the issues to be addressed and the methodology of the studies, to ensure that it adheres to the highest standards of quality. The panel shall submit to the Secretary, relevant committees of Congress, and the Library of Congress an independent analysis of the findings and recommendations from the assessment. Members of the advisory panel shall consist of:

- educators, administrators, state directors of CTE, and chief executives, including those with expertise in the integration of academic and career and technical education;

- experts in evaluation, research and assessment;

- representatives of labor organizations and businesses, including small businesses, economic development entities and workforce investment entities;

- parents;

- career guidance and academic counseling professionals; and

The Secretary shall carry out a demonstration partnership project involving a four-year, accredited postsecondary institution in cooperation with local public education organizations, volunteer groups, and private sector business participants to provide program support and facilities for education, training, tutoring, counseling, employment preparation, specific skills training in emerging and established professions, and for retraining of military medical personnel, individuals displaced by corporate or military restructuring, migrant workers, and others who otherwise do not have access to such services, through multisite, multistate distance learning technologies. The project may be carried out directly or through grants, contracts, cooperative agreements, or through the national center(s). *[Section 114(c)(6)(B)]*

National Activities— NAVE

The Secretary shall appoint an independent advisory panel, consisting of vocational and technical education administrators, educators, researchers and representatives of labor organizations, businesses, parents, guidance and counseling professionals, and other relevant groups, to advise the Secretary on implementation of the assessment, including the issues to be addressed, the methodology of the studies involved, and the findings and recommendations resulting from the assessment. The panel shall submit to the Committee on Education and the Workforce of the House of Representatives, the Committee on Labor and Human Resources of the Senate, and the Secretary, an independent analysis of the findings and recommendations resulting from the assessment. *[Section 114(c)(2)]*

ANALYSIS

Topics	1998 Perkins Act	2006 Perkins Act
National Activities— NAVE, (cont'd)		• other individuals and intermediaries with relevant expertise. *[Section 114(d)(1)]*
	The Secretary shall provide for the conduct of an independent evaluation and assessment of vocational and technical education programs under this Act through studies and analyses conducted independently through competitive grants, contracts, and cooperative agreements. *[Section 114(c)(3)(A)]*	Same as previous law, except specifies that the study should also consider the "implementation" of the 2006 Perkins Act, to the extent practicable. *[Section 114(d)(2)(A)]*
	The Secretary shall submit to the Committee on Education and the Workforce of the House of Representatives and the Committee on Labor and Human Resources of the Senate an interim report regarding the assessment on or before January 1, 2002, and a final report on or before July 1, 2002. *[Section 114(c)(3)(C)]*	The Secretary shall submit to Congress an interim report on or before January 1, 2010, and a final report on or before July 1, 2011. *[Section 114(d)(2)(C)]*
	The assessment must include descriptions and evaluations of—	
	• The extent to which state, local and tribal entities have developed, implemented or improved state and local vocational and technical education programs and the programs' effect on development, implementation or improvement, including the capacity of state, tribal and local vocational and technical education systems to achieve the purpose of this Act.	• The extent to which state, local and tribal entities have developed, implemented or improved state and local CTE programs assisted under the Perkins Act.
	• The extent to which expenditures at the federal, state, tribal and local levels address program improvement in vocational and technical education, including the impact of federal allocation requirements on the delivery of services.	• Eliminated.
	• The preparation and qualifications of teachers of vocational and technical and academic curricula in vocational and technical education programs, as well as shortages of such teachers.	• The preparation and qualifications of teachers and faculty of CTE (such as meeting state established teacher certification or licensing requirements), as well as shortages of such teachers and faculty.
	• Participation of students in vocational and technical education programs.	• Same as previous law.

- Academic and employment outcomes of vocational and technical education, including analyses of—

  » the number of vocational and technical education and Tech Prep students who meet state adjusted levels of performance

  » the extent and success of integration of academic and vocational and technical education for students participating in vocational and technical education programs

  » the extent to which vocational and technical education programs prepare students for subsequent employment in high-wage, high-skill careers or participation in postsecondary education.

- Employer involvement in, and satisfaction with, vocational and technical education programs.

- The use and impact of educational technology and distance learning with respect to vocational and technical education and Tech Prep programs.

- The effect of state adjusted levels of performance and state levels of performance on the delivery of vocational and technical education services.

[Section 114(c)(3)(B)]

National Activities—
Research and
Dissemination

The Secretary shall award competitive grants, contracts or cooperative agreements to an institution of higher education, a public or private nonprofit organization or agency, or a consortium of thereof, to establish a national research center or centers to carry out research—

- For developing, improving and identifying the most successful methods for addressing the education, employment and training needs of participants in vocational and technical education programs, including in research and evaluation in such activities—

- Academic and CTE achievement and employment outcomes of CTE, including analyses of—

  » the extent and success of the integration of rigorous and challenging academic and career and technical education for students participating in CTE programs, including a review of the effect of such integration on the academic and technical achievement of students (including the number of students receiving a secondary school diploma); and

  » the extent to which CTE programs prepare students, including special populations, for subsequent employment in high-skill, high-wage occupations (including those in which math and science skills are critical), or for participation in postsecondary education.

- Employer involvement in, and satisfaction with, CTE programs and CTE students' preparation for employment.

- "Impact" is eliminated.

- The effect of state and local adjusted levels of performance and state and local levels of performance on the delivery of CTE services, including the percentage of CTE and Tech Prep students meeting the adjusted levels of performance.

[Section 114(d)(2)(B)]

Same as previous law, except there can only be one "center", and it must carry out "scientifically based research and evaluation."

- Same as previous law, but specifically mentions including "special populations."

ANALYSIS

Topics	1998 Perkins Act	2006 Perkins Act
National Activities— Research and Dissemination, (cont'd)	» integration of vocational and technical instruction and academic, secondary and postsecondary instruction;	• Same as previous law.
	» effective education technology and distance learning approaches and strategies;	• Same as previous law.
	» state adjusted levels of performance and state levels of performance that serve to improve vocational and technical education programs and student achievement; and	• Same as previous law.
	» academic knowledge and vocational and technical skills required for employment or postsecondary education.	• Same as previous law.
		» Preparation for occupations in high-skill, high-wage or high-demand business and industry, including examination of collaboration between CTE programs and business and industry; and academic and technical skills required for a regional or sectoral workforce, including small business.
		• References CTE programs that are integrated with coherent and rigorous content aligned with challenging academic standards.
	• To increase the effectiveness and improve the implementation of vocational and technical education programs, including conducting research and development and studies providing longitudinal information or formative evaluation.	• Same as previous law, except research should address the integration of teacher education programs with academic standards and coordinating technical education with industry-recognized certification requirements; and recruitment and retention of CTE professionals.
	• That can be used to improve teacher training and learning in the vocational and technical education classroom, including	
	» effective inservice and preservice teacher education systems	
	» dissemination and training activities related to applied research and demonstration activities, which may also include a repository for information on vocational and technical skills, state academic standards, and related materials	

	• That the Secretary deems appropriate to assist states and local programs. *[Section 114(c)(5)(A)]*	• Additional research must be consistent with the purposes of the Act. *[Section 114 (d)(4)(A)]*
	The research center(s) shall annually prepare a report of key research findings and submit copies to the Secretary, the Committee on Education and the Workforce of the House of Representatives, the Committee on Labor and Human Resources of the Senate, the Library of Congress, and each state. *[Section 114(c)(5)(B)]*	Same as previous law, except Committee language is updated.
	The center(s) shall conduct dissemination and training activities based upon the research they conduct. *[Section 114(c)(5)(C)]*	Same as previous law.
National Activities— Authorization	"Such sums as necessary" for FY 1999 and each of the four succeeding fiscal years are authorized. *[Section 114(c)(8)]*	"Such sums as necessary" for each of fiscal years 2007–2012 are authorized for all activities. *[Section 114(e)]*
Assistance to Outlying Areas	Secretary shall reserve 0.2 percent of the total federal appropriation for grants to outlying areas. *[Section 111(a)(1)(A)]* From these funds, the Secretary shall: • Make a $500,000 grant to Guam • Make a $190,000 grant each to American Samoa and the Northern Mariana Islands *[Section 115(a)]* The remainder shall be allocated to the Pacific Region Educational Laboratory to make grants for vocational education and training in Guam, American Samoa, Palau, Northern Mariana Islands, Micronesia, and Marshall Islands. *[Section 115(b)]*	Secretary shall reserve 0.13 percent of the total federal appropriation for grants to outlying areas. *[Section 111(a)(1)(A)]* From these funds, the Secretary shall: • Make a $660,000 grant to Guam • Make a $350,000 grant each to American Samoa and the Northern Mariana Islands • Make a $160,000 grant to Palau *[Section 115(a)]* Same as previous law for first fiscal year, except that Micronesia and the Marshall Islands are no longer eligible. After that, grants will be made in equal proportion directly to Guam, American Samoa, and the Northern Mariana Islands. *[Section 115(b)]*

Topics	1998 Perkins Act	2006 Perkins Act
Assistance to Outlying Areas, (cont'd)	Grants are to be used to provide direct vocational and technical educational services, including teacher and counselor training and retraining, curriculum development, and improving vocational and technical education and training programs in secondary schools and institutions of higher education, or improving cooperative education programs at the secondary and postsecondary levels. *[Section 115(b)]*	Same as previous law.
	The Pacific Region Educational Laboratory may not use more than 5 percent of grant funds for administrative costs. *[Section 115(c)]*	Same as previous law.
	No funds may be provided to the Marshall Islands, Micronesia, and Palau in FY 2002 and subsequent fiscal years. *[Section 115(d)]*	The Republic of Palau shall cease to be eligible to receive funding upon entering into an agreement for extension of U.S. educational assistance under the Compact of Free Association. *[Section 115(d)]*
Native American Programs	Secretary shall reserve 1.25 percent of the federal appropriation for Native American vocational and technical education programs. *[Section 111(a)(1)(B)]*	This entire section remains the same as in previous law.
	Secretary may make grants to, or enter into contracts with:	
	• Any Indian tribe or tribal organization eligible under the Indian Self-Determination Act or the Johnson-O'Malley Act	
	• Any Alaska Native entity eligible under the Alaska Native Claims Settlement Act	
	[Section 116(b)(1)]	
	No grants or contracts may be awarded to secondary school programs in BIA-funded schools. Such programs may receive assistance from an Indian tribe or tribal organization or Alaska Native entity that receives a grant or contract. *[Section 116(b)(1)]*	
	Any regulations relating to the application of the Indian Self-Determination Act and the Johnson-O'Malley Act to grants and contracts shall be promulgated through negotiated rule-making. *[Section 116(b)(5)(b)]*	

If sufficient funding is available, BIA shall expend for vocational education an amount equal to the amount made available under Perkins for Indian programs. In each fiscal year, BIA must expend not less than 100 percent of what it expended in the previous fiscal year to support vocational education, except that such funding may not be provided from accounts that support other Indian education programs. *[Section 116(b)(4)]*

The Secretary and Assistant Secretary of the Interior for Indian Affairs shall jointly prepare a plan for the expenditure of funds and evaluation of assisted programs. Program is administered by the Secretary of Education with assistance from BIA. *[Section 116(b)(4)]*

Those desiring grants under this section may apply individually or as part of a consortium. The organization, tribe or entity shall submit an application to the Secretary assuring compliance with grant requirements. *[Section 116(b)(6)]*

Grant funds may be used to provide reasonable stipends to students who are enrolled in vocational and technical education programs and who have acute economic needs that cannot be met through work-study programs. *[Section 116(c)(2)]*

The Secretary shall ensure that the grants and contracts awarded will improve vocational and technical education programs, and shall give special consideration to programs that involve or encourage tribal economic development plans, and applications from tribally controlled colleges or universities that are accredited or seeking accreditation, or that have accredited programs and issue certificates for completion of programs. *[Section 116(e)]*

Secretary may not impose any additional restrictions relating to programs or outcomes beyond those imposed on states under the Basic State Grant program. *[Section 116(e)]*

Recipients of funds may consolidate funds with funds received from related programs in accordance with the Indian Employment, Training, and Related Services Demonstration Act. *[Section 116(f)]*

Topics	1998 Perkins Act	2006 Perkins Act
Native American Programs, (cont'd)	These grants shall not limit the eligibility of a tribe, organization, or entity to participate in activities offered under the Basic State Grant or to preclude or discourage agreements between organizations, tribes, or entities and states or other local programs receiving Perkins funding. *[Section 116(g)]*	
Hawaiian Native Program	The Secretary shall reserve 0.25 percent of the federal appropriation to award grants to, or enter into contracts with, organizations primarily serving and representing Hawaiian Natives, which are recognized by the Governor of Hawaii. These grants can be used to plan, conduct and administer vocational and technical education programs consistent with the provisions or the Native American Programs section. *[Section 116(h)]*	The Secretary shall reserve 0.25 percent of the federal appropriation to award grants to, or enter into contracts with, community-based organizations primarily serving and representing Native Hawaiians, to plan, conduct and administer programs consistent with provisions of the Native American Programs section. *[Section 116(h)]*
Tribally Controlled Postsecondary Career and Technical Institutions—Authorization	Authorizes $4 million for grants to tribally controlled postsecondary vocational and technical institutions in FY 99 and each of the four succeeding years to provide basic support for the education and training of Indian students. *[Section 117(a) and Section 117(l)]*	Authorizes appropriations for FY 2007–2012 to provide basic support for the education and training of Indian students in tribally controlled postsecondary CTE institutions. Institutions that receive assistance under the Tribally Controlled College or University Assistance Act or the Navajo Community College Act are not eligible for funds. *[Section 117(a) and (l)]*
Tribally Controlled Postsecondary Career and Technical Institutions—Eligibility	To be eligible for funds, an institution must be: • Formally controlled, sanctioned or chartered by the governing body of an Indian tribe or tribes and offer technical degrees or certificate granting programs • Governed by board of directors/trustees, a majority of whom are Indians • Demonstrate adherence to goals, philosophy or plan of operation which fosters individual Indian economic and self-sufficiency opportunity, including programs which are appropriate to tribal goals of developing individual entrepreneurships and self-sustaining economic infrastructures on reservations	Same as previous law.

- In operation at least three years

- Accredited or candidate for accreditation

- Enroll 100 FTE, majority of whom are Indians

- Institution must be an institution of higher education as defined by Section 101 of HEA (excluding paragraph (2) of that Section)

[Section 3(28)]

Eligibility for assistance under this program shall not preclude an institution from receiving assistance under the Higher Education Act or any other program that benefits institutions of higher education or vocational education. [Section 117(f)(1)]

Funds must be used for vocational and technical education. [Section 117(b)]

Same as previous law, except as otherwise specified in subsection (a).

Funds must be used for CTE programs for Indian students and for the institutional support costs of the grant. [Section 117(b)]

Tribally Controlled Postsecondary Career and Technical Institutions— Distribution of Funds

Any institution desiring a grant under this section must submit an application to the Secretary at the time and manner specified by the Secretary. [Section 117(d)]

For each institution with an approved application, the Secretary shall provide an amount necessary to pay expenses associated with:

- Maintenance and operation of the program, including costs of development, basic and special instruction, materials, boarding, transportation, student services, day care and family support programs for students and their families (including contributions to the costs of education for dependents); student costs and stipends; and administrative expenses

- Capital expenditures, including operations and maintenance and minor improvements and repair, and physical plant maintenance costs

Same as previous law.

Same as previous law, except "institutional support of CTE" is added. [Section 117(e)(1)(D)]

Topics	1998 Perkins Act	2006 Perkins Act
Tribally Controlled Postsecondary Career and Technical Institutions— Distribution of Funds, (cont'd)	• Repair, upkeep, replacement and upgrading of instructional equipment *[Section 117(e)(1)]*	
	If federal appropriations are insufficient to pay the full amount to which all approved applicants are eligible to receive, the grant amount will be determined on the basis of each institution's Indian student count and prior grant amounts. *[Section 117(c)]*	Same as previous law.
	The grant amount for currently funded applicants shall be equal to per capita payment received during previous year multiplied by Indian student count, plus an increase to the per capita payment resulting from inflationary costs beyond institution's control. *[Section 117(c)]*	Same as previous law, expect that restricted indirect costs rates are not required for grants. *[Section 117(c)(3)]*
	Indian student count is the number of Indian students enrolled as of October 1. Credits toward a certificate earned during a summer term are included in student count in the succeeding fall term. Credits earned toward secondary/GED degree may not be counted. Continuing education credit hours shall be included in the student count. *[Section 117(h)(2)]*	Indian student count is determined by enrollments in the third week of the fall or summer term, and by dividing the total number of credits earned by 12. Credits earned in the summer term shall be counted in the succeeding fall term. Continuing education credit hours shall be included in student count, but credits earned toward a secondary education degree shall not be included. *[Section 117(h)(2)(b)]*
	Each institution receiving a grant shall provide an annual report to the Secretary detailing the institution's operating and maintenance expenses. *[Section 117(e)(2)]*	Same as previous law.
		A complaint resolution procedure must be established by the Secretary in consultation with tribally controlled postsecondary CTE institutions for grant determinations and calculations. *[Section 117(g)]*
Tribally Controlled Postsecondary Career and Technical Institutions—Needs Assessment	The Secretary is required to prepare an actual budget needs estimate for all eligible institutions and submit the estimate to Congress to be considered during the appropriations process. *[Section 117(g)(1)]*	Needs estimate and report on facilities, training and housing needs is eliminated.

	A detailed study of housing, training equipment, and immediate facilities needs of each eligible institution must be conducted by the Secretary by July 1, 2000, and reported to Congress. *[Section 117(g)(2)]* A long-term study of facilities, equipment and housing needs with five-year projections must also be conducted by the Secretary and reported to Congress 18 months after the law is enacted. *[Section 117(g)(3)]*	
Occupational and Employment Information—Authorization	Funding for this program is provided through a separate authorization. Authorization is such sums as may be necessary for FY 1999 – FY 2003. *[Section 118(f)]*	Authorization is for such sums as necessary for each of years FY 2007 through FY 2012. *[Section 118(f)]*
Occupational and Employment Information—National Activities	In consultation with appropriate federal agencies, the Secretary is authorized to provide assistance to an entity to: • Provide technical assistance to states to enable them to carry out activities under this section • Disseminate information that promotes the replication of high-quality practices • Develop and disseminate products and services • Award grants to states to carry out activities authorized under this section *[Section 118(a)]* No more than 15 percent of the federal appropriation can be used to carry out these activities. *[Section 118(d)(1)]* The Secretary shall report annually to Congress on assisted activities and functions. *[Section 118(e)]*	Same as previous law.
Occupational and Employment Information—State Activities	To receive a grant, the eligible agency and the Governor of a state shall jointly designate a state entity to carry out state level activities. *[Section 118(b)]*	Same as previous law.

Topics	1998 Perkins Act	2006 Perkins Act
Occupational and Employment Information—State Activities, (cont'd)		The jointly designated state agency shall submit an application to the Secretary at the same time the state submits its plan for Basic State Grant activities. At a minimum, the application should describe how the jointly designated entity will provide information based on trends provided pursuant to Section 15 of the Wagner-Peyser Act to inform program development, and may require other information as reasonably determined by the Secretary. *[Section 118(b)]*
	State Level Activities:	State Level Activities:
	Provide support for a career guidance and academic counseling program designed to promote improved career and education decision-making by individuals, especially in areas of career information delivery and use. *[Section 118(b)(1)]*	Provide support for career guidance and academic counseling programs designed to promote improved career and education decision-making by students (and parents, as appropriate) regarding education (including postsecondary education) and training options and preparations for high-skill, high-wage or high-demand occupations, and nontraditional fields. *[Section 118(c)(1)]*
	Make available to students, parents, teachers, administrators and counselors, and to improve accessibility with respect to information and planning resources that relate educational preparation to career goals and expectations. *[Section 118(b)(2)]*	Make available to students, parents, teachers, administrators, faculty and career guidance and academic counselors, and to improve accessibility to information and planning resources that relate academic and career and technical educational preparation to career goals and expectations. *[Section 118(c)(2)]*
	Equip teachers, administrators and counselors with the knowledge and skills needed to assist students and parents with career exploration, educational opportunities, and education financing. *[Section 118(b)(3)]*	Provide academic and CTE teachers, faculty, administrators and career guidance and academic counselors with the knowledge, skills and occupational information needed to assist parents and students, especially special populations, with career exploration, educational opportunities, education financing, and exposure to high-skill, high-wage or high-demand occupations and nontraditional fields, including occupations and fields requiring a baccalaureate degree. *[Section 118(c)(3)]*
	Assist appropriate state entities in tailoring career-related educational resources and training for use by such entities. *[Section 118(b)(4)]*	Assist appropriate state entities in tailoring career-related educational resources and training for use by such entities, including information on high-skill, high-wage or high-demand occupations in current or emerging professions and on career ladder information. *[Section 118(c)(4)]*

Improve coordination in use of program and employment data among Perkins and employment service program administrators at federal, state, and local levels to ensure nonduplication of efforts and the appropriate use of shared information and data. *[Section 118(b)(5)]*	Same as previous law.
Provide ongoing means for customers, such as students and parents, to provide comments and feedback on products and services and to update resources, as appropriate, to better meet customer requirements. *[Section 118(b)(6)]*	Same as previous law.
	Provide readily available occupational information such as information relative to employment sectors, information on occupation supply and demand, and other information provided pursuant to Section 15 of the Wagner-Peyser Act as is considered relevant. *[Section 118(c)(7)]*
At least 85 percent of the federal allocation must be distributed to designated state entities for these activities. *[Section 118(d)(2)]*	Same as previous law.
The state entity may use funds to supplement Wagner-Peyser Section 15 activities only to the extent that such activities do not duplicate activities assisted under Section 15. None of the assisted functions and activities may duplicate functions and activities assisted under the Workforce Investment Act. *[Section 118(c)]*	Same as previous law.

Eligible State Agency

"Eligible agency" means a state board designated or created consistent with state law as the sole state agency responsible for the administration or supervision of the administration of the state vocational and technical education program. *[Section 3(10)]*	Same as previous law.

Role of State Agency

The eligible agency develops and implements the state plan; evaluates activities; consults with interested parties on the planning, administration and evaluation of programs; distributes funds; and coordinates activities with the state workforce development board. *[Section 121(a)]*	Same as previous law.

Topics	1998 Perkins Act	2006 Perkins Act
State Plan— Duration and Date of Submission	Five-year plan, with annual revisions as necessary. After second year of plan, state shall review activities assisted under Part B and submit any necessary revisions to the plan. The date of submission is determined by the Secretary. *[Section 122(a)]*	A six-year plan must be submitted, except that a transition plan may be submitted during the first fiscal year after the law's enactment. *[Section 122(a)(1)]*
State Plan— Development	In developing the state plan, the state is required to conduct public hearings to permit members of the public and interested groups, including employers, labor organizations, and parents, to present their views and make recommendations on the state plan. A summary of recommendations and the board's response must be included in state plan. *[Section 122(a)(3)]*	Charter school authorizers and organizers, students and community organizations are added to the groups that should be included in public hearings. *[Section 122(a)(3)]*
	The state shall develop its plan in consultation with teachers, eligible recipients, parents, students, interested community members, representatives of special populations, representatives of business and industry, representatives of labor organizations in the state, and the state's Governor. *[Section 122(b)(1)]*	The state plan shall be developed in consultation with academic and CTE teachers, faculty and administrators; career guidance and academic counselors; eligible recipients; charter school authorizers and organizers; parents and students; institutions of higher education; the state Tech Prep coordinator and representatives of Tech Prep consortia (if applicable); entities participating in state workforce investment boards; interested community members (including parent and community organizations); representatives of special populations; representatives of business and industry (including small business); representatives of labor organizations in the state, and the state's Governor. *[Section 122(b)(1)]*
	The state must develop "effective activities and procedures" to enable these publics to participate in state and local decision-making related to plan. *[Section 122(b)(2)]*	Same as previous law.
	The eligible agency shall consult with the state agency responsible for community colleges and the state agency responsible for secondary education on the development of the plan. Any agency objections and comments, as well as board response, must be included in the state plan. *[Section 122(e)(3)]*	Same as previous law.
State Plan Contents	The state plan shall include information that:	The state plan shall include information that:

Describes the CTE activities to be assisted under Perkins that are designed to meet or exceed the state adjusted levels of performance, including a description of—

- The career and technical programs of study, which may be adopted by local educational agencies and postsecondary institutions to be offered as an option to students (and their parents as appropriate) when planning for and completing future coursework, for career and technical content areas that—

    » Incorporate secondary education and postsecondary education elements;

    » Include coherent and rigorous content aligned with challenging academic standards and relevant career and technical content in a coordinated, nonduplicative progression of courses that align secondary and postsecondary education to adequately prepare students to succeed in postsecondary education;

    » May include the opportunity for secondary students to participate in dual or concurrent enrollment programs or acquire postsecondary credit in other ways;

    » Lead to an industry-recognized credential or certificate at the postsecondary level, or an associate or baccalaureate degree.

[Section 122(c)(1)(A)]

- How the eligible agency, in consultation with eligible recipients, will develop and implement the career and technical programs of study. [Section 122(c)(1)(B)]

- How the eligible agency will support eligible recipients in developing and implementing articulation agreements between secondary and postsecondary education institutions. [Section 122(c)(1)(C)]

Describes the vocational and technical education activities to be assisted under Perkins that are designed to meet or exceed the state adjusted levels of performance, including a description of—

- Secondary and postsecondary programs to be carried out, including programs to develop, improve and expand access to quality, state-of-the-art technology in vocational and technical education programs. [Section 122(c)(1)(A)]

- The criteria used in approving applications for funds from eligible recipients. [Section 122(c)(1)(B)]

- How programs will prepare students for postsecondary education opportunities or entry into high-skill, high-wage jobs in current and emerging occupations. [Section 122(c)(1)(C)]

- How funds will be used to improve or develop new courses. [Section 122(c)(1)(D)]

Topics	1998 Perkins Act	2006 Perkins Act
State Plan Contents, (cont'd)		• How the eligible agency will make available information about career and technical programs of study offered by eligible recipients. *[Section 122(c)(1)(D)]* • Secondary and postsecondary programs to be carried out, including programs to develop, improve and expand access to appropriate technology in CTE programs. *[Section 122(c)(1)(E)]* • The criteria used in approving applications for funds from eligible recipients, including criteria to assess the extent to which the local plan will promote continuous improvement in academic achievement and technical skill attainment and address current or emerging occupational opportunities. *[Section 122(c)(1)(F)]* • How secondary programs will prepare CTE students, including special populations, to graduate with a diploma. *[Section 122(c)(1)(G)]* • How programs will prepare students, including special populations, academically and technically, for postsecondary education opportunities or entry into high-skill, high-wage or high-demand occupations in current and emerging occupations, and how participating students will be made aware of such opportunities *[Section 122(c)(1)(H)]* • How funds will be used to improve or develop new CTE courses at the secondary level that are aligned with rigorous and challenging academic content and achievement standards, at the postsecondary level that are relevant and challenging, and that lead to employment in high-skill, high-wage or high-demand occupations. *[Section 122(c)(1)(I)]* • How the communication of best practices will be facilitated and coordinated among successful Tech Prep programs and eligible recipients to improve program quality and student achievement. *[Section 122(c)(1)(J)]*

- How funds will be used to link secondary and postsecondary academic and career and technical education in a way that increases achievement. *[Section 122(c)(1)(K)]*

- How the state will report the integration of coherent and rigorous content aligned with challenging academic standards in CTE programs in order to adequately evaluate the extent of such integration. *[Section 122(c)(1)(L)]*

Describes how comprehensive professional development (including initial teacher preparation and activities that support recruitment) for CTE teachers, faculty, administrators, and career guidance and academic counselors will be provided, especially that:

- Promotes integration of coherent and rigorous academic content standards and CTE curricula, including through opportunities for the appropriate academic and CTE teachers to jointly develop and implement curricula and pedagogical strategies, as appropriate. *[Section 122(c)(2)(A)]*

- Increases the percentage of teachers that meet teacher certification or licensing requirements. *[Section 122(c)(2)(B)]*

- Is high quality, sustained, intensive and focused on instruction, and increases the academic knowledge and understanding of industry standards, as appropriate, of CTE teachers. *[Section 122(c)(2)(C)]*

- Encourages applied learning that contributes to academic and career and technical knowledge of the student. *[Section 122(c)(2)(D)]*

- Provides the knowledge and skills needed to work with and improve instruction for special populations. *[Section 122(c)(2)(E)]*

- Assists in accessing and utilizing data, including occupational and employment information, and student achievement and assessment data. *[Section 122(c)(2)(F)]*

- Promotes integration with activities that the state carries out under Title II of ESEA and Title II of HEA. *[Section 122(c)(1)(G)]*

Describes how comprehensive professional development (including initial teacher preparation) for vocational and technical, academic, guidance and administrative personnel will be provided. *[Section 122(c)(2)]*

Topics	1998 Perkins Act	2006 Perkins Act
State Plan Contents, (cont'd)	Describes how the state will actively involve parents, teachers, businesses and labor organizations in planning, development, implementation and evaluation of local programs. *[Section 122(c)(3)]*	Describes how the state will actively involve parents, academic and CTE teachers, administrators, faculty, career guidance and academic counselors, business, and labor organizations in planning, development, implementation and evaluation of local programs. *[Section 122(c)(5)]*
	Describes how funds will be allocated among secondary, postsecondary and adult programs, and consortia among secondary schools and postsecondary institutions, including the rationale for such allocations. *[Section 122(c)(4)]*	Same as previous law.
	Describes how the state will:	Describes how the state will:
	• Improve the academic and technical skills of participating students, including through integration of academic and vocational education, and provide students with strong experience in, and understanding of, all aspects of an industry. *[Section 122(c)(5)(A)]*	• Improve the academic and technical skills of participating students, including through integration of academic with CTE to ensure learning in the core academic subjects and CTE subjects. *[Section 122(c)(7)(A)]*
	• Ensure that participating students are taught to the same challenging academic proficiencies as other students. *[Section 122(c)(5)(B)]*	• Provide students with strong experience in, and understanding of, all aspects of an industry. *[Section 122(c)(7)(B)]*
		• Ensure that participating students are taught to the same challenging academic proficiencies as other students. *[Section 122(c)(7)(C)]*
	Describes how the state will annually evaluate the effectiveness of local programs and how, to the extent practicable, the state is coordinating local programs with other federal programs to ensure nonduplication. *[Section 122(c)(6)]*	Same as previous law.
	Describes program strategies for special populations. *[Section 122(c)(7)]*	Eliminated and incorporated into other elements.
	Describes how special populations will be provided with equal access to Perkins activities, not discriminated against, and provided with programs designed to enable attainment of state performance levels and prepare for further learning and high-skill, high-wage careers. *[Section 122(c)(8)]*	Describes program strategies for special populations, including a description of how special populations—
		• Will be provided with equal access to activities. *[Section 122(c)(9)(A)]*
		• Will not be discriminated against. *[Section 122(c)(9)(B)]*

• Will be provided with programs designed to enable them to meet or exceed state performance levels, and prepare for further learning and for high-skill, high-wage or high-demand occupations. *[Section 122(c)(9)(C)]*	
Describes—	
• The state's efforts to ensure eligible recipients are given an opportunity to provide input in determining the state adjusted levels of performance. *[Section 122(c)(10)(A)]*	
• How the state, in consultation with eligible recipients, will develop a process for the negotiation of local adjusted levels of performance. *[Section 122(c)(10)(B)]*	Same as previous law.
Describes steps the state will take to involve representatives of local programs in the development of state adjusted levels of performance. *[Section 122(c)(9)]*	Same as previous law.
Assures the state will comply with requirements of the Title and the provisions of the state plan, including an audit of funds received (which may be included as part of audit of other federal or state programs). *[Section 122(c)(10)]*	Same as previous law, also adds content from previous law Section 122(c)(20).
Assures that no funds will be used to acquire equipment/software that results in direct financial benefit to any organization representing the interests of the purchasing entity or its employees or affiliates. *[Section 122(c)(11)]*	Same as previous law.
Describes how the state will report data relating to students participating in vocational and technical education in order to adequately measure student progress, including special populations. *[Section 122(c)(12)]*	Same as previous law.
Describes how the state will adequately address the needs of students in alternative education programs, if appropriate. *[Section 122(c)(13)]*	Same as previous law.
Describes how the state will provide local programs with technical assistance. *[Section 122(c)(14)]*	Same as previous law.
Describes how vocational and technical education relates to state and regional occupational opportunities. *[Section 122(c)(15)]*	
Describes methods proposed for joint planning and coordination with other federal education programs. *[Section 122(c)(16)]*	

ANALYSIS

Topics	1998 Perkins Act	2006 Perkins Act
State Plan Contents, (cont'd)	Describes how funds will be used to promote preparation for nontraditional training employment. *[Section 122(c)(17)]*	Describes how funds will be used to promote preparation for high-skill, high-wage or high-demand occupations and non-traditional fields. *[Section 122(c)(18)]*
	Describes how funds will be used to serve individuals in state correctional institutions. *[Section 122(c)(18)]*	Same as previous law.
	Describes how funds will be used to effectively link secondary and postsecondary education. *[Section 122(c)(19)]*	Incorporated earlier as Section 122(c)(1)(K).
	Describes how the state will ensure locally-reported data and data reported to the Secretary are complete, accurate and reliable. *[Section 122(c)(20)]*	Incorporated earlier into Section 122(c)(13).
	Describes the involvement of students in postsecondary institutions and school dropout programs in the Workforce Investment Act one-stop delivery system. *[Section 122(c)(21)]*	Same as previous law.
		New Content Requirements:
		Describe efforts to improve the recruitment and retention of CTE teachers, faculty, and career guidance and academic counselors, including underrepresented groups, and the transition to teaching from business and industry, including small business. *[Section 122(c)(3)]*
		Describe effort to facilitate the transition of subbaccalaureate CTE students into baccalaureate degree programs. *[Section 122(c)(4)]*
Plan Submission	The state may submit a unified plan under Section 501 of the Workforce Investment Act in lieu of a separate Perkins state plan. Contents of the unified plan relating to the Perkins Act must meet all of the requirements of the Act. *[Section 122(d), Workforce Investment Act Section 501]*	Same as previous law.
		A state that does not choose to consolidate Tech Prep and Basic State Grant funds under Section 202 must submit a single state plan for Tech Prep and Basic State Grant activities. In such case, the state may allow local recipients to submit a single local plan. *[Section 122(d)(1)]*

Accountability— State Program Improvement and Sanctions	If a state fails to meet agreed upon levels of performance, the state shall develop and implement a program improvement plan in consultation with various groups for the first program year succeeding the program year in which the state failed to meet the levels of performance. *[Section 123(a)]*	If a state fails to meet at least 90 percent of an agreed upon state adjusted level of performance for any of the core indicators, the state shall develop and implement a program improvement plan in consultation with various groups (with special consideration to performance gaps between subgroups) during the first program year succeeding the program year for which the state failed to meet the performance level. *[Section 123(a)(1)]*
	The Secretary will work with the states to implement improvement activities. *[Section 123(d)(1)]*	Same as previous law.
	After providing notice and an opportunity for a hearing, the Secretary may withhold all or a portion of the state's allotment if: • The state fails to meet the agreed upon levels of performance and has not implemented an improvement plan or has shown no improvement within one year of implementing an improvement plan OR • The state has failed to meet the agreed upon levels of performance for two or more consecutive years *[Section 123(d)(2)]*	After providing notice and opportunity for a hearing, the Secretary may withhold all or a portion of the state's administrative and leadership funds if: • The state fails to implement an improvement plan. • The state fails to make any improvement in meeting performance levels within the first program year of implementation of the improvement plan. • The state fails to meet at least 90 percent of an agreed upon state adjusted level of performance for three consecutive years. *[Section 123(a)(3)(A)]*
	Sanctions may be waived due to exceptional or uncontrollable circumstances. *[Section 123(d)(2)]*	Same as previous law.
	The Secretary shall use withheld funds to support services and activities within the state through alternative arrangements. If the Secretary cannot satisfactorily use withheld funds, funds may be redistributed by formula to other states. *[Section 123(d)(3)]*	The Secretary shall use withheld funds to provide the state with technical assistance, to assist in the development of an improved state improvement plan, or for other improvement activities consistent with Perkins requirements. *[Section 123(a)(4)]*
Accountability— Local Performance Evaluation and Program Improvement	The state shall annually evaluate the performance of each local recipient of funds in meeting the agreed upon state levels of performance. *[Section 123(b)]*	Same as previous law, except eligible agencies shall use the local adjusted performance levels instead of state adjusted levels to evaluate performance. *[Section 123(b)(1)]*

Topics	1998 Perkins Act	2006 Perkins Act
Accountability— Local Performance Evaluation and Program Improvement, (cont'd)	If the state determines the local recipient of funds is not making substantial progress in achieving the state levels of performance, the state shall: • Conduct an assessment of the educational needs that the recipient shall address to overcome performance deficiencies. *[Section 123(c)(1)(A)]* • Enter into an improvement plan that includes instructional and other programmatic innovations of demonstrated effectiveness, and where necessary, strategies for appropriate staffing and staff development. *[Section 123(c)(1)(B)]* • Conduct regular evaluations of the recipient's progress toward reaching state performance levels. *[Section 123(c)(1)(C)]* The state shall conduct these activities in consultation with teachers, parents, other school staff, appropriate agencies, and other individuals and organizations. *[Section 123(c)(2)]*	A new subsection is added establishing sanctions for local programs. If a local recipient fails to meet at least 90 percent of an agreed upon local adjusted level of performance for any of the core indicators, the local recipient shall develop and implement a program improvement plan in consultation with various groups (with special consideration to performance gaps between subgroups) during the first program year succeeding the program year for which the local recipient failed to meet the performance level. *[Section 123(b)(2)]* The state will work with the local recipient to implement improvement activities. *[Section 123(b)(3)]* After providing notice and opportunity for a hearing, the state may withhold all or a portion of a local recipient's funding if: • The recipient fails to implement an improvement plan. • The recipient fails to make any improvement in meeting performance levels within the first program year of implementation of the improvement plan. • The recipient fails to meet at least 90 percent of an agreed upon state adjusted level of performance for three consecutive years. *[Section 123(b)(4)(A)]* Sanctions may be waived due to exceptional or uncontrollable circumstances, or based on the impact of the small size of CTE programs offered by the local recipient. *[Section 123(b)(4)(B)]* The state shall use withheld funds to provide (through alternative arrangements) services and activities to students within the area served by the local recipient in order to meet the purposes of the Act. *[Section 123(b)(5)]*

**State Uses of Funds—
Required State
Leadership Activities**

Each eligible agency must conduct the following leadership activities:

An assessment of the vocational and technical education programs carried out with funds under this title that includes an assessment of how the needs of special populations are being met and how such programs are designed to enable special populations to meet state adjusted levels of performance and prepare for further learning or for high-skill, high-wage careers. *[Section 124(b)(1)]*

Developing, improving or expanding the use of technology in vocational and technical education that may include—

• Training of vocational and technical education personnel to use state-of-the-art technology, including distance learning.

• Providing vocational and technical education students with the academic and vocational and technical skills that lead to entry into the high technology and telecommunications fields.

• Encouraging schools to work with high technology industries to offer voluntary internships and mentoring programs.

[Section 124(b)(2)]

Professional development programs, including providing comprehensive professional development (including initial teacher preparation) for vocational and technical, academic, guidance and administrative personnel, that—

• Will provide inservice and preservice training in state-of-the-art vocational and technical education programs and techniques, effective teaching skills based on research, and effective practices to improve parental and community involvement

Each eligible agency must conduct the following leadership activities:

An assessment of the CTE programs carried out with funds under this title that includes an assessment of how the needs of special populations are being met and how CTE programs are designed to enable special populations to meet state adjusted levels of performance and prepare for further education, further training, or for high-skill, high-wage or high-demand occupations. *[Section 124(b)(1)]*

Developing, improving or expanding the use of technology in career and technical education that may include—

• Training of CTE teachers, faculty, career guidance and academic counselors, and administrators to use technology, including distance learning.

• Providing CTE students with the academic and career and technical skills (including the mathematics and science knowledge that provides a strong basis for such skills) that lead to entry into technology fields, including nontraditional fields.

• Encouraging schools to collaborate with technology industries to offer voluntary internships and mentoring programs.

[Section 124(b)(2)]

Professional development programs, including providing comprehensive professional development (including initial teacher preparation) for CTE teachers, faculty, administrators, and career guidance and academic counselors at the secondary and postsecondary levels, that support activities described in the state plan and—

• Provide inservice and preservice training in CTE programs

  » on effective integration and use of challenging academic and career and technical education provided jointly with academic teachers to the extent practicable;

Topics	1998 Perkins Act	2006 Perkins Act
State Uses of Funds— Required State Leadership Activities, (cont'd)	• Will help teachers and personnel to assist students in meeting the state adjusted levels of performance established under Section 113 (Accountability)	» on effective teaching skills based on research that includes promising practices;
	• Will support education programs for vocational and technical education teachers in public schools and other public school personnel who are involved in the direct delivery of educational services to vocational and technical students to ensure that such teachers stay current with the needs, expectations and methods of industry	» on effective practices to improve parental and community involvement; and
		» on effective use of scientifically based research and data to improve instruction.
	• Is integrated with the professional development activities that the state carries out under Title II of ESEA	• Are high quality, sustained, intensive, and classroom focused in order to have a positive and lasting impact on classroom instruction and the teachers performance in the classroom, and are not one-day or short-term workshops or conferences.
	[Section 124(b)(3)]	• Will help teachers and personnel improve student achievement in order to meet the state adjusted levels of performance.
		• Will support education programs for CTE teachers and other public school personnel who are involved in the direct delivery of educational services to CTE students to ensure that teachers and personnel—
		» stay current with the needs, expectations and methods of industry;
		» can effectively develop rigorous and challenging integrated academic and CTE curriculum jointly with academic teachers, to the extent practicable;
		» develop a higher level of academic and industry knowledge and skills in CTE; and
		» effectively use applied learning that contributes to the academic and career and technical knowledge of the student.

- Are coordinated with the teacher certification or licensing and professional development activities that the state carries out under Title II of ESEA and Title II of HEA.

[Section 124(b)(3)]

Same as previous law, but emphasizes coherent and relevant content aligned with challenging academic standards and defines core academic subjects as in ESEA. [Section 124(b)(4)]

Providing preparation for nontraditional fields in current and emerging professions, and other activities that expose students, including special populations, to high-skill, high-wage occupations. [Section 124(b)(5)]

Supported partnerships must also enable students to complete career and technical programs of study. [Section 124(b)(6)]

Same as previous law.

Support for programs for special populations that lead to high-skill, high-wage or high-demand occupations. [Section 124(b)(8)]

Technical assistance for eligible recipients is added as a required use of state funds (rather than a permissible use as in previous law.) [Section 124(b)(9)]

Leadership activities may include:

Technical assistance is made a required use of funds.

Support for vocational and technical education programs that improve the academic, and vocational and technical skills of students participating in the programs by strengthening the academic and vocational and technical components of such programs through the integration of academics with vocational and technical education to ensure learning in the core academic and vocational and technical subjects. [Section 124(b)(4)]

Providing preparation for nontraditional training and employment. [Section 124(b)(5)]

Supporting partnerships among LEA's, institutions of higher education, adult education providers, and, as appropriate, other entities such as employers, labor organizations, parents, and local partnerships, to enable students to achieve state academic standards and vocational and technical skills. [Section 124(b)(6)]

Serving individuals in state institutions, such as state correctional institutions and those that serve individuals with disabilities. [Section 124(b)(7)]

Support for programs for special populations that lead to high-skill, high-wage careers [Section 124(b)(8)]

Leadership activities may include:

Technical assistance for eligible recipients. [Section 124(c)(1)]

State Uses of Funds—Permissible Uses

Topics	1998 Perkins Act	2006 Perkins Act
State Uses of Funds— Permissible Uses, (cont'd)	Improvement of career guidance and academic counseling programs that assist students in making informed academic and vocational and technical education decisions. *[Section 124(c)(2)]*	Same as previous law, but adds that programs should encourage secondary and postsecondary students to graduate with a diploma or degree, and expose students to high-skill, high-wage occupations and nontraditional fields. *[Section 124(c)(1)]*
	Establishment of agreements between secondary and postsecondary vocational and technical education programs in order to provide postsecondary education and training opportunities for students participating in vocational and technical education programs, such as Tech Prep programs. *[Section 124(c)(3)]*	Same as previous law, but specifically mentions "articulation agreements" as an example. *[Section 124(c)(2)]*
	Support for cooperative education. *[Section 124(c)(4)]*	Incorporated into Section 124(c)(8).
	Support for VSOs, especially with respect to efforts to increase the participation of students who are members of special populations. *[Section 124(c)(5)]*	Same as previous law.
	Support for public charter schools operating secondary vocational and technical education programs. *[Section 124(c)(6)]*	Same as previous law.
	Support for vocational and technical education programs that offer experience in, and understanding of, all aspects of an industry for which students are preparing to enter. *[Section 124(c)(7)]*	Same as previous law.
	Support for family and consumer sciences programs. *[Section 124(c)(8)]*	Same as previous law.
	Support for education and business partnerships. *[Section 124(c)(9)]*	Support for partnerships between education and business or intermediaries, including cooperative education and adjunct faculty arrangements at the secondary and postsecondary levels. *[Section 124(c)(8)]*
	Support to improve or develop new vocational and technical education courses. *[Section 124(c)(10)]*	Support to improve or develop new CTE courses and initiatives, including career clusters, career academies, and distance education, that prepare individuals academically and technically for high-skill, high-wage or high-demand occupations. *[Section 124(c)(9)]*

Providing vocational and technical education programs for adults and school dropouts to complete their secondary school education. [Section 124(c)(11)]

Providing assistance to students who have participated in services and activities under this Title in finding an appropriate job and continuing their education. [Section 124(c)(12)]

Same as previous law, but specifies that the assistance should be coordinated, to the extent practicable, with activities under the Adult Education and Family Literacy Act. [Section 124(c)(12)]

Same as previous law, and provides the example of referring students to the one-stop system established under the Workforce Investment Act. [Section 124(c)(13)]

NEW PERMISSIBLE USES OF FUNDS:

Support for initiatives to facilitate the transition of subbaccalaureate CTE students into baccalaureate degree programs, including—

- Statewide articulation agreements between subbaccalaureate degree granting career and technical postsecondary educational institutions and baccalaureate degree granting institutions

- Postsecondary dual and concurrent enrollment programs;

- Academic and financial aid counseling; and

- Other initiatives to overcome barriers to participation in baccalaureate degree programs, including geographic and other barriers affecting rural students and special populations.

[Section 124(c)(3)]

Awarding incentive grants to local recipients for exemplary performance in carrying out programs under this Act, which awards shall be based on—

- Exceeding the local adjusted levels of performance in a manner that reflects sustained or significant improvement.

- Effectively developing connections between secondary and postsecondary education and training.

- Adoption and integration of coherent and rigorous content aligned with challenging academic standards and technical coursework.

Topics	1998 Perkins Act	2006 Perkins Act
State Uses of Funds— Permissible Uses, (cont'd)		• An eligible recipient's progress in having special populations participating in CTE programs meet local adjusted performance levels.
		• Other performance factors as the state determines appropriate.
		Or, if a local recipient elects to use funds as permitted under Section 135(c)(19), pooling for innovative programs.
		[Section 124(c)(10)]
		Providing for activities to support entrepreneurship education and training. *[Section 124(c)(11)]*
		Developing valid and reliable assessments of technical skills. *[Section 124(c)(14)]*
		Developing and enhancing data systems to collect and analyze data on secondary and postsecondary academic and employment outcomes. *[Section 124(c)(15)]*
		Improving the recruitment and retention of CTE teachers, faculty, administrators, and career guidance and academic counselors, including individuals in groups underrepresented in the teaching profession; and the transition to teaching from business and industry, including small business. *[Section 124(c)(16)]*
		Support for occupational and employment information resources, such as those described in Section 118. *[Section 124(c)(17)]*
Within-State Formula— Allocation Between Secondary/ Postsecondary	State determines allocation of basic grant funds between LEAs and postsecondary institutions. *[Section 112(a)(1), Section 122(c)(4)(A)]*	Same as previous law
Within-State Secondary Formula	In FY 99, secondary funds are distributed by the state based on Title I (70 percent), IDEA (20 percent), and the number of students enrolled in LEAs and adults enrolled in training programs (10 percent). *[Section 131(a)]*	Provision is no longer needed.

Under the 1998 Perkins Act, data was never available for the 15- to 19-year-old population. Therefore states received a waiver to distribute funds based on the 5- to 17-year-old population. The 2006 Act updates the language in statute to require funds to be distributed based on 5- to 17-year-olds. This population must be determined by the Census report determining eligibility under Title I of ESEA, or from student membership data collected by the National Center for Education Statistics. Data on the number of these youth in families below the poverty line should be obtained from Section 1124(c)(1)(A) of ESEA. Data shall be adjusted to reflect any change in school district boundaries that occurred since the data were collected, and to include LEAs without geographic boundaries, such as charter schools and BIA funded schools. *[Section 131(a)]*

Same as previous law.

Same as previous law.

Same as previous law.

In FY 2000 and each of the succeeding FYs, secondary funds are distributed by the state based on youth population (ages 15 through 19) within the LEA (30 percent) and low-income youth population within the LEA (70 percent). *[Section 131(b)]*

The state may allocate funds using an alternative formula that more effectively targets funds on the basis of poverty, if waiver is approved by the Secretary. *[Section 131(c)]*

Minimum award of $15,000. LEAs may enter into consortia for the purposes of meeting the minimum allocation. The state shall waive the minimum allocation rule if the LEA:

- Is located in a rural, sparsely-populated area; OR

- Is a public charter school that operates a secondary vocational and technical education program

AND

- Demonstrates it is unable to enter into a consortium

[Section 131(d)]

Within-State Formula— Area CTE Schools and Intermediate Agencies

Area vocational schools and intermediate educational agencies shall be eligible to receive secondary school funds if the school or agency has entered into a consortium or cooperative agreement with the LEA concerned. *[Section 131(f)]*

ANALYSIS

Topics	1998 Perkins Act	2006 Perkins Act
Within-State Formula— Area CTE Schools and Intermediate Agencies	Funding allocation is based on each school's/agency's relative share of students who are attending vocational and technical education programs (based on average three-year enrollment). *[Section 131(f)]*	Same as previous law.
Within-State Formula— Postsecondary	Postsecondary funds are distributed by the state to eligible institutions or consortia based on the number of Pell Grant and BIA-assistance recipients enrolled in vocational and technical education programs. *[Section 135(a)]*	Same as previous law.
	If approved by the Secretary, an alternative formula is allowed by waiver if the specified formula does not adequately target resources to areas with the highest numbers of economically disadvantaged individuals, and the alternative will result in such a distribution. *[Section 132(b)]*	Same as previous law.
	Minimum grant award of $50,000 to institutions or consortia of institutions. *[Section 132(c)]*	Same as previous law.
Contents of Local Plan	Each local plan shall:	Each local plan shall:
	Describe how the required vocational and technical program elements will be carried out with Perkins funds. *[Section 134(b)(1)]*	Same as previous law.
	Describe how programs will be carried out with respect to meeting state adjusted levels of performance. *[Section 134(b)(2)]*	Same as previous law, except meeting local performance levels is added. *[Section 134(b)(2)]*
	Describe how the eligible recipient will:	Describe how the eligible recipient will:
		• Offer the appropriate courses of not less than one of the career and technical programs of study described in the state plan.

- Improve academic and technical skills of students in vocational and technical education by integrating academics with vocational and technical education programs through a coherent sequence of courses to ensure learning in core academic and vocational and technical subjects.

- Provide students with strong experience in, and understanding of, all aspects of an industry.

- Ensure students participating in vocational and technical education are taught to the same challenging academic proficiencies as all other students.

[Section 134(b)(3)]

Describe how parents, students, teachers, representatives of business and industry, labor organizations, representatives of special populations, and other interested individuals are involved in development, implementation and evaluation of Perkins programs, and how such individuals and entities are informed about and assisted in understanding the requirements of Perkins. [Section 134(b)(4)]

Assure that the program is such size, scope and quality to improve the quality of vocational and technical education. [Section 134(b)(5)]

Describe the process that will be used to independently evaluate and improve local program performance. [Section 134(b)(6)]

- Improve academic and technical skills of CTE students by integrating coherent and rigorous content aligned with challenging academic standards and relevant CTE programs to ensure learning in core academic subjects (as defined by ESEA) and CTE subjects.

- Provide students with strong experience in, and understanding of, all aspects of an industry.

- Ensure students participating in CTE are taught to the same coherent and rigorous content aligned with challenging academic standards as all other students.

- Encourage CTE students at the secondary level to enroll in rigorous and challenging courses in core academic subjects (as defined by ESEA).

[Section 134(b)(3)]

Describe how parents, students, academic and CTE teachers, faculty, administrators, career guidance and academic counselors, representatives of Tech Prep consortia (if applicable), representatives of entities participating in state workforce investment boards (if applicable), representatives of business (including small business) and industry, labor organizations, representatives of special populations, and other interested individuals are involved in development, implementation and evaluation of programs supported by Perkins, and how such individuals and entities are informed about and assisted in understanding the requirements of Perkins, including career and technical programs of study. [Section 134(b)(5)]

Same as previous law.

Same as previous law, except evaluation no longer has to be independent. [Section 134(b)(7)]

ANALYSIS

Topics	1998 Perkins Act	2006 Perkins Act
Contents of Local Plan, (cont'd)	Describe the process for reviewing programs and identifying and adopting strategies to overcome barriers that lower special populations' rates of access to, or success in, vocational and technical education programs; and how programs will be provided that are designed to enable special populations to meet state performance levels. *[Section 134(b)(7)]*	Same as previous law, but adds that the plan must describe how activities will be provided that prepare special populations, including single parents and displaced homemakers, for high-skill, high-wage or high-demand occupations that will lead to self-sufficiency. *[Section 134(b)(8)]*
	Describe how special populations will not be discriminated against. *[Section 134(b)(8)]*	Same as previous law.
	Describe how funds will be used to promote preparation for nontraditional training and employment. *[Section 134(b)(9)]*	Same as previous law.
	Describe how comprehensive professional development (including initial teacher preparation) for vocational, academic, guidance and administrative personnel will be provided. *[Section 134(b)(10)]*	Describe how comprehensive professional development (including initial teacher preparation) for CTE, academic, guidance and administrative personnel will be provided that promotes the integration of coherent and rigorous content aligned with challenging academic standards and relevant CTE (including curriculum development). *[Section 134(b)(4)]*
		NEW LOCAL PLAN REQUIREMENTS:
		Describe how career guidance and academic counseling will be provided to CTE students, including linkages to future education and training opportunities. *[Section 134(b)(11)]*
		Describe efforts to improve the recruitment and retention of CTE teachers, faculty, and counselors, including individuals in groups underrepresented in the teaching profession, and the transition to teaching from business and industry. *[Section 134(b)(12)]*
Local Uses of Funds— Required	Strengthen the academic and vocational and technical skills of students in vocational and technical education through the integration of academics with vocational and technical education programs through a coherent sequence of courses to ensure learning in the core academic and vocational and technical subjects. *[Section 135(b)(1)]*	Strengthen the academic and career and technical skills of CTE students through the integration of academics with CTE programs through a coherent sequence of courses, such as career and technical programs of study described in the state plan, to ensure learning in the core academic subjects as defined by ESEA, and CTE subjects. *[Section 135(b)(1)]*

Provide students with strong experience in and understanding of all aspects of an industry. *[Section 135(b)(2)]*

Develop, improve or expand the use of technology in vocational and technical education, which may include:

- Training of vocational and technical education personnel to use state-of-the-art technology, which may include distance learning

- Providing vocational and technical education students with the academic and vocational and technical skills that lead to entry into the high technology and telecommunications fields

- Encouraging schools to work with high technology industries to offer voluntary internships and mentoring programs

[Section 135(b)(3)]

Provide professional development programs to teachers, counselors and administrators, including:

- Inservice and preservice training in state-of-the-art vocational and technical education programs and techniques, in effective teaching skills based on research, and in effective practices to improve parental and community involvement

---

Same as previous law, except adds that this may include work-based learning experiences. *[Section 135(b)(3)]*

Develop, improve or expand the use of technology in career and technical education, which may include:

- Training of CTE teachers, faculty and administrators to use technology, which may include distance learning.

- Providing CTE students with the academic and career and technical skills (including the math and science knowledge that provides a strong basis for such skills) that lead to entry into the technology fields.

- Encouraging schools to collaborate with technology industries to offer voluntary internships and mentoring programs, including programs that improve the math and science knowledge of students.

[Section 135(b)(4)]

Provide professional development programs consistent with the state plan to secondary and postsecondary teachers, faculty, administrators, and career guidance and academic counselors who are involved in integrated CTE programs, including:

- Inservice and preservice training on—

  » effective integration and use of challenging academic and career and technical education provided jointly with academic teachers to the extent practicable;

  » effective teaching skills based on research that includes promising practices;

  » effective practices to improve parental and community involvement; and

  » effective use of scientifically based research and data to improve instruction.

Topics	1998 Perkins Act	2006 Perkins Act
Local Uses of Funds— Required, (cont'd)	• Support education programs for teachers and other public school personnel who are involved with the direct delivery of education to vocational and technical education students, to ensure that such personnel stay current with all aspects of an industry.	• Support of education programs for CTE teachers and other public school personnel who are involved in the direct delivery of educational services to CTE students, to ensure that such teachers and personnel stay current with all aspects of industry.
	Internship programs that provide business experience to teachers	Internship programs that provide relevant business experience.
	• Programs designed to train teachers in the use and application of technology *[Section 135(b)(4)]*	• Programs designed to train teachers in the effective use and application of technology to improve instruction. *[Section 135(b)(5)]*
	Develop and implement evaluations of vocational and technical education programs being carried out with Perkins funds, including an assessment of how the needs of special populations are being met. *[Section 135(b)(5)]*	Same as previous law.
	Initiate, improve, expand and modernize quality vocational and technical education programs. *[Section 135(b)(6)]*	Same as previous law, except adds, "including relevant technology." *[Section 135(b)(7)]*
	Provide services and activities that are of sufficient size, scope and quality to be effective. *[Section 135(b)(7)]*	Same as previous law.
	Link secondary and postsecondary vocational and technical education, including implementing Tech Prep programs. *[Section 135(b)(8)]*	Link secondary and postsecondary CTE programs, including by offering the relevant elements of not less than one career and technical program of study described in the state plan. *[Section 135(b)(2)]*
		NEW REQUIRED USE OF FUNDS:
		Provide activities to prepare special populations, including single parents and displaced homemakers who are enrolled in CTE programs, for high-skill, high-wage or high-demand occupations that will lead to self-sufficiency. *[Section 135(b)(9)]*

Local Uses of Funds— Permissive

Involving parents, businesses and labor organizations in the design, implementation and evaluation of programs. *[Section 135(c)(1)]*	Same as previous law.
Providing career guidance and academic counseling to students participating in vocational and technical education. *[Section 135(c)(2)]*	Providing career guidance and academic counseling, which may include information described in Section 118, for students participating in CTE programs, that— • Improves graduation rates and provides information on postsecondary and career options, including baccalaureate degree programs, for secondary students, which may include the use of graduation and career plans. • Provides assistance for postsecondary students, including for adult students who are changing careers or updating skills. *[Section 135(c)(2)]*
Providing work-related experiences, such as internships, cooperative education, school-based enterprises, entrepreneurship, and job shadowing that are related to vocational and technical education programs. *[Section 135(c)(3)]*	Local education and business (including small business) partnerships, including for— • Work-related experiences for students, such as internships, cooperative education, school-based enterprises, entrepreneurship, and job shadowing that are related to CTE programs. • Adjunct faculty arrangements for qualified industry professionals. • Industry experience for teachers and faculty. *[Section 135(c)(3)]*
Providing programs for special populations. *[Section 135(c)(4)]*	Same as previous law.
Local education and business partnerships. *[Section 135(c)(5)]*	Incorporated into Section 135(c)(3).
Assisting vocational and technical student organizations. *[Section 135(c)(6)]*	Same as previous law.
Providing mentoring and support services. *[Section 135(c)(7)]*	Same as previous law.

Topics	1998 Perkins Act	2006 Perkins Act
Local Uses of Funds— Permissive, (cont'd)	Leasing, purchasing, upgrading, or adapting equipment, including instructional aides. *[Section 135(c)(8)]*	Leasing, purchasing, upgrading or adapting equipment, including instructional aids and publications (including support for library resources) designed to strengthen and support academic and technical skill achievement. *[Section 135(c)(7)]*
	Providing teacher preparation programs that assist individuals (including those with experience in business and industry) who are interested in becoming vocational and technical education instructors. *[Section 135(c)(9)]*	Same as previous law, but teacher preparation programs must address integration of academic and career and technical education. *[Section 135(c)(9)]*
	Improving or developing new vocational and technical education courses. *[Section 135(c)(10)]*	Improving or developing new CTE courses, including development of new proposed career and technical programs of study for state approval and courses that prepare individuals academically and technically for high-skill, high-wage or high-demand occupations and dual or concurrent enrollment opportunities by which CTE students at the secondary level could obtain postsecondary credit to count toward an associate or baccalaureate degree. *[Section 135(c)(12)]*
	Supporting family and consumer sciences programs. *[Section 135(c)(11)]*	Same as previous law.
	Providing vocational and technical education programs for adults and school dropouts to complete their secondary education. *[Section 135(c)(12)]*	Same as previous law, except adds a focus on upgrading technical skills. *[Section 135(c)(15)]*
	Assisting participating students in finding employment and continuing their education. *[Section 135(c)(13)]*	Same as previous law, but provides the example of referring students to the one-stop system established under the Workforce Investment Act. *[Section 135(c)(16)]*
	Supporting nontraditional training and employment activities. *[Section 135(c)(14)]*	Supporting training and activities (such as mentoring and outreach) in nontraditional fields. *[Section 135(c)(17)]*
	To support other vocational and technical education activities that are consistent with the purpose of the Act. *[Section 135(c)(15)]*	Same as previous law.

NEW PERMISSIVE USES OF FUNDS:

Developing and expanding postsecondary program offerings at times and in formats that are accessible for students, including working students, including through the use of distance education. *[Section 135(c)(9)]*

Developing initiatives that facilitate the transition of subbaccalaureate CTE students into baccalaureate degree programs, including—

- Articulation agreements between subbaccalaureate degree granting CTE postsecondary educational institutions and baccalaureate degree granting institutions.

- Postsecondary dual and concurrent enrollment programs.

- Academic and financial aid counseling for subbaccalaureate CTE students that inform the students of the opportunities for pursuing a baccalaureate degree and advise the students on how to meet any transfer requirements.

- Other initiatives to encourage the pursuit of a baccalaureate degree and to overcome barriers to enrollment in and completion of baccalaureate degree programs, including geographic and other barriers affecting rural students and special populations.

[Section 135(c)(10)]

Providing activities to support entrepreneurship education and training. *[Section 135(c)(11)]*

Developing and supporting small, personalized career-themed learning communities. *[Section 135(c)(13)]*

Providing support for training programs in automotive technologies. *[Section 135(c)(18)]*

Pooling a portion of such funds with a portion of funds available to not less than one other eligible recipient for innovative initiatives, which may include—

Topics	1998 Perkins Act	2006 Perkins Act
Local Uses of Funds— Permissive, (cont'd)		• Improving the initial preparation and professional development of CTE teachers, faculty, administrators, and counselors. • Establishing, enhancing or supporting systems for accountability data collection or reporting under Perkins. • Implementing CTE programs of study described in the state plan. • Implementing technical assessments. *[Section 135(c)(19)]*
Local Uses of Funds— Administration	Local programs may use not more than 5 percent of grant funds for administrative costs. *[Section 135(d)]*	Same as previous law.
Tech Prep— Title	Title II of the Carl D. Perkins Vocational and Technical Education Act of 1998 is titled the "Tech Prep Education Act." *[Section 201]*	While the title is not specifically included in Section 201, the title remains "Tech Prep Education."
Tech Prep— Authorization	The authorization for Tech Prep is "such sums as may be necessary for fiscal year 1999 and each of the four succeeding fiscal years." *[Section 208]*	The authorization for Tech Prep is "such sums as may be necessary for fiscal year 2007 and each of the five succeeding fiscal years." *[Section 206]*
Tech Prep— Allotment	Funds are allotted to states on the same formula basis as the Basic State Grant. *[Section 203(a)]*	Same as previous law.
Tech Prep— State Application	Each eligible agency desiring Tech Prep funds shall submit an application to the Secretary of Education at the time and manner the Secretary requires. After the approval of the state application, the Secretary will award funds to the state's eligible agency. *[Section 203(b),(c)]*	Each eligible agency desiring Tech Prep funds shall submit an application as part of its state plan under Section 122. The application should describe how Tech Prep activities will be coordinated, to the extent practicable, with activities under the Basic State Grant, and contain such other information as the Secretary requires. After the approval of the state application, the Secretary will award funds to the state's eligible agency. *[Section 201(b), (c)]*

A state may choose to combine all, or a portion, of its Tech Prep allotment with funds received under the Basic State Grant. A state that chooses this consolidation option shall notify the Secretary in the state plan, and funds consolidated shall be considered as funds allocated under Section 111 and shall be distributed in accordance with Section 112.

Tech Prep— State Report	Each state that receives a grant must submit an annual report to the Secretary on the effectiveness of the Tech Prep programs in the state, including a description of how grants were awarded. *[Section 206]*	Same as previous law.
Tech Prep— Distribution of Funds to Local Programs	States award sub-grants to local consortia for Tech Prep education programs either competitively or by a formula determined by the state. *[Section 204(a)(1)]*	Same as previous law.
	Each consortium desiring a Tech Prep grant shall submit an application to the state at the time and manner specified by the state. *[Section 205(a)]*	Same as previous law.
	The application shall contain a five-year plan for the development and implementation of Tech Prep programs. The plan shall be reviewed after the second year of the program. *[Section 205(b)]*	Plans submitted during the application process must be six years instead of five years. *[Section 143(b)]*
	The state shall approve applications based on the potential of the activities described to create effective Tech Prep programs. *[Section 205(c)]*	Same as previous law.
	In awarding grants, the state shall give special consideration to applications which:	The list of special considerations is amended:
	• Provide for effective employment placement activities or the transfer of students to baccalaureate degree programs.	• Provide for effective employment placement activities or the transfer of students to baccalaureate or advanced degree programs.
	• Are developed in consultation with business, industry, institutions of higher education, and labor organizations.	• Are developed in consultation with business, industry, institutions of higher education and labor organizations.
	• Address effectively the issues of school dropout prevention and re-entry and the needs of special populations.	• Address effectively the issues of school dropout prevention and re-entry and the needs of special populations.

ANALYSIS

Topics	1998 Perkins Act	2006 Perkins Act
Tech Prep— Distribution of Funds to Local Programs, (cont'd)	• Provide education and training in areas or skills in which there are significant workforce shortages, including the information technology industry. • Demonstrate how Tech Prep programs will help students meet high academic and employability competencies. *[Section 205(d)]* The state shall ensure an equitable distribution of grants between urban and rural area consortia. *[Section 205(e)]*	• Provide education and training in an area or skill, including an emerging technology, in which there is a significant workforce shortage based on the data provided by the entity in the state under Section 118. • Demonstrate how Tech Prep programs will help students meet high academic and employability competencies. • Demonstrate success in, or provide assurances of, coordination and integration with local recipients of the Basic State Grant. *[Section 204(d)]* Same as previous law.
Tech Prep— Eligible Consortia	Eligible entities are consortia of: • An LEA, intermediate educational agency, area vocational school, or BIA-funded secondary school AND • A nonprofit institution of higher education that offers a two-year associate degree or two-year certificate program and meets the requirements of Section 102 of the Higher Education Act, including tribally controlled postsecondary institutions; or that offers a two-year apprenticeship program OR • A proprietary institution of higher education that offers a two-year associate degree program and meets the requirements of Section 102 of the Higher Education Act, if such institution is not subject to a default management plan. *[Section 204(a)(1)]*	• Same as previous law, except adds "educational service agency." • Same as previous law. • Same as previous law.

	Consortia may also include institutions of higher education that award baccalaureate degrees, and employer and labor organizations. *[Section 204(a)(2)]*	Small businesses and business intermediaries are added. *[Section 203(a)(2)]*

Tech Prep—Program Elements	Each consortium receiving a grant shall develop and operate a four- or six-year Tech Prep program which shall:
	
	• Be carried out under an articulation agreement among consortia participants.
	
	• Consist of at least two years of secondary school preceding graduation and two or more years of higher education or an apprenticeship program of at least two years after secondary school.
	
	• Have a common core of required proficiency in math, science, reading, writing, communications and technologies.
	
	• Be designed to lead to an associate degree or a postsecondary certificate in a specific career field.
	
	• Include the development of program elements for both secondary and postsecondary participants that meet academic standards developed by the state and link secondary schools and two-year postsecondary institutions and, if possible and practicable, four-year institutions of higher education through nonduplicative sequences of courses in career fields, including the investigation of opportunities for Tech Prep secondary students to enroll concurrently in secondary and postsecondary coursework.
	
	• Use, if appropriate and available, work-based or worksite learning in conjunction with business and all aspects of an industry.
	
	• Use educational technology and distance learning, as appropriate.
	
	• Include inservice training for teachers that—
	  » is designed to train vocational and technical education teachers to effectively implement Tech Prep programs
		Each consortium receiving a grant shall develop and operate a four- or six-year Tech Prep program which shall:
		
		• Be carried out under an articulation agreement between the participants in a consortium.
		
		• Consist of a program of study that—
		  » combines a minimum of two years of secondary education with a minimum of two years of postsecondary education in a nonduplicative, sequential course of study, or an apprenticeship program of at least two years following secondary instruction;
		  » integrates academic and CTE instruction, and utilizes work-based and worksite learning experience where appropriate and available;
		  » provides technical preparation in a career field, including high-skill, high-wage or high-demand occupations;
		  » builds student competence in technical skills and in core academic subjects (as defined by ESEA) as appropriate, through applied, contextual and integrated instruction, in a coherent sequence of courses;
		  » leads to technical skill proficiency, an industry-recognized credential, a certificate, or a degree, in a specific career field;
		  » leads to placement in high-skill or high-wage employment, or to further education; and
		  » utilizes career and technical programs of study, to the extent practicable.
		
		• Include the development of Tech Prep programs for secondary and postsecondary education that—

Topics	1998 Perkins Act	2006 Perkins Act
Tech Prep—Program Elements, (cont'd)	» provides for joint training for teachers in the consortia » is designed to ensure that teachers and administrators stay current with the needs, expectations and methods of business and all aspects of an industry » focuses on training postsecondary faculty in use of contextual and applied curricula and instruction » provides training in the use of technology. • Include training programs designed to enable counselors to more effectively— » provide information to students on Tech Prep programs and related employment opportunities » support student progress in completing programs » ensure that students are placed in appropriate employment » stay current with the needs, expectations and methods of business and all aspects of an industry » provide equal access to special populations. • Provide equal access to the full range of technical preparation programs to special populations, including the development of program elements to meet the needs of special populations. • Provide for preparatory services that assist program participants. *[Section 204(c)]*	» meet academic standards developed by the state; » link secondary schools and two-year postsecondary institutions, and if possible, four-year institutions of higher education, through nonduplicative sequences of courses in career fields, the use of articulation agreements, and opportunities for concurrent enrollment; » use, if appropriate and available, work-based or work-site learning experiences in conjunction with business and all aspects of an industry; and » use educational technology and distance learning, as appropriate, to involve all the consortium partners more fully in the development and operation of programs. • Include inservice professional development for teachers, faculty and administrators that— » supports effective implementation of Tech Prep programs; » supports joint training in the consortia; » supports the needs, expectations and methods of business and all aspects of an industry; » supports the use of contextual and applied curricula, instruction and assessment; » supports the use and application of technology; and » assists in accessing and utilizing data, information available pursuant to Section 118, and information on student achievement, including assessments. • Include professional development programs for counselors designed to enable them to more effectively— » provide information to students regarding Tech Prep programs;

» support student progress in completing programs, which may include the use of graduation and career plans;

» provide information on related employment opportunities;

» ensure that students are placed in appropriate employment or further education opportunities;

» stay current with the needs, expectations and methods of business and all aspects of an industry; and

» provide comprehensive career guidance and academic counseling to participating students, including special populations.

• Provide equal access to the full range of technical preparation programs (including pre-apprenticeship programs) to special populations, including the development of Tech Prep program services appropriate to the needs of special populations.

• Provide for preparatory services that assist participants.

• Coordinate with activities conducted under Title I of the Perkins Act.

[Section 203(c)]

Same as previous law, plus the addition of the following:

• Improvement of career guidance and academic counseling for participating students through the development and implementation of graduation and career plans.

• Development of curriculum that supports effective transitions between secondary and postsecondary CTE programs.

[Section 203(d)]

Additional authorized activities:

• Acquisition of Tech Prep program equipment.

• Acquisition of technical assistance from entities that have designed and operated Tech Prep programs that have effectively used educational technology and distance learning.

• Establishment of articulation agreements with institutions of higher education, labor organizations, or businesses, especially with regard to using distance learning.

[Section 204(d)]

Topics	1998 Perkins Act	2006 Perkins Act
Tech Prep Accountability	No similar provisions.	Each consortium shall establish and report to the eligible agency indicators of performance for each Tech Prep program. The indicators of performance shall include the following:

Under **2006 Perkins Act**:

- The number of secondary education Tech Prep students and postsecondary education Tech Prep students served.

- The number and percent of secondary education Tech Prep students enrolled in the program who—

  » enroll in postsecondary education;

  » enroll in postsecondary education in the same field or major as the students were enrolled in at the secondary level;

  » complete a state or industry-recognized certification or licensure;

  » successfully complete, as a secondary student, courses that award postsecondary credit; and

  » enroll in remedial mathematics, writing or reading courses upon entering postsecondary education.

- The number and percent of postsecondary education Tech Prep students who—

  » are placed in a related field of employment not later than 12 months after graduation from the Tech Prep program;

  » complete a state or industry-recognized certification or licensure;

  » complete a two-year degree or certificate program within the normal time for completion of such program; and

  » complete a baccalaureate degree program within the normal time for completion of such program.

[Section 203(e)(1)]

Each consortium must enter into an agreement with the eligible agency to meet a minimum level of performance for each of the above performance indicators and the indicators in Section 113(b). *[Section 204(e)(1)]*

An eligible agency shall require consortia that do not meet the agreed upon performance levels for three consecutive years to resubmit an application for a Tech Prep program grant; and may choose to terminate the funding for the Tech Prep program that does not meet the performance levels for three consecutive years, including when the grants are made on the basis of a formula. *[Section 204(e)(2)]*

The Tech Prep Demonstration program is eliminated.

Tech Prep Demonstration Program

Authorizes $25 million in FY 1999 and each of the four succeeding fiscal years for competitive federal grants to support Tech Prep programs that involve the location of a secondary school on the campus of a community college. *[Section 207(e)]*

Consortia desiring demonstration grants must submit an application to the Secretary of Education at the time, in the manner, and accompanied by such information as specified by the Secretary. *[Section 207(c)]*

Consortium eligibility requirements are the same as those for the Tech Prep program. *[Section 207(d)(1)]*

Required program elements are the same as those for the Tech Prep program, except that linkages with four-year institutions of higher education are not specifically encouraged. In addition, consortia must include business as a participant, and programs may offer summer internships at a business for students or teachers. Participation of students in the program shall be voluntary. *[Section 207(d)(2), Section 207(b)]*

In awarding grants, the Secretary shall give special consideration to applications that—

- Provide for effective employment placement activities

- Address effectively the issues of school dropout prevention and re-entry and the needs of special populations

ANALYSIS

Topics	1998 Perkins Act	2006 Perkins Act
Tech Prep Demonstration Program, (cont'd)	• Provide education and training in areas or skills in which there are significant workforce shortages, including the information technology industry • Demonstrate how Tech Prep programs will help students meet high academic and employability competencies *[Section 207(d)(3)]*	
Supplement Not Supplant	Perkins funds shall supplement, and not supplant, non-federal funds expended for vocational and technical education, including Tech Prep activities. *[Section 311(a)]*	Same as previous law.
Maintenance of Effort	No payments may be made under the Perkins Act for vocational and technical education programs or Tech Prep programs to a state unless its non-federal expenditures for vocational and technical education during the fiscal or program year prior to the grant year were equal to or greater than its non-federal expenditures during the second year prior to the grant year. Maintenance of effort may be calculated on a per student or total expenditure basis. *[Section 311(b)(1)(A)]* Capital expenditures, special one-time project costs, and the costs of pilot programs shall be excluded from the computation of maintenance of effort. *[Section 311(b)(1)(B)]* In any fiscal year in which appropriations for the Act are less than appropriations made during the preceding fiscal year, the required maintenance of effort for a state shall be reduced by the same percentage by which appropriations were reduced. *[Section 311(b)(1)(C)]* The Secretary may waive requirement for up to 5 percent of expenditures for one year if the reduction in expenditures was due to "exceptional or uncontrollable circumstances." *[Section 311(b)]*	Same as previous law.

Participation of Private School Personnel and Children

An eligible agency or local recipient that uses funds under this Act for inservice and preservice vocational and technical education professional development programs for vocational and technical teachers, administrators, and other personnel may, upon request, permit the participation in such programs of vocational and technical education teachers, administrators and other personnel in nonprofit private schools offering vocational and technical education programs that are located in the geographical area served by such agency or recipient. *[Section 318]*

An eligible agency or eligible recipient that uses funds under this Act for inservice and preservice CTE professional development programs for CTE teachers, administrators and other personnel shall, to the extent practicable, upon written request, permit the participation in such programs of CTE secondary school teachers, administrators and other personnel in nonprofit private schools offering CTE programs, located in the geographical area served by such eligible agency or eligible recipient. *[Section 317(a)]*

Except as prohibited by state or local law, an eligible recipient may, upon written request, use funds made available under this Act to provide for the meaningful participation, in CTE programs and activities receiving funding under this Act, of secondary school students attending nonprofit private schools who reside in the geographical area served by the eligible recipient. *[Section 317(b)(1)]*

An eligible recipient shall consult, upon written request, in a timely and meaningful manner with representatives of nonprofit private schools in the geographical area served by the eligible recipient regarding the meaningful participation, in CTE programs and activities receiving funding under this Act, of secondary school students attending nonprofit private schools. *[Section 317(b)(2)]*

ANALYSIS

ANALYSIS

SECTION-BY-SECTION SUMMARY OF 2006 PERKINS ACT

SECTION 1
SHORT TITLE; TABLE OF CONTENTS

This Act amends the Carl D. Perkins Vocational and Technical Education Act of 1998. The amendments rename the law. The new name is the "Carl D. Perkins Career and Technical Education Act of 2006."

SECTION 2
PURPOSE

This section gives an overview of congressional intent regarding the legislation. The purposes are described to develop more fully the academic and career and technical skills of secondary and postsecondary students who enroll in CTE by developing and assisting students in meeting high standards, integrating academic and career and technical instruction, linking secondary and postsecondary education, increasing state and local flexibility, collecting and disseminating research and information on best practices, providing technical assistance and professional development, supporting partnerships among diverse stakeholders, and providing individuals with the knowledge and skills to keep the U.S. competitive. These purposes are significantly expanded to reflect increased congressional priorities in key areas, such as partnerships, professional development, and economic competitiveness.

SECTION 3
DEFINITIONS

In this section are 34 definitions of words and phrases used in the Act. These definitions are critical to understanding the provisions of the Act in a consistent manner. Most of the definitions are maintained from the 1998 Perkins Act, and four new terms and definitions are added—for "Articulation Agreement," "Scientifically Based Research," "Secondary Education Tech Prep Student," and "Postsecondary Education Tech Prep Student."

Among terms already defined in current law, the most significant change in this section is to the definition of "Vocational and Technical Education," which is now "Career and Technical Education." The clause in the first part of the definition restricting preparation for careers to those not requiring a baccalaureate, master's or doctoral degree is eliminated. This allows for CTE programs that prepare students for careers eventually requiring baccalaureate degrees, such as engineering. Two additional clauses are also added to the definition. One states that CTE "provides technical skill proficiency, an industry-recognized credential, a certificate, or an associate degree" and the other specifies that CTE may include prerequisite courses that meet the

Purposes of the 2006 Perkins Act

- Build on the efforts of states and localities to develop challenging academic and technical standards and to assist students in meeting such standards, including preparation for high-skill, high-wage or high-demand occupations in current or emerging professions;
- Promote the development of services and activities that integrate rigorous and challenging academic and career and technical instruction, and that link secondary education and postsecondary education for participating career and technical education students;
- Increase state and local flexibility in providing services and activities designed to develop, implement and improve career and technical education, including Tech Prep education;
- Conduct and disseminate national research and disseminate information on best practices that improve career and technical education programs, services and activities;
- Provide technical assistance that promotes leadership, initial preparation, and professional development at the state and local levels; and improves the quality of career and technical education teachers, faculty, administrators and counselors;
- Support partnerships among secondary schools, postsecondary institutions, baccalaureate degree granting institutions, area career and technical education schools, local workforce investment boards, business and industry, and intermediaries; and
- Provide individuals with opportunities throughout their lifetimes to develop, in conjunction with other education and training programs, the knowledge and skills needed to keep the United States competitive.

requirements of the definition, as long as they are not remedial in nature. These additional clauses maintain the targeting of Perkins funds at the post-secondary level to programs that provide associate degrees or certificates.

Another significant change is to the definition of an "eligible institution." At the postsecondary level, the change ensures that only public or nonprofit private institutions of higher education that offer CTE courses qualify for funding under the 2006 Perkins Act.

In the definition of "special populations," the broad category of "individuals with other barriers to educational achievement" has been eliminated, so this category will not have to be used when disaggregating accountability data.

SECTION 4
TRANSITION PROVISIONS

Congress directs the Secretary of Education to ensure an orderly transition from the 1998 Perkins Act provisions to those of the 2006 Perkins Act. This section requires that the Secretary give each state the opportunity to submit a transition plan for the first fiscal year following the date of enactment of the Carl D. Perkins Career and Technical Education Improvement Act of 2006. Since the Perkins Act was enacted August 12, 2006, the first full fiscal year would be Fiscal Year 2007 (which begins on October 1, 2006), and the corresponding program year applicable to education programs like Perkins would be July 1, 2007–June 30, 2008. States will be allowed to submit a one-year transition plan for the 2007–2008 program year, to be followed by a five-year plan for the 2008–2013 program years.

SECTION 5
PRIVACY

Parents and students have privacy protections afforded to them through Section 444 of the General Education Provisions Act (GEPA), as amended by the Family Educational Rights and Privacy Act of 1974. The text of these provisions may be found in *Appendix C* of this Guide. Nothing in the 2006 Perkins Act is permitted to violate these protections. Further, this section prohibits the use of this Act to create a national database containing personally identifiable information about individuals who receive services under this Act.

SECTION 6
LIMITATION

This section specifies that all of the funds made available under Perkins shall be used in accordance with the requirements of the Act. Previous limitations related to the School-to-Work Opportunities

Act have been eliminated in favor of this more straightforward language.

SECTION 7
SPECIAL RULE

Labor organizations are referenced in several instances in the 2006 Perkins Act, such as in the state plan provisions that require that labor organizations be included in the development, implementation and evaluation of career and technical education programs funded under this Act. This section allows for other employee representatives to be substituted for labor organizations in communities where labor organizations do not exist.

SECTION 8
PROHIBITIONS

The Act adds a new section of prohibitions that includes provisions to ensure local control and clarify that nothing in the Act shall authorize the federal government to mandate, direct or control a state, local educational agency, or school's curriculum, program of instruction, or allocation of state or local resources; or mandate a state to spend any funds or incur any costs not paid for under this Act (an unfunded mandate provision). The new section also ensures that a state's refusal to apply for funds under the 2006 Perkins Act does not prevent that state from receiving funds under other federal education programs, that states are not required to have academic or career and technical content or achievement standards approved by the federal government in order to receive Perkins funds, and that "coherent and rigorous content" shall be determined by each state consistent with activities under the Elementary and Secondary Education Act. However, these prohibitions do not exempt a state or local program from the accountability provisions in the Act, or the matching and maintenance of effort requirements.

SECTION 9
AUTHORIZATION OF APPROPRIATIONS

This section allows federal funds to be appropriated for the Act for each of the fiscal years 2007 through 2012, except for specific sections in the Act that have their own funding authorizations (National Activities, Tribally Controlled Postsecondary Career and Technical Institutions, Occupational and Employment Information, and Tech Prep). This section provides no specific dollar amount and therefore creates no limitations on the appropriations amount, instead leaving funding determinations to the appropriations committees of Congress each year.

ANALYSIS

CAREER AND TECHNICAL EDUCATION ASSISTANCE TO THE STATES

PART A—Allotment and Allocation

SECTION 111
RESERVATIONS AND STATE ALLOTMENT

This section describes how the federal appropriation provided under Section 9 is to be allocated. "Reservations" refers to the amounts reserved for use at the national level and "state allotment" refers to how much each state will receive from the remaining funds once the "reservations" are subtracted from the total appropriation.

Reservations

Of the funds appropriated under Section 9 of this Act, the following will be reserved by the Secretary of Education:

- 0.13 percent to carry out Section 115, Assistance for the Outlying Areas; and
- 1.50 percent to carry out Section 116, Native American Programs. This is further divided as follows:

  » 1.25 percent of the sum shall be available to carry out Section 116(b), the Native American program; and

  » 0.25 percent of the sum shall be available to carry out Section 116(h), the Native Hawaiian Program.

Due to the reduction in funds for the Outlying Areas and the elimination of the reservation that was set aside for incentive grants in the 1998 Perkins Act, a higher percentage of the appropriation will be available for the state allotment as described below.

State Allotment

The Act uses the same state allotment formula as the 1998 Perkins Act for fiscal years for which there are no additional funds above the FY 2006 levels. The formula determines how much money each state will receive in a fiscal year. The "populations" listed refer to those in the state in the fiscal year preceding the fiscal year for which the allotment determination is made, as determined by the Department of Education. All ages listed are inclusive (meaning that, in the case of the first age group listed, all 15-year-olds will be included as well as all 19-year-olds, and all those whose ages fall between 15 and 19.) The term "state" refers to each of the states in the United States, plus the District of Columbia, the Commonwealth of Puerto Rico and the U.S. Virgin Islands. The factors used in determining the amount that each state will receive are as follows:

Factors: 50 percent—population aged 15–19
20 percent—population aged 20–24
15 percent—population aged 25–65

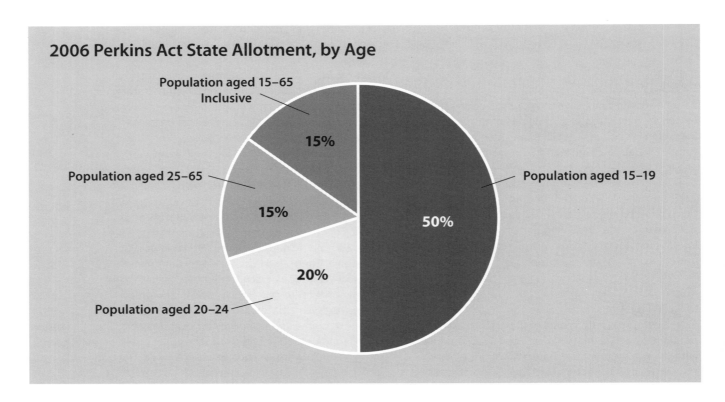

2006 Perkins Act State Allotment, by Age

Population aged 15–65 Inclusive — 15%

Population aged 25–65 — 15%

Population aged 20–24 — 20%

Population aged 15–19 — 50%

15 percent—population aged 15–65 inclusive

This formula includes a minimum allocation of 0.5 percent for each state, commonly known as the "small state minimum." However, because of additional requirements, such as the fact that no state can receive more than 150 percent of the national average-per-pupil payment of Perkins funds, many small states were not receiving the full 0.5 percent. To work toward correcting this, the 2006 Act contains new allotment provisions for years in which new funds are appropriated. Of any new money appropriated, small states would receive one-third of the new money until they reach the small state minimum. These funds would go first to those states that are farthest away from 0.5 percent of the total allocation. The remaining two-thirds of new money would go out by the same formula as described above.

A hold harmless provision is maintained from the 1998 Perkins Act that ensures a state receives an allotment that is at least as much as the allotment that the state received under Part A of Title I (the Basic State Grant) of the 1990 Perkins Act for Fiscal Year 1998. However, if total appropriations are reduced, thereby prohibiting each state from receiving such an amount, the payments to states will be reduced proportionately (referred to in the text of the law as "ratably" reduced).

If the Secretary of Education determines that any amount of a state's allotment will not be required by that state for carrying out activities under the 2006 Perkins Act, the Secretary of Education must make such amount available for reallotment. Any such reallotment will be made available to other states on the basis of criteria established by regulation, and will remain available for obligation during the next fiscal year. Such allotment should occur on the basis of need, defined as per capita income.

SECTION 112
WITHIN-STATE ALLOCATION

This section stipulates how a state will allocate its state allotment between state and local activities.

State Funds
State Leadership: Up to 10 percent of the state

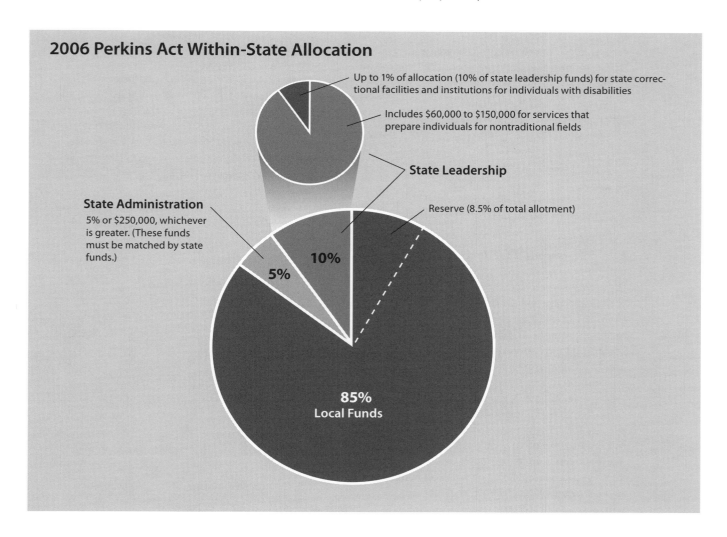

2006 Perkins Act Within-State Allocation

Up to 1% of allocation (10% of state leadership funds) for state correctional facilities and institutions for individuals with disabilities

Includes $60,000 to $150,000 for services that prepare individuals for nontraditional fields

State Leadership

State Administration
5% or $250,000, whichever is greater. (These funds must be matched by state funds.)

Reserve (8.5% of total allotment)

5%

10%

85%
Local Funds

allotment may be used for the required and permissible state leadership activities that are described in Section 124. From this pool of funds, two other requirements must be satisfied.

- Serving individuals in state institutions—Of the leadership funds, up to 1 percent of the total state allotment must be used for serving individuals in state institutions, such as correctional facilities or institutions serving individuals with disabilities. Although no minimum amount is included, the Secretary requires states to spend some dollar amount on this set aside.
- Preparing individuals for nontraditional fields—At least $60,000 and no more than $150,000 of a state's leadership funds must be used for services that prepare individuals for nontraditional fields (defined as fields in which one gender accounts for less than 25 percent of those employed in the occupation or field of work.)

State Administration: A state may reserve up to 5 percent of the total state allotment, or $250,000, whichever is greater, for the administration of the state plan. The state MUST provide matching funds on a dollar-for-dollar basis from non-federal sources for any 2006 Perkins Act funds used for administration. Administrative funds may only be used for the following activities:

- developing the state plan
- reviewing a local plan
- monitoring and evaluating program effectiveness
- assuring compliance with all applicable federal laws
- providing technical assistance
- supporting and developing state data systems relevant to the provisions of the 2006 Perkins Act

Local Funds
At least 85 percent of funds made available under the state allotment must flow to local eligible recipients (secondary and postsecondary career and technical education programs) The state determines the split between secondary and postsecondary recipients, and these funds must be distributed according to the formulas described in Sections 131 and 132, the in-state secondary and postsecondary distribution formulas.

Reserve Option: Of the minimum 85 percent of funds that must flow to the local level, up to 10 percent (or 8.5 percent of the total state allotment), may be distributed to local eligible recipients in an alternative manner determined by the state, for uses described in Section 135 (Local Uses of Funds). These funds may be made available to career and technical education programs in

- rural areas
- areas with high percentages of CTE students
- areas with high numbers of CTE students.

SECTION 113
ACCOUNTABILITY
This section establishes and supports a state and local performance accountability system designed to assess the effectiveness of the state and local funding recipients in achieving progress in CTE. The local component of this system is new in the 2006 Act.

The state-developed performance measures must consist of core indicators, any additional indicators that the state determines, and the "state adjusted levels of performance" for the indicators. They must be developed with input from local recipients.

Performance Indicators
Core indicators of performance must be defined for secondary and postsecondary CTE students in the state plan. These indicators must be valid and reliable, and at a minimum, must include the following:

SECONDARY INDICATORS:
Student attainment of challenging academic content standards and student academic achievement standards, as adopted by a state under the Elementary and Secondary Education Act (ESEA), and measured by the state determined proficient levels on the academic assessments under ESEA. *(See Appendix A)*
Student attainment of career and technical skill proficiencies, including student achievement on technical assessments, that are aligned with industry-recognized standards, if available and appropriate.
Student rates of attainment of each of the following: • A secondary school diploma • A GED credential, or other state-recognized equivalent (including recognized alternative standards for individuals with disabilities) • A proficiency credential, certificate, or degree, in conjunction with a secondary school diploma (if offered by the state)
Student graduation rates as described in the ESEA. *(See Appendix A)*
Student placement in postsecondary education or advanced training, in military service, or in employment.
Student participation in and completion of CTE programs that lead to nontraditional fields.

Student attainment of challenging career and technical skill proficiencies, including student achievement on technical assessments, that are aligned with industry-recognized standards, if available and appropriate.

Student attainment of an industry-recognized credential, a certificate, or a degree.

Student retention in postsecondary education or transfer to a baccalaureate degree program.

Student placement in military service or apprenticeship programs or placement or retention in employment, including placement in high-skill, high-wage or high-demand occupations or professions.

Student participation in, and completion of, CTE programs that lead to employment in nontraditional fields.

A state, with input from local recipients, may identify additional indicators of performance for CTE activities, such as the attainment of self-sufficiency (a standard of economic independence adopted, calculated, or commissioned by a local area or State.) Existing state performance measures that meet the requirements of this section may also be used. To the greatest extent possible, indicators should be aligned with information collection efforts for other state and federal programs to reduce the collection burden.

The Act emphasizes that the state must establish performance indicators on its own, with input from eligible recipients.

State Adjusted Levels of Performance

With input from eligible recipients, the state must establish and include in the state plan levels of performance for each of the core indicators of performance above, as well as any additional indicators. These levels of performance must be expressed in percentage or numerical form, and must require continual improvement in the performance of CTE students.

The first set of levels will apply to the first two years of the state plan. The Secretary and the state must reach agreement on these levels, with the Secretary's role being limited to negotiating agreement on the numbers or percentages. The agreement must take into account how the state's levels of performance compare to those of other states, and the extent to which the levels of performance promote continuous improvement. Prior to the third and fifth program years, agreement must be reached on levels for the corresponding subsequent years of the state plan. Levels may be revised if unforeseen circumstances arise.

Local Adjusted Levels of Performance

In a manner almost identical to the adjusted performance level negotiations between the Secretary of Education and states, local recipients must also establish performance goals. Each local recipient must agree to accept the state adjusted levels of performance as their own local adjusted levels of performance, or negotiate with the state for new levels for each of the core indicators established by the state. Local levels must also be expressed in percentage or numerical form, and require continuous improvement. Local levels must be identified in the local plan submitted under Section 134.

Reports

State Report: Each state must submit a report to the Secretary each year regarding the state's progress in achieving its performance levels, including the performance of special populations. Data must be disaggregated for each indicator of performance by the subcategories of students described in the Elementary and Secondary Education Act (see *Appendix A*) and the categories of special populations identified in Perkins. The state must identify and quantify gaps in performance between groups of students, and describe the progress of these students.

The Secretary will make state-by-state comparisons of the data and will issue a report to Congress, as well as make information available to the public in a variety of formats.

Local Report: Each local recipient must submit a report to the state each year regarding the progress the recipient has made in achieving its performance levels. The data must be disaggregated for each indicator of performance by the subcategories of students described in the Elementary and Secondary Education Act (see *Appendix A*) and the categories of special populations identified in Perkins. Local recipients must identify and quantify gaps in performance between groups of students. The report should be made available to the public in a variety of formats.

SECTION 114
NATIONAL ACTIVITIES

This section authorizes activities by the Secretary that are national in scope, or that provide assistance to states in implementing the provisions of the Act. A separate authorization of "such sums as necessary" for these specific activities is provided for fiscal years 2007–2012.

Program Performance Information

The Secretary is required to collect performance information and report on the condition of CTE and on the effectiveness of state and local programs, services and activities covered under this title. The Secretary will report to Congress annually on the aggregate performance information of all states, including the performance of special populations. The collection of performance information should, to the extent feasible, be compatible with other federal efforts to collect similar information and must be done at a reasonable cost. All states receiving assistance under the 2006 Perkins Act must cooperate with the Secretary in implementing the information systems.

The National Center for Education Statistics must collect and report information regarding CTE for a nationally representative sample of students. International comparisons are permissible in the aggregate.

Secretary's Plan

Under the requirements of this section, the Secretary must develop a single plan to carry out any research, development, dissemination, evaluation, and assessment, capacity building, and technical assistance with regard to CTE programs under the Act. The plan will describe activities to be conducted under this section and how activities will be evaluated.

National Assessment

From the funds made available for this section, the Secretary shall conduct an independent evaluation and assessment of CTE programs, including the implementation of the 2006 Perkins Act, to the extent possible. This assessment should be accomplished through studies and analyses conducted independently through grants, contracts and cooperative agreements that are awarded on a competitive basis. The Secretary must submit an interim report on the findings of the assessment by January 1, 2010, and the final report by July 1, 2011.

The assessment should include descriptions and evaluations of:

- the extent to which state, local, and tribal entities have developed, implemented or improved CTE programs funded under this Act;
- the preparation and qualifications of teachers and faculty of CTE, including teacher and faculty shortages;
- academic and CTE achievement, and employment outcomes of CTE, including:
  » the extent and success of the integration of academic and career and technical education in CTE programs, including the effect of such integration on the achievement of students (including the number of students receiving a diploma); and
  » the extent to which CTE programs prepare students, including special populations, for high-skill, high-wage occupations (including those in which mathematics and science skills are critical), or for postsecondary education;

- employer involvement in, and satisfaction with, CTE and students' preparation for employment;
- the participation of students in CTE programs;
- the use of educational technology and distance learning with respect to CTE and Tech Prep programs; and
- the effect of state and local performance levels on the delivery of CTE services, including the percentage of CTE and Tech Prep students meeting the performance goals described in Section 113.

Advisory Panel

An independent advisory panel must be appointed by the Secretary to advise the Secretary on how to conduct the evaluation and assessment of CTE described above. Advisement should be provided on the issues to be addressed and the methodology of the studies involved to ensure the highest standards of quality. The panel must submit an independent analysis of the findings and recommendations of the assessment to the Secretary, Congress, and the Library of Congress.

The panel shall consist of:

- educators, administrators, state directors of CTE and chief executives, including those with expertise in the integration of academics and CTE;
- experts in evaluation, research and assessment;
- representatives of labor organizations and businesses, including small businesses, economic development entities and workforce investment entities;
- parents;
- career guidance and academic counseling professionals; and
- other individuals and intermediaries with relevant expertise.

National Research Center

From the funds made available under this section, the Secretary shall award a grant, contract or cooperative agreement, on a competitive basis, to an institution of higher education, a public or private nonprofit organization or agency, or a consortium of such entities, to establish a national research center.

The requirements for center activities are more prescriptive and detailed than in the 1998 Act, but in general, the center shall carry out scientifically based research and evaluation:

- for the purpose of developing, improving, and identifying the most successful methods for addressing the education, employment and training needs of participants, including special populations, in CTE programs;
- to increase the effectiveness and improve the implementation of CTE programs that are integrated

with coherent and rigorous content aligned with challenging academic standards, including conducting research that provides longitudinal information or formative evaluation with respect to CTE programs and student achievement; and

- that can be used to improve the preparation and professional development of teachers, faculty and administrators, and to improve student learning in the CTE classroom.

The center shall also carry out such other research and evaluation, consistent with the purposes of this Act, as the Secretary determines appropriate to assist state and local recipients and conduct dissemination and training activities based upon the above research. An annual report on key research findings shall be submitted to the Secretary, Congress, the Library of Congress, and each state.

Demonstration and Dissemination

In order to assist in the improvement of CTE programs, the Secretary may carry out demonstration CTE programs to replicate model programs, disseminate best practices information and provide technical assistance to the states. The purpose of these activities must be to develop, improve, and identify the most successful methods and techniques for providing CTE programs funded under the 2006 Perkins Act.

SECTION 115
ASSISTANCE FOR THE OUTLYING AREAS

From the appropriation authorized under Section 9, 0.13 percent of the total must be reserved for the outlying areas. This section establishes the distribution and uses of reserve funds for the outlying areas, which currently include Guam, American Samoa, the Commonwealth of the Northern Mariana Islands, and the Republic of Palau.

SECTION 116
NATIVE AMERICAN PROGRAMS

From the appropriation authorized under Section 9, 1.5 percent of the total is used for this section. Using 1.25 percent of the total, the Secretary will make grants to and enter into contracts with Indian tribes, tribal organizations, and Alaska Native groups to carry out CTE programs consistent with the purposes of the Act. Secondary school programs funded by the Bureau of Indian Affairs are not eligible to receive funds directly under this section. Instead, these programs are eligible for funds under Section 131(h). However, these secondary school programs may receive support under this section indirectly through a grant or contract with an Indian tribe, tribal organization, or an Alaska Native entity that receives funds under this section to assist the secondary school in carrying out

CTE programs. The Bureau of Indian Affairs will pay a part of the costs of programs funded under this section, if sufficient funding is available.

Using 0.25 percent of the overall appropriation, the Secretary shall award grants or enter into contracts with community-based organizations serving and representing Native Hawaiians to plan, conduct and administer CTE programs.

SECTION 117
TRIBALLY CONTROLLED POSTSECONDARY CAREER AND TECHNICAL INSTITUTIONS

The Secretary of Education will make grants to tribally controlled postsecondary career and technical institutions for the purpose of providing basic support for the education and training of Indian students. Only institutions not receiving support under the Tribally Controlled College or University Assistance Act or the Navajo Community College Act are eligible. Grants made available under this section shall be used for CTE programs for Indian students and for the institutional support costs of the grant. Tribally controlled career and technical institutions wishing to receive a grant must submit an application to the Secretary of Education. This section has a separate authorization of "such sums as necessary" for fiscal years 2007–2012.

This section requires that if funds appropriated for these activities are not sufficient to allow the per-pupil expenditure at each institution to remain equal to that of the previous fiscal year, with adjustments for inflation, the Secretary will allocate to the institution the amount necessary to meet these costs, adjusted for inflation.

SECTION 118
OCCUPATIONAL AND EMPLOYMENT INFORMATION

This section authorizes the Secretary of Education to designate an entity at the national level to carry out activities relating to occupational and employment information for CTE programs, including (1) providing technical assistance to state information entities, (2) disseminating information that promotes the replication of high-quality practices, and (3) developing and disseminating products and services. This entity is to be chosen by the Secretary in consultation with other appropriate federal agencies. Fifteen percent of the appropriation for this section is reserved for use by the national entity.

In addition, this section reserves at least 85 percent of the appropriation for state level occupational and employment information functions. No specific distribution formula is included. For a state to receive funds under this section, the eligible agency and Governor must jointly designate an entity at the state level. This entity must submit an application to the Secretary of Education at the same time as the state plan is submitted. The state entity should conduct the following activities:

- provide support for career guidance and academic counseling programs
- make available to students, parents, teachers, administrators, faculty, and career guidance and academic counselors, information and planning resources that relate academic and career and technical educational preparation to career goals
- provide academic and career and technical education teachers, faculty, administrators, and career guidance and academic counselors with the knowledge, skills and occupational information needed to assist parents and students
- assist appropriate state entities in tailoring career-related educational resources and training for use by such entities
- improve coordination and communication among administrators and planners of programs authorized by this Act and by Section 15 of the Wagner-Peyser Act to ensure nonduplication of efforts
- provide ongoing means for customers, such as students and parents, to provide comments and feedback on products and services and to update resources
- provide readily available occupational information

The state entity designated to carry out these functions may use the funds allocated to them to supplement activities under the Wagner-Peyser Act, as long as such funds do not duplicate activities under Wagner-Peyser or WIA. The Secretary must report to Congress annually on the activities funded under this section.

The section includes a separate authorization of "such sums as necessary" for fiscal years 2007–2012 to carry out this section. However, Congress did not include funding for the program in the last year of the 1998 Perkins Act authorization. If this continues to be the case, states can use leadership funds (Section 124) to carry out the activities described in this section.

PART B—State Provisions

SECTION 121
STATE ADMINISTRATION
This section details the responsibilities of the eligible agency, which include:

- coordinating the development, submission and implementation of the state plan, as well as the evaluation of programs, services and activities carried out under Title I of the 2006 Perkins Act,

including preparation for nontraditional fields
- consulting with the Governor and other agencies, groups and individuals including parents, students, teachers, teacher and faculty preparation programs, representatives of businesses (including small businesses), labor organizations, eligible recipients, state and local officials, and local program administrators
- convening and meeting as an eligible agency at least four times annually
- adopting procedures to coordinate with the state workforce investment boards authorized in WIA (Section 111 of P.L. 105–220, see *Appendix B*) and make available to the one-stop delivery system authorized under WIA (Section 121 of P.L. 105–220, see *Appendix B*) a listing of all school dropout, postsecondary and adult programs assisted under this title

As in the 1998 Act, responsibilities of the eligible agency other than those above may be delegated to one or more other appropriate state agencies (which might be a state education agency, a state agency responsible for postsecondary education or community colleges, or a state agency responsible for workforce development, among others.) This allows the designation of a state entity to administer the funds and activities authorized under this Act.

SECTION 122
STATE PLAN
Each state seeking funding under this title must submit a six-year plan to the Secretary of Education. However, states may take advantage of the transition provisions in Section 4 and submit a one-year transition plan followed by a complete five-year plan. After the second year of the six-year period, the state shall conduct a review of the activities assisted under the title and submit any revisions necessary to the Secretary. Additional annual revisions may be made as needed, at the discretion of the state.

Development
The state shall conduct public hearings for the purpose of giving all segments of the public and interested organizations (including charter school authorizers and organizers consistent with state law, employers, labor organizations, parents, students and community organizations), an opportunity to present views and make recommendations on the state plan. A summary of the recommendations collected, and the state's response, should be included in the state plan.

In addition, the state must consult with the Governor of the state with respect to plan development. In addition, it must develop activities and procedures to consult with and allow for input into state plan deci-

State Plan Checklist

☐ Describe the CTE activities to be assisted that are designed to meet or exceed the state adjusted levels of performance, including:

- CTE programs of study.
- How the state, in consultation with eligible recipients, will develop and implement the CTE programs of study.
- How the state will support the development and implementation of articulation agreements.
- How the state will make available information about CTE programs of study.
- The secondary and postsecondary CTE programs to be carried out, including those that will develop, improve and expand access to appropriate technology in CTE programs.
- The criteria that will be used by the state to approve eligible recipients for funds under this Act.
- How programs at the secondary level will prepare CTE students, including special populations, to graduate from secondary school with a diploma.
- How programs will prepare CTE students, including special populations, academically and technically for opportunities in postsecondary education or entry into high-skill, high-wage or high-demand occupations in current or emerging occupations, and how students will be made aware of such opportunities.
- How funds will be used to improve or develop new CTE courses.
- How the state will facilitate and coordinate communication on best practices among successful Tech Prep programs and other eligible recipients.
- How funds will be used effectively to link academic and career and technical education at the secondary level and at the postsecondary level.
- How the state will report on the integration of coherent and rigorous content aligned with challenging academic standards in CTE programs.

☐ Describe how comprehensive professional development (including initial teacher preparation and activities that support recruitment) for CTE teachers, faculty, administrators, and career guidance and academic counselors will be provided.

☐ Describe efforts to improve the recruitment and retention of CTE teachers, faculty, and career guidance and academic counselors, including individuals in underrepresented groups, and the transition to teaching from business and industry.

☐ Describe efforts to facilitate the transition of subbaccalaureate CTE students into baccalaureate degree programs.

☐ Describe how the state will actively involve parents, academic and CTE teachers, administrators, faculty, career guidance and academic counselors, local business (including small businesses) and labor organizations in the planning, development, implementation and evaluation of CTE programs.

☐ Describe how funds received by the state will be allocated among CTE at the secondary, postsecondary and adult levels, and among any consortia.

☐ Describe how the state will improve the academic and technical skills of students participating in CTE; provide students with strong experience in, and understanding of, all aspects of an industry; and ensure that students who participate in CTE programs are taught to the same challenging academic proficiencies as are taught to all other students.

☐ Describe how the state will annually evaluate the effectiveness of CTE programs, and ensure nonduplication with other federal programs.

☐ Describe the state's program strategies for special populations, including a description of how individuals who are members of the special populations will be provided with equal access to activities, will not be discriminated against, and will be provided with programs designed to enable them to meet or exceed state adjusted levels of performance, and prepare for further learning and for high-skill, high-wage or high-demand occupations.

☐ Describe how eligible recipients will be given the opportunity to provide input in determining the state adjusted levels of performance; and how the state, in consultation with eligible recipients, will develop a process for the negotiation of local adjusted levels of performance.

☐ Provide assurances that the state will comply with all of the requirements of the Act and the provisions of the state plan, including a financial audit.

☐ Provide assurances that none of the funds expended under the Act for equipment or software will be used to result in a direct financial benefit to any organization representing the interests of the purchasing entity.

☐ Describe how the state will report data to adequately measure the progress of CTE students, including special populations, and how the state will ensure that the data reported to the state from local educational agencies and eligible institutions, and the data the state reports to the Secretary, are complete, accurate and reliable.

☐ Describe how the state will adequately address the needs of students in alternative education programs, if appropriate.

☐ Describe how the state will provide local educational agencies, area CTE schools, and eligible institutions in the state with technical assistance.

☐ Describe how CTE relates to state and regional occupational opportunities.

☐ Describe the methods proposed for the joint planning and coordination of programs carried out under this title with other federal education programs.

☐ Describe how funds will be used to promote preparation for high-skill, high-wage or high-demand occupations and nontraditional fields.

☐ Describe how funds will be used to serve individuals in state correctional institutions.

☐ Meet the requirements of WIA in Sections 112(b)(8) and 121(c) regarding coordination of services for postsecondary students and school dropouts, including providing information to the one-stop delivery system established under WIA (see *Appendix B*).

ANALYSIS

sions by a broad array of groups, including:

- academic and CTE teachers, faculty and administrators
- career guidance and academic counselors
- eligible recipients
- charter school authorizers and organizers consistent with state law
- parents and students
- institutions of higher education
- the state Tech Prep coordinator and representatives of Tech Prep consortia (if applicable)
- entities participating in the State Workforce Development Board
- interested community members (including parent and community organizations)
- representatives of special populations, business and industry (including representatives of small business), and labor organizations in the state

In developing the state plan, each eligible agency must consult with other state agencies responsible for secondary, postsecondary, and adult CTE, and Tech Prep (including the state agency responsible for community and technical colleges and the state agency responsible for secondary education) on portions of the state plan relevant to their areas of responsibility, including amount and uses of funding. Any of these agencies may file objections to the state plan and the eligible agency must include a response to such objections in the plan submitted for approval.

Contents
The state plan must address 20 requirements identified in Section 122(c). While many of these requirements are the same as in the 1998 Perkins Act, several are much more prescriptive, requiring more detailed descriptions and assurances. This is especially true in the areas of professional development and new requirements for CTE programs of study.

Plan Submission
If a state does not consolidate Tech Prep and Basic State Grant funds (as described in Section 202), the state must still submit a single state plan to cover requirements of this section and Tech Prep (Section 201). The state may also allow recipients to submit a single local plan covering all activities.

The state may also develop and submit the state plan as part of a unified plan authorized under WIA (Section 501 of Public Law 105–220, see *Appendix B*). Under these provisions, a state may include plans for postsecondary CTE in a unified plan, but inclusion of secondary CTE programs requires the prior approval of the state legislature. In addition, under a unified plan, all requirements of the 2006 Perkins Act must be met.

Approval
The Secretary of Education must approve a state plan, or amendments to a plan, unless it does not meet requirements of the Act, or if performance indicators are not rigorous enough to meet the purposes of the Act. Before disapproving a state plan, the Secretary must give the state notice and opportunity for a hearing. A state plan shall be deemed "approved" if the Secretary has not responded to a state within 90 days after receiving a plan.

SECTION 123
IMPROVEMENT PLANS
In the 2006 Perkins Act, new language is added related to local improvement plans and sanctions, and Section 123 is separated into two subsections— "State Program Improvement" and "Local Program Improvement."

State Program Improvement
If a state fails to meet at least 90 percent of an agreed upon performance level for any of the indicators of performance, it will have to develop and implement an improvement plan, with special consideration to performance gaps between population subgroups. This plan must be developed and implemented during the first program year after the year the performance level was not met. The Secretary of Education shall work with the state to implement improvement activities and provide technical assistance.

The Secretary may, after opportunity for a hearing, withhold all or part of a state's administration and leadership activity funding if the state meets any one of the three criteria below:

- Fails to implement the required improvement plan.
- Makes no improvement within one year of implementing the improvement plan.
- Fails to meet at least 90 percent of a performance level for the same performance indicator three years in a row.

For example, if a state's adjusted level of performance for student graduation rates was 95 percent, the state must not fall below 90 percent of that target (which would be 85.5 percent) for three years in a row.

The Secretary may waive this sanction due to exceptional or uncontrollable circumstances, such as a natural disaster or financial decline. If funds are withheld from a state, the Secretary must use them to provide technical assistance, assist in the development of a new state improvement plan, or for other improvement activities in the state.

Local Program Improvement
Language related to local program improvement closely mirrors language related to state program

improvement. Each state will annually evaluate local programs based on their performance on account-ability indicators. If the local recipient fails to meet at least 90 percent of an agreed upon performance level for any of the indicators of performance, it will have to develop and implement an improvement plan, with special consideration to performance gaps between population subgroups.

This plan must be developed in consultation with the state and implemented during the first program year after the year the performance level was not met. The state shall work with the local recipient to implement improvement activities and provide technical assistance.

The state may, after opportunity for a hearing, withhold all or part of a local recipient's funding if the local meets any one of the three criteria below:

- Fails to implement the required improvement plan.
- Makes no improvement within one year of implementing the improvement plan.
- Fails to meet at least 90 percent of a performance level for the same performance indicator three years in a row.

A state may waive this sanction due to exceptional or uncontrollable circumstances, such as a natural disaster or financial decline, or if the local recipient's performance was impacted by the small size of CTE programs offered. If a state withholds funds from a local program, it must use them to provide, through alternative arrangements, services and activities to students within the area served by the local program. Alternate arrangements should be provided by the state agency or another eligible recipient.

SECTION 124
STATE LEADERSHIP ACTIVITIES

From the amount made available to states for leadership activities (up to 10 percent of a state's allocation), each state must determine how much to spend on each of the nine required and 17 permissive activities. There are numerous additions to this section in the 2006 Perkins Act, and the full text should be consulted for complete details. These funds may not be spent on administrative activities.

Required Uses of Funds

1. An assessment of the CTE programs carried out with Perkins funds under this title, including specific focus on meeting the needs of special populations.
2. Developing, improving or expanding the use of technology in CTE, that may include personnel training, providing CTE students the skills needed for entry into technology fields, or encouraging

schools to collaborate with technology industries to offer internships and mentoring programs.
3. Professional development programs, including initial teacher preparation, for CTE teachers, faculty, administrators, and career guidance and academic counselors at all levels, that:
   - Provide inservice and preservice training on effective integration (provided jointly with academic teachers to the extent practicable), teaching skills based on research, practices to improve parental and community involvement; and use of scientifically based research and data.
   - Are high-quality, sustained, intensive and classroom-focused in order to have a impact on classroom instruction , and are not one-day or short-term workshops or conferences.
   - Will help teachers and personnel to improve student achievement.
   - Will ensure that teachers and personnel stay current with the needs, expectations, and methods of industry; can effectively develop rigorous and challenging integrated curricula (jointly with academic teachers, to the extent practicable), develop a higher level of academic and industry knowledge and skills, and effectively use applied learning.
   - Are coordinated with the teacher certification or licensing and professional development activities that the state carries out under the Elementary and Secondary Education Act and the Higher Education Act.
4. Supporting CTE programs that improve the academic and career and technical skills of CTE students through the integration of academics and CTE.
5. Providing preparation for nontraditional fields in current and emerging professions, and other activities that expose students, including special populations, to high-skill, high-wage occupations.
6. Supporting partnerships among local educational agencies, institutions of higher education, adult education providers, and, as appropriate, other entities, such as employers, labor organizations, intermediaries, parents and local partnerships, to enable students to achieve state academic standards, and career and technical skills, or complete programs of study.
7. Serving individuals at state correctional institutions and institutions that serve individuals with disabilities.
8. Supporting programs for special populations that lead to high-skill, high-wage or high-demand occupations.
9. Technical assistance for local recipients.

Permissible Uses of Funds

1. Improvement of career guidance and academic counseling programs that assist students in making informed decisions, including encouraging secondary and postsecondary students to graduate with a diploma or degree; and exposing students to high-skill, high-wage occupations and nontraditional fields.
2. Establishment of agreements, including articulation agreements, between secondary and postsecondary CTE programs in order to provide postsecondary opportunities for students, such as through Tech Prep programs.
3. Support for initiatives that facilitate the transition of subbaccalaureate CTE students into baccalaureate degree programs, including articulation agreements, dual enrollment programs, academic and financial aid counseling and other initiatives to overcome barriers and encourage enrollment and completion.
4. Support for career and technical student organizations.
5. Support for public charter schools operating CTE programs.
6. Support for career and technical education programs that offer experience in, and understanding of, all aspects of an industry.
7. Support for family and consumer sciences programs.
8. Support for partnerships between education and business or business intermediaries, including cooperative education and adjunct faculty arrangements.
9. Support to improve or develop new CTE courses and initiatives, including career clusters, career academies, and distance education, that prepare individuals for high-skill, high-wage or high-demand occupations.
10. Awarding incentive grants to eligible recipients for exemplary performance.
11. Providing activities to support entrepreneurship education and training.
12. Providing CTE programs for adults and school dropouts to complete secondary education, in coordination, to the extent practicable, with activities under the Adult Education and Family Literacy Act.
13. Providing assistance to individuals who have participated in CTE to continue their education or training or find jobs.
14. Developing valid and reliable assessments of technical skills.
15. Developing and enhancing data systems to collect and analyze data on academic and employment outcomes.
16. Improving the recruitment and retention of CTE teachers, faculty, administrators, and career guidance and academic counselors, including individuals in underrepresented groups, and transition to teaching from business and industry.
17. Support for occupational and employment information resources, such as those described in Section 118.

PART C—Local Provisions

SECTION 131
DISTRIBUTION OF FUNDS TO SECONDARY EDUCATION PROGRAMS

While in practice, the state-to-local formula for secondary programs remains the same as under the 1998 Act, the statute is updated to reflect how it was actually being implemented at the state level. Instead of basing the secondary formula on individuals ages 15–19, information that is not available, the new Act would codify the practice of basing the formula on individuals ages 5–17, which states were already receiving a waiver to use.

The formula includes the following:

- 30 percent allocated to local educational agencies (LEAs) based on the number of 5- to 17-year-olds who reside in the school district.
- 70 percent allocated to LEAs based on the number of 5- to 17-year-olds in families below the poverty line, based on data collected under ESEA (see *Appendix A*).

Population counts must come from the most recent satisfactory data from the National Center for Education Statistics or have been provided by the Census Bureau for ESEA Title I eligibility purposes. A state should adjust this data for any changes in school district boundaries since that data was collected, and include LEAs without geographic boundaries, such as charter schools and schools funded by the Bureau of Indian Affairs.

The Secretary of Education will collect data from states regarding the distribution of funds under this section to LEAs, area CTE schools, and educational service agencies.

Waiver
As in the 1998 Act, a state is allowed to apply to the Secretary of Education for a waiver on the implementation of the prescribed formula. To qualify for a waiver, an alternative formula must be submitted that more effectively targets funds on the basis of poverty.

Minimal Allocation
An LEA must qualify for a grant of at least $15,000

under the formula to receive an allocation, or it must enter into a consortium that meets the minimum allocation requirement. A state may waive this minimum allocation requirement in any case in which the LEA is in a rural, sparsely populated area or is a public charter school operating CTE programs, and demonstrates that it is unable to enter a consortium to provide CTE activities.

Consortia

Any LEA receiving an allocation that is not sufficient to meet the requirements of the Act is encouraged to form a consortium or enter into a cooperative agreement with an area CTE school or educational service agency, transfer its allocation to the area CTE school or educational service agency, and operate programs that are of sufficient size, scope and quality to be effective. Funds allocated to consortia must be used only for purposes and programs that are mutually beneficial to all members of the consortium, and cannot be reallocated to individual members of the consortium.

Allocation to Area CTE Schools

In instances in which an area CTE school or education service agency has joined with an LEA in a consortium or cooperative agreement, the state must distribute funds for which the LEA qualifies to the appropriate area CTE school or education service agency. The amount to be distributed to the area CTE school or service agency will be based on the relative share of students in CTE programs. Thus, the money "follows" the students to the institution at which they are participating in CTE programs. The Act requires an appeals procedure to be set up to handle any dispute regarding these allocations.

Any consortia formed for the purposes of this section must comply with the requirements of Section 135 (Local Uses of Funds), transfer its allocation to the AVTS or ESA, and operate programs that are of sufficient size, scope and quality to be effective. Funds allocated to consortia must be used to benefit all members of the consortium.

SECTION 132
DISTRIBUTION OF FUNDS FOR POSTSECONDARY EDUCATION PROGRAMS

The 2006 Act uses the same postsecondary within-state distribution formula as the 1998 Act, basing the allocation on the number of individuals receiving federal Pell grants and number of recipients of assistance from the Bureau of Indian Affairs.

Waiver

A state is allowed to apply to the Secretary for a waiver on the implementation of the prescribed formula. To qualify for a waiver, the state must show that the prescribed formula does not send funds to institutions or consortia that have the higher numbers of economically disadvantaged individuals. An alternative formula must effectively target funds to these individuals.

Minimal Allocation

An eligible institution must qualify for a grant of at least $50,000 to receive an allocation, or they must join a consortium that qualifies for that amount.

Consortia

Eligible institutions may enter into a consortium for the purposes of receiving funds. Such consortia must operate joint projects that:

- Provide services to all postsecondary institutions participating in the consortium (unless the eligible institution is in a rural, sparsely populated area and the state waives this requirement), and
- Are of sufficient size, scope and quality to be effective.

Funds allocated to consortia must be used only for purposes and programs that are mutually beneficial to all members of the consortium, and cannot be reallocated to individual members of the consortium.

SECTION 133
SPECIAL RULES FOR CAREER AND TECHNICAL EDUCATION

Special Rule for Minimal Allocation

As in the 1998 Act, if 15 percent or less of the state's allocation that must be distributed locally (the amount made available for local distribution in Section 112(a)(1)) is made available to either secondary or postsecondary CTE, the state may distribute the funding on a competitive basis or based on another alternative method. In other words, if the state, in determining its secondary/postsecondary split of funds, decides to give 15 percent or less to either secondary or postsecondary programs, the requirements regarding the distribution formulas described above are waived.

Special Rule for Redistribution

As in the 1998 Act, if any Basic State Grant funds are not expended at the local level within the academic year for which they are provided, they must be returned to the state for redistribution in that same year. If the funds are returned late in the year, they may be retained by the state for distribution locally in the next program year.

Secondary/Postsecondary Consortia

As in the 1998 Act, secondary and postsecondary eligible recipients can work together to provide secondary and postsecondary CTE services that comply with the title. However, secondary schools or consortia thereof must apply to the state for funds dedicated to secondary programs, and postsecondary institutions or consortia must apply to the state for funds dedicated to postsecondary programs. In working together, the secondary and postsecondary members must qualify for funds independently of one another, as this provision does not give them the ability to apply jointly for funds. This is different from Tech Prep funding, which does get distributed jointly to consortia of secondary and postsecondary partners.

Charter Schools

As in the 1998 law, a public charter school providing CTE is not required by the provisions in Sections 131 and 132 to take any additional steps to establish its eligibility beyond the requirements already imposed by a state. Thus, a charter school that is considered an LEA by the state would be eligible if it provided CTE and otherwise meets the requirements of the Act, unless other provisions in state law would prohibit its participation. Charter schools providing CTE programs can receive funds just as any other qualifying school, as long as programs offered are of sufficient size, scope and quality to be effective.

SECTION 134
LOCAL PLAN FOR CAREER AND TECHNICAL EDUCATION PROGRAMS

Each local secondary or postsecondary eligible recipient needs to submit a local plan in order to qualify to receive Perkins funds. The plan must correspond to the time period covered by the state plan described in Section 122 (either a six-year plan or a transition plan followed by a five-year plan). The state will establish requirements for the submission of the local plan.

Contents

The local plan must address at least the 12 specific requirements identified in Section 134(b). While many of these requirements are the same as in the 1998 Perkins Act, several are much more prescriptive, requiring more detailed descriptions and assurances. This is especially true in the area of professional development.

SECTION 135
LOCAL USES OF FUNDS

Each local recipient receiving funds under Perkins may not use more than five percent for administrative purposes. This balance of the funds must be used to improve CTE programs as described below.

Required Uses of Funds

1. Strengthen the academic and career and technical skills of students participating in CTE programs

through the integration of academics with CTE programs.
2. Link CTE at the secondary level and the postsecondary level, including by offering the relevant elements of not less than one program of study described in Section 122(c)(1)(A).
3. Provide students with strong experience in and understanding of all aspects of an industry, which may include work-based learning experiences.
4. Develop, improve, or expand the use of technology in CTE, which may include training to use technology, providing students with the skills needed to enter technology fields, and encouraging schools to collaborate with technology industries to offer internships and mentoring programs.
5. Provide inservice and preservice professional development programs to teachers, faculty, administrators, and career guidance and academic counselors who are involved in integrated CTE programs, on topics including effective integration of academics and CTE, effective teaching skills based on research, effective practices to improve parental and community involvement, effective use of scientifically based research and data to improve instruction. Professional development should also ensure that teachers and personnel stay current with all aspects of an industry; involve internship programs that provide relevant business experience; and train teachers in the effective use and application of technology.
6. Develop and implement evaluations of the CTE programs carried out with Perkins funds, including an assessment of how the needs of special populations are being met.
7. Initiate, improve, expand and modernize quality CTE programs, including relevant technology.
8. Provide services and activities that are of sufficient size, scope and quality to be effective.
9. Provide activities to prepare special populations, including single parents and displaced homemakers who are enrolled in CTE programs, for high-skill, high-wage or high-demand occupations that will lead to self-sufficiency.

Permissible Uses of Funds

1. Involving parents, businesses and labor organizations, in the design, implementation and evaluation of CTE programs.
2. Providing career guidance and academic counseling, which may include information described in Section 118, for students participating in CTE programs, that improves graduation rates and provides information on postsecondary and career options, and provides assistance for postsecondary students and adults.
3. Local education and business partnerships,

including for work-related experiences for students, adjunct faculty arrangements for qualified industry professionals and industry experience for teachers and faculty.

4. Providing programs for special populations.
5. Assisting career and technical student organizations.
6. Mentoring and support services.
7. Leasing, purchasing, upgrading or adapting equipment, including instructional aids and publications (including support for library resources) designed to strengthen and support academic and technical skill achievement.
8. Teacher preparation programs that address the integration of academic and CTE and that assist individuals who are interested in becoming CTE teachers and faculty, including individuals with experience in business and industry.
9. Developing and expanding postsecondary program offerings at times and in formats that are accessible for all students, including through the use of distance education.
10. Developing initiatives that facilitate the transition of subbaccalaureate career and technical education students into baccalaureate degree programs, including articulation agreements, dual enrollment programs, academic and financial aid counseling and other initiatives to overcome barriers and encourage enrollment and completion.
11. Providing activities to support entrepreneurship education and training.
12. Improving or developing new CTE courses, including the development of programs of study for consideration by the state and courses that prepare individuals academically and technically for high-skill, high-wage or high-demand occupations and dual or concurrent enrollment opportunities.
13. Developing and supporting small, personalized career-themed learning communities.
14. Providing support for family and consumer sciences programs.
15. Providing CTE programs for adults and school dropouts to complete secondary education or upgrade technical skills.
16. Providing assistance to individuals who have participated in services and activities under this Act in continuing their education or training or finding an appropriate job.
17. Supporting training and activities (such as mentoring and outreach) in nontraditional fields.
18. Providing support for training programs in automotive technologies.
19. Pooling a portion of such funds with a portion of

Local Plan Checklist

☐ Describe how CTE programs will be carried out.

☐ Describe how CTE activities will meet state and local adjusted levels of performance.

☐ Describe how the recipient will—
  • Offer the appropriate courses of not less than one of the career and technical programs of study.
  • Improve the academic and technical skills of students participating in CTE programs through integration.
  • Provide students with strong experience in, and understanding of, all aspects of an industry.
  • Ensure that students who participate in CTE programs are taught to the same coherent and rigorous content aligned with challenging academic standards as are taught to all other students;
  • Encourage CTE students at the secondary level to enroll in rigorous and challenging courses in core academic subjects.

☐ Describe how comprehensive professional development (including initial teacher preparation) for CTE, academic, guidance and administrative personnel will be provided that promotes the integration of coherent and rigorous content aligned with challenging academic standards and relevant CTE (including curriculum development).

☐ Describe how a wide variety of stakeholders are involved in the development, implementation and evaluation of CTE programs, and how such individuals and entities are informed about, and assisted in understanding, the requirements of Perkins, including CTE programs of study.

☐ Provide assurances that programs are of such size, scope and quality to bring about improvement in the quality of CTE.

☐ Describe the process that will be used to evaluate and continuously improve performance.

☐ Describe how the recipient will review CTE programs, identify and adopt strategies to overcome barriers that result in lower access or success for special populations, provide programs that enable special populations to meet local performance levels, and provide activities to prepare special populations, including single parents and displaced homemakers, for high-skill, high-wage or high-demand occupations that will lead to self-sufficiency.

☐ Describe how individuals who are members of special populations will not be discriminated against based on this status.

☐ Describe how funds will be used to promote preparation for nontraditional fields.

☐ Describe how career guidance and academic counseling will be provided to CTE students, including linkages to future education and training opportunities.

☐ Describe efforts to improve the recruitment and retention of CTE teachers, faculty, and career guidance and academic counselors, including underrepresented groups; and the transition to teaching from business and industry.

funds available to other recipients for innovative initiatives.

20. Supporting other CTE activities consistent with the purpose of the Act.

TITLE II
TECH PREP EDUCATION

SECTION 201
STATE ALLOTMENT AND APPLICATION

States will receive Tech Prep funds based on the same Basic State Grant allotment formula used in Title I, with funding being administered by the state eligible agency. The state must submit an application as part of its state plan to the Secretary with accompanying information as required by the Secretary. The application must describe how Tech Prep activities will be coordinated with Basic State Grant activities described in the state plan.

SECTION 202
CONSOLIDATION OF FUNDS

While the Tech Prep program is maintained as a separate title and federal funding stream under the Act, states will have the flexibility to consolidate all or part of their Tech Prep grants with funds received under the Basic State Grant. States must make this choice in their state plans. If states use this flexibility, all combined funds must be distributed and used in accordance with Basic State Grant funds, using the formulas described in Sections 131 and 132. Since these funds "shall be considered as funds" allotted under the Basic State Grant, the remainder of the requirements of this title will not apply. If states do not use this flexibility, the provisions of Title II will apply to funds received from the Tech Prep grant.

SECTION 203
TECH PREP PROGRAM

As in the 1998 Act, local grants may be awarded within a state on a competitive basis or on the basis of a formula determined by the state. Grants must be awarded to consortia of one or more secondary providers (LEA, intermediate education agency, educational service agency, area CTE school, or school funded by the Bureau of Indian Affairs) of CTE and:

- One or more nonprofit institutions of higher education that are not prohibited from receiving funds under the federal student loan program and offer:

  » A two-year associate degree or certificate program and are permitted to receive funds under Section 102 of HEA (which allows institutions that meet certain eligibility requirements to participate in the federal student aid

programs, see *Appendix C*), including institutions receiving assistance under the Tribally Controlled College or University Assistance Act and tribally controlled postsecondary CTE institutions; or

  » A two-year apprenticeship program that follows secondary instruction; or

- One or more proprietary institutions of higher education that offer a two-year associate degree program, are qualified to receive funds under Section 102 of HEA, and are not subject to default management plan required by the Secretary of Education.

In addition, the consortia may include postsecondary institutions that offer baccalaureate degrees and employers, business intermediaries, or labor organizations. These entities, however, would not qualify to receive funding to support programs unless, in the case of postsecondary institutions, they also qualified to be in the consortia by virtue of providing two-year programs.

Duration
Grant recipients must use funds to develop and operate four- or six-year Tech Prep programs.

Tech Prep Program Requirements
Tech Prep programs must:

1. Be carried out under an articulation agreement between the participants in the consortium.
2. Consist of a program that combines a minimum of two years of secondary education with a minimum of two years of postsecondary education or an apprenticeship program in a nonduplicative, sequential course of study; and
   - integrates academic and CTE instruction, and utilizes work-based and worksite learning experiences where possible;
   - provides technical preparation in a career field;
   - builds student competence in technical skills and in core academic subjects;
   - leads to technical skill proficiency, an industry-recognized credential, a certificate, or a degree in a specific career field;
   - leads to placement in high-skill or high-wage employment, or to further education; and
   - utilizes career and technical education programs of study (as defined in Title I), to the extent practicable.
3. Include the development of Tech Prep programs that meet academic standards developed by the state; link secondary schools and two-year postsecondary institutions, and if possible, four-year institutions, through nonduplicative sequences of

courses, the use of articulation agreements, and dual and concurrent enrollment; use, if appropriate and available, work-based learning experiences in conjunction with business and all aspects of an industry; and use educational technology and distance learning, as appropriate, to more fully involve all the participants in the consortium.

4. Include inservice professional development for teachers, faculty and administrators that supports effective implementation, joint training within the consortium, the needs, expectations and methods of business and all aspects of an industry, the use of contextual and applied curricula, instruction and assessment, the use and application of technology; and assists in accessing and utilizing data and information.

5. Include professional development programs for counselors that enable them to more effectively provide information to students regarding Tech Prep programs; support student progress in completing programs (which may include the use of graduation and career plans); provide information on related employment opportunities; ensure that students are placed in appropriate employment or further education; stay current with the needs, expectations, and methods of business and all aspects of an industry; and provide comprehensive career guidance and academic counseling to Tech Prep students, including special populations.

6. Provide equal access to members of special populations, including the development of appropriate services.

7. Provide for preparatory services that assist Tech Prep participants.

8. Coordinate with activities conducted under the Basic State Grant.

Additionally, Tech Prep programs may also be used to purchase equipment, acquire technical assistance from state and local entities with experience in Tech Prep, establish articulation agreements with a broader array of postsecondary institutions and employers using distance learning and educational technology, improve career guidance and academic counseling for participating students through the use of graduation and career plans, and develop curriculum that supports effective transitions between secondary and postsecondary programs.

Accountability

Each Tech Prep consortium must report on the performance indicators in Section 113(b) of the Basic State Grant, and a separate set of performance indicators under Section 203(e) of Tech Prep. This new set of indicators in Section 203(e) requires each consortium that receives a Tech Prep grant to report on the

following indicators of performance:

- The number of secondary and postsecondary Tech Prep students served.
- The number and percent of secondary Tech Prep students who:
  » Enroll in postsecondary education;
  » Enroll in postsecondary education in the same field;
  » Complete a state or industry-recognized certification or licensure;
  » Complete courses that earn postsecondary credit; and
  » Enroll in remedial math, writing or reading courses upon entering postsecondary education.
- The number and percent of postsecondary Tech Prep students who:
  » Are placed in a related field of employment within 12 months of graduation;
  » Complete a state or industry-recognized certification or licensure;
  » Complete a two-year degree or certificate program within the normal time; and
  » Complete a baccalaureate degree program within the normal time.

To aid in specifying which students should be included in this accountability reporting, two new definitions are included in the "Definitions" section of the Act—for secondary and postsecondary Tech Prep students. A "Secondary Education Tech Prep Student" is defined as a student who has enrolled in two courses in the secondary component of a Tech Prep program. A "Postsecondary Education Tech Prep Student" is defined as a student who has completed the secondary component of a Tech Prep program and has enrolled in the postsecondary component at an institution of higher education.

SECTION 204
CONSORTIUM APPLICATIONS

Each consortium must submit an application containing a six-year plan for Tech Prep education, and other required information, to the state at a state-specified time. The plan will be reviewed after the second year.

Approval is at the discretion of the state, which shall make this approval based on the potential of activities to create effective Tech Prep programs. Special consideration must be given to applications that:

- Provide for employment placement services or the transfer of students to baccalaureate or advanced degree programs.
- Are developed with business and industry, institutions of higher education, and labor organizations.
- Address dropout prevention, re-entry, and the

needs of special populations.
- Provide education in areas where there are workforce shortages.
- Show how students will meet high academic and employability competencies.
- Demonstrate success in or provide assurances of coordination of activities with local recipients of Basic State Grant funds.

The distribution of funds within a state must include an equitable distribution between urban and rural consortium participants.

Each consortium that receives a Tech Prep grant shall enter into an agreement with the state to meet a minimum level of performance for each of the required Tech Prep and Basic State Grant performance indicators. A state shall require consortia that do not meet the levels specified in the agreement for three years in a row to resubmit their grant applications, and the state may choose to terminate funding (even if Tech Prep grants are made by formula).

SECTION 205
REPORT
As in the 1998 Act, each state that receives a Tech Prep grant must submit an annual report to the Secretary regarding the effectiveness of Tech Prep programs and how funds are distributed within the state.

SECTION 206
AUTHORIZATION OF APPROPRIATIONS
This section authorizes appropriations for Tech Prep programs as described in this title at "such sums as necessary" for fiscal years 2007–2012. The Tech Prep Demonstration Program that received a separate authorization under the 1998 Act has been eliminated.

TITLE III
GENERAL PROVISIONS

PART A—Federal Administrative Provisions

SECTION 311
FISCAL REQUIREMENTS

Supplement Not Supplant
As in the 1998 Act, provisions are included to prohibit states from using federal Perkins funds to replace state and local funds for CTE activities, including Tech Prep.

Maintenance of Effort
The Act uses the same "maintenance of effort" language as the 1998 Act to ensure that states continue to provide funding for CTE programs at least at the level of support of the previous year. The Secretary may grant a waiver of up to 5 percent of expenditures for exceptional or uncontrollable circumstances (such as a natural disaster or a dramatic financial decline) that affect the state's ability to continue funding at the prior year's levels. The waiver would not allow for decreases in required funding levels in subsequent years.

A state continues to be allowed to make reductions in state funding proportionate to any federal reduction in support. The Secretary is required to omit from the computation of maintenance of effort special one-time expenditures within a state, such as capital expenditures and pilot projects.

SECTION 312
AUTHORITY TO MAKE PAYMENTS
As in the 1998 Act, this section states that any authority to make payments or enter into contracts under this Act will be limited to amounts that are provided in advance in appropriations Acts.

SECTION 313
CONSTRUCTION
As in the 1998 Act, this section states that there will be no federal control over any aspect of private, religious or home schools, regardless of whether a home school is treated as private or public under the law.

This section clearly states that no students attending such a school will be excluded from participation in activities funded under this Act on the basis of provisions in the 2006 Perkins Act. Therefore, state and local decision-making about such students' participation in public school activities, including CTE, will not be overruled by any provision of the 2006 Perkins Act.

SECTION 314
VOLUNTARY SELECTION AND PARTICIPATION
As in the 1998 Act, no funds under this Act may be used to require secondary school students to choose or pursue a specific career path or major. Also prohibited is any mandate that any individual participate in a CTE program, including a program that requires the attainment of a federally-funded skill level, standard or certificate of mastery.

SECTION 315
LIMITATION FOR CERTAIN STUDENTS
As in the 1998 Act, no funds may be used to provide CTE programs to students prior to the seventh grade. However, students below grade seven are not prohibited from using equipment and facilities purchased with funds under the 2006 Perkins Act.

SECTION 316
FEDERAL LAWS GUARANTEEING CIVIL RIGHTS

As in the 1998 Act, this section states that nothing in the 2006 Perkins Act will be construed to be inconsistent with applicable federal law prohibiting discrimination on the basis of race, color, sex, national origin, age or disability in the provision of federal programs or services.

SECTION 317
PARTICIPATION OF PRIVATE SCHOOL PERSONNEL AND CHILDREN

This section is amended to make allowing the participation of private school personnel in professional development programs supported by the Act required (instead of optional) to the extent practical and upon written request. A new subsection also requires local school districts to consult with representatives of private nonprofit schools, upon written request, regarding the meaningful participation of their students in CTE programs. Local school districts may then use Perkins funds to provide for this participation. This provision is consistent with many agreements already in place around the country allowing private school students to participate in CTE programs.

SECTION 318
LIMITATION ON FEDERAL REGULATIONS

As in the 1998 Act, the Secretary of Education may issue regulations under the 2006 Perkins Act "only to the extent necessary" to administer and ensure compliance with the specific requirements of the Act.

PART B—State Administrative Provisions

SECTION 321
JOINT FUNDING

As in the 1998 Act, states may use Perkins funds (except matching funds) for programs under the Wagner-Peyser Act and WIA if the programs:

- Meet the requirements of the 2006 Perkins Act and the other federal program.
- Serve the same individuals that are served under the 2006 Perkins Act.
- Provide services in a coordinated manner with services provided under the 2006 Perkins Act.
- Use funds to supplement, not supplant, funds provided from non-federal sources.

SECTION 322
PROHIBITION ON USE OF FUNDS TO INDUCE OUT-OF-STATE RELOCATION OF BUSINESSES

As in the 1998 Act, this section continues the requirement that no funds provided under the 2006 Perkins Act can be used to provide incentives or inducements to an employer to relocate a business enterprise from one state to another state, if the move would result in a reduction in the number of jobs available in the state where the business enterprise was originally located.

SECTION 323
STATE ADMINISTRATIVE COSTS

This section continues the requirement that the funding a state contributes to administrative costs must be equal to the amount provided by the state in the previous year. If the federal amount is reduced, the state may reduce its expenditures by the same rate (although matching requirements still apply to all federal administrative funding.)

SECTION 324
STUDENT ASSISTANCE AND OTHER FEDERAL PROGRAMS

As in the 1998 Act, this section stipulates that any funds under the 2006 Perkins Act that are provided to a student for the purpose of meeting attendance costs for a program will not count as income for that student for the purposes of the student's eligibility for other financial assistance from federally supported sources. Attendance costs include normal tuition and fees (including costs for equipment, materials or supplies that are required of all students), an allowance for books, supplies, transportation, dependent care and miscellaneous personal expenses for students attending at least half time.

In addition, this section permits the use of Perkins funds for meeting the costs of CTE services required in the individualized education programs of students with disabilities developed under the Individuals with Disabilities Education Act as well as services necessary to meet the requirements of Section 504 of the Rehabilitation Act of 1973 with respect to ensuring equal access to CTE.

ANALYSIS

COMPLETE TEXT OF THE CARL D. PERKINS CAREER AND TECHNICAL EDUCATION IMPROVEMENT ACT OF 2006*

SECTION 1. SHORT TITLE; TABLE OF CONTENTS.

(a) **Short Title.**—This Act may be cited as the 'Carl D. Perkins Career and Technical Education Act of 2006'.

(b) **Table of Contents.**—The table of contents for this Act is as follows:

* Pages 92–150 of this publication follow the federal government's editorial style.

SEC. 2. PURPOSE.

The purpose of this Act is to develop more fully the academic and career and technical skills of secondary education students and postsecondary education students who elect to enroll in career and technical education programs, by—

(1)   building on the efforts of States and localities to develop challenging academic and technical standards and to assist students in meeting such standards, including preparation for high skill, high wage, or high demand occupations in current or emerging professions;

(2)   promoting the development of services and activities that integrate rigorous and challenging academic and career and technical instruction, and that link secondary education and postsecondary education for participating career and technical education students;

(3)   increasing State and local flexibility in providing services and activities designed to develop, implement, and improve career and technical education, including tech prep education;

(4)   conducting and disseminating national research and disseminating information on best practices that improve career and technical education programs, services, and activities;

(5)   providing technical assistance that—

    (A)   promotes leadership, initial preparation, and professional development at the State and local levels; and

    (B)   improves the quality of career and technical education teachers, faculty, administrators, and counselors;

(6)   supporting partnerships among secondary schools, postsecondary institutions, baccalaureate degree granting institutions, area career and technical education schools, local workforce investment boards, business and industry, and intermediaries; and

(7)   providing individuals with opportunities throughout their lifetimes to develop, in conjunction with other education and training programs, the knowledge and skills needed to keep the United States competitive.

TEXT OF LAW

SEC. 3. DEFINITIONS.

Unless otherwise specified, in this Act:

(1) **Administration.**—The term 'administration', when used with respect to an eligible agency or eligible recipient, means activities necessary for the proper and efficient performance of the eligible agency or eligible recipient's duties under this Act, including the supervision of such activities. Such term does not include curriculum development activities, personnel development, or research activities.

(2) **All Aspects of an Industry.**—The term 'all aspects of an industry' means strong experience in, and comprehensive understanding of, the industry that the individual is preparing to enter, including information as described in section 118.

(3) **Area Career and Technical Education School.**— The term 'area career and technical education school' means—
   (A) a specialized public secondary school used exclusively or principally for the provision of career and technical education to individuals who are available for study in preparation for entering the labor market;
   (B) the department of a public secondary school exclusively or principally used for providing career and technical education in not fewer than 5 different occupational fields to individuals who are available for study in preparation for entering the labor market;
   (C) a public or nonprofit technical institution or career and technical education school used exclusively or principally for the provision of career and technical education to individuals who have completed or left secondary school and who are available for study in preparation for entering the labor market, if the institution or school admits, as regular students, individuals who have completed secondary school and individuals who have left secondary school; or
   (D) the department or division of an institution of higher education, that operates under the policies of the eligible agency and that provides career and technical education in not fewer than 5 different occupational fields leading to immediate employment but not necessarily leading to a baccalaureate degree, if the department or division admits, as regular students, both individuals who have completed secondary school and individuals who have left secondary school.

(4) **Articulation Agreement.**—The term 'articulation agreement' means a written commitment—
   (A) that is agreed upon at the State level or approved annually by the lead administrators of—
      (i) a secondary institution and a postsecondary educational institution; or
      (ii) a subbaccalaureate degree granting postsecondary educational institution and a baccalaureate degree granting postsecondary educational institution; and
   (B) to a program that is—
      (i) designed to provide students with a non-duplicative sequence of progressive achievement leading to technical skill proficiency, a credential, a certificate, or a degree; and
      (ii) linked through credit transfer agreements between the 2 institutions described in clause (i) or (ii) of subparagraph (A) (as the case may be).

(5) **Career and Technical Education.**—The term 'career and technical education' means organized educational activities that—
   (A) offer a sequence of courses that—
      (i) provides individuals with coherent and rigorous content aligned with chal-

lenging academic standards and relevant technical knowledge and skills needed to prepare for further education and careers in current or emerging professions;

    (ii)   provides technical skill proficiency, an industry-recognized credential, a certificate, or an associate degree; and

    (iii)   may include prerequisite courses (other than a remedial course) that meet the requirements of this subparagraph; and

  (B)   include competency-based applied learning that contributes to the academic knowledge, higher-order reasoning and problem-solving skills, work attitudes, general employability skills, technical skills, and occupation-specific skills, and knowledge of all aspects of an industry, including entrepreneurship, of an individual.

  (6) **Career and Technical Student Organization.**—

    (A)   **In General.**—The term 'career and technical student organization' means an organization for individuals enrolled in a career and technical education program that engages in career and technical education activities as an integral part of the instructional program.

    (B)   **State and National Units.**—An organization described in subparagraph (A) may have State and national units that aggregate the work and purposes of instruction in career and technical education at the local level.

  (7) **Career Guidance and Academic Counseling.**—The term 'career guidance and academic counseling' means guidance and counseling that—

    (A)   provides access for students (and parents, as appropriate) to information regarding career awareness and planning with respect to an individual's occupational and academic future; and

    (B)   provides information with respect to career options, financial aid, and postsecondary options, including baccalaureate degree programs.

  (8) **Charter Schools.**—The term 'charter school' has the meaning given the term in section 5210 of the Elementary and Secondary Education Act of 1965.

  (9) **Cooperative Education.**—The term 'cooperative education' means a method of education for individuals who, through written cooperative arrangements between a school and employers, receive instruction, including required rigorous and challenging academic courses and related career and technical education instruction, by alternation of study in school with a job in any occupational field, which alternation—

    (A)   shall be planned and supervised by the school and employer so that each contributes to the education and employability of the individual; and

    (B)   may include an arrangement in which work periods and school attendance may be on alternate half days, full days, weeks, or other periods of time in fulfilling the cooperative program.

  (10) **Displaced Homemaker.**—The term 'displaced homemaker' means an individual who—

    (A) (i)   has worked primarily without remuneration to care for a home and family, and for that reason has diminished marketable skills;

        (ii)   has been dependent on the income of another family member but is no longer supported by that income; or

        (iii)   is a parent whose youngest dependent child will become ineligible to receive assistance under part A of title IV of the Social Security Act (42 U.S.C. 601 et seq.) not later than 2 years after the date on which the parent applies for assistance under such title; and

    (B)   is unemployed or underemployed and is experiencing difficulty in obtaining or upgrading employment.

TEXT OF LAW

(11) Educational Service Agency.—The term 'educational service agency' has the meaning given the term in section 9101 of the Elementary and Secondary Education Act of 1965.

(12) Eligible Agency.—The term 'eligible agency' means a State board designated or created consistent with State law as the sole State agency responsible for the administration of career and technical education in the State or for the supervision of the administration of career and technical education in the State.

(13) Eligible Institution.—The term 'eligible institution' means—

    (A) a public or nonprofit private institution of higher education that offers career and technical education courses that lead to technical skill proficiency, an industry-recognized credential, a certificate, or a degree;

    (B) a local educational agency providing education at the postsecondary level;

    (C) an area career and technical education school providing education at the postsecondary level;

    (D) a postsecondary educational institution controlled by the Bureau of Indian Affairs or operated by or on behalf of any Indian tribe that is eligible to contract with the Secretary of the Interior for the administration of programs under the Indian Self-Determination and Education Assistance Act (25 U.S.C. 450 et seq.) or the Act of April 16, 1934 (25 U.S.C. 452 et seq.);

    (E) an educational service agency; or

    (F) a consortium of 2 or more of the entities described in subparagraphs (A) through (E).

(14) Eligible Recipient.—The term 'eligible recipient' means—

    (A) a local educational agency (including a public charter school that operates as a local educational agency), an area career and technical education school, an educational service agency, or a consortium, eligible to receive assistance under section 131; or

    (B) an eligible institution or consortium of eligible institutions eligible to receive assistance under section 132.

(15) Governor.—The term 'Governor' means the chief executive officer of a State.

(16) Individual with Limited English Proficiency.— The term 'individual with limited English proficiency' means a secondary school student, an adult, or an out-of-school youth, who has limited ability in speaking, reading, writing, or understanding the English language, and—

    (A) whose native language is a language other than English; or

    (B) who lives in a family or community environment in which a language other than English is the dominant language.

(17) Individual with a Disability.—

    (A) In General.—The term 'individual with a disability' means an individual with any disability (as defined in section 3 of the Americans with Disabilities Act of 1990 (42 U.S.C. 12102)).

    (B) Individuals with Disabilities.—The term 'individuals with disabilities' means more than 1 individual with a disability.

(18) Institution of Higher Education.—The term 'institution of higher education' has the meaning given the term in section 101 of the Higher Education Act of 1965.

(19) Local Educational Agency.—The term 'local educational agency' has the meaning given the term in section 9101 of the Elementary and Secondary Education Act of 1965.

(20) Non-traditional Fields.—The term 'non-traditional fields' means occupations or fields of

TEXT OF LAW

work, including careers in computer science, technology, and other current and emerging high skill occupations, for which individuals from one gender comprise less than 25 percent of the individuals employed in each such occupation or field of work.

(21) **Outlying Area.**—The term 'outlying area' means the United States Virgin Islands, Guam, American Samoa, the Commonwealth of the Northern Mariana Islands, and the Republic of Palau.

(22) **Postsecondary Educational Institution.**—The term 'postsecondary educational institution' means—

    (A) an institution of higher education that provides not less than a 2-year program of instruction that is acceptable for credit toward a bachelor's degree;

    (B) a tribally controlled college or university; or

    (C) a nonprofit educational institution offering certificate or apprenticeship programs at the postsecondary level.

(23) **Postsecondary Education Tech Prep Student.**—The term 'postsecondary education tech prep student' means a student who—

    (A) has completed the secondary education component of a tech prep program; and

    (B) has enrolled in the postsecondary education component of a tech prep program at an institution of higher education described in clause (i) or (ii) of section 203(a)(1)(B).

(24) **School Dropout.**—The term 'school dropout' means an individual who is no longer attending any school and who has not received a secondary school diploma or its recognized equivalent.

(25) **Scientifically Based Research.**—The term 'scientifically based research' means research that is carried out using scientifically based research standards, as defined in section 102 of the Education Sciences Reform Act of 2002 (20 U.S.C. 9501).

(26) **Secondary Education Tech Prep Student.**—The term 'secondary education tech prep student' means a secondary education student who has enrolled in 2 courses in the secondary education component of a tech prep program.

(27) **Secondary School.**—The term 'secondary school' has the meaning given the term in section 9101 of the Elementary and Secondary Education Act of 1965.

(28) **Secretary.**—The term 'Secretary' means the Secretary of Education.

(29) **Special Populations.**—The term 'special populations' means—

    (A) individuals with disabilities;

    (B) individuals from economically disadvantaged families, including foster children;

    (C) individuals preparing for non-traditional fields;

    (D) single parents, including single pregnant women;

    (E) displaced homemakers; and

    (F) individuals with limited English proficiency.

(30) **State.**—The term 'State', unless otherwise specified, means each of the several States of the United States, the District of Columbia, the Commonwealth of Puerto Rico, and each outlying area.

(31) **Support Services.**—The term 'support services' means services related to curriculum modification, equipment modification, classroom modification, supportive personnel, and instructional aids and devices.

TEXT OF LAW

(32) **Tech Prep Program.**—The term 'tech prep program' means a tech prep program described in section 203(c).

(33) **Tribally Controlled College or University.**—The term 'tribally controlled college or university' has the meaning given the term in section 2(a) of the Tribally Controlled College or University Assistance Act of 1978 (25 U.S.C. 1801(a)).

(34) **Tribally Controlled Postsecondary Career and Technical Institution.**—The term 'tribally controlled postsecondary career and technical institution' means an institution of higher education (as defined in section 101 of the Higher Education Act of 1965, except that subsection (a)(2) of such section shall not be applicable and the reference to Secretary in subsection (a)(5) of such section shall be deemed to refer to the Secretary of the Interior) that—

  (A) is formally controlled, or has been formally sanctioned or chartered, by the governing body of an Indian tribe or Indian tribes;

  (B) offers a technical degree or certificate granting program;

  (C) is governed by a board of directors or trustees, a majority of whom are Indians;

  (D) demonstrates adherence to stated goals, a philosophy, or a plan of operation, that fosters individual Indian economic and self-sufficiency opportunity, including programs that are appropriate to stated tribal goals of developing individual entrepreneurships and self-sustaining economic infrastructures on reservations;

  (E) has been in operation for at least 3 years;

  (F) holds accreditation with or is a candidate for accreditation by a nationally recognized accrediting authority for postsecondary career and technical education; and

  (G) enrolls the full-time equivalent of not less than 100 students, of whom a majority are Indians.

SEC. 4. TRANSITION PROVISIONS.

The Secretary shall take such steps as the Secretary determines to be appropriate to provide for the orderly transition to the authority of this Act (as amended by the Carl D. Perkins Career and Technical Education Improvement Act of 2006) from any authority under the provisions of the Carl D. Perkins Vocational and Technical Education Act of 1998, as in effect on the day before the date of enactment of the Carl D. Perkins Career and Technical Education Improvement Act of 2006. The Secretary shall give each eligible agency the opportunity to submit a transition plan for the first fiscal year following the date of enactment of the Carl D. Perkins Career and Technical Education Improvement Act of 2006.

SEC. 5. PRIVACY.

(a) **GEPA.**—Nothing in this Act shall be construed to supersede the privacy protections afforded parents and students under section 444 of the General Education Provisions Act (20 U.S.C. 1232g).

(b) **Prohibition on Development of National Database.**—Nothing in this Act shall be construed to permit the development of a national database of personally identifiable information on individuals receiving services under this Act.

SEC. 6. LIMITATION.

All of the funds made available under this Act shall be used in accordance with the requirements of this Act.

SEC. 7. SPECIAL RULE.

In the case of a local community in which no employees are represented by a labor organization, for purposes of this Act, the term 'representatives of employees' shall be substituted for 'labor organization'.

SEC. 8. PROHIBITIONS.

(a) **Local Control.**—Nothing in this Act shall be construed to authorize an officer or employee of the Federal Government to mandate, direct, or control a State, local educational agency, or school's curriculum, program of instruction, or allocation of State or local resources, or mandate a State or any subdivision thereof to spend any funds or incur any costs not paid for under this Act, except as required under sections 112(b), 311(b), and 323.

(b) **No Preclusion of Other Assistance.**—Any State that declines to submit an application to the Secretary for assistance under this Act shall not be precluded from applying for assistance under any other program administered by the Secretary.

(c) **Prohibition on Requiring Federal Approval or Certification of Standards.**—Notwithstanding any other provision of Federal law, no State shall be required to have academic and career and technical content standards or student academic and career and technical achievement standards approved or certified by the Federal Government, in order to receive assistance under this Act.

(d) **Rule of Construction.**—Nothing in this section shall be construed to affect the requirements under section 113.

(e) **Coherent and Rigorous Content.**—For the purposes of this Act, coherent and rigorous content shall be determined by the State consistent with section 1111(b)(1)(D) of the Elementary and Secondary Education Act of 1965.

SEC. 9. AUTHORIZATION OF APPROPRIATIONS.

There is authorized to be appropriated to carry out this Act (other than sections 114, 117, and 118, and title II) such sums as may be necessary for each of the fiscal years 2007 through 2012.

T I T L E **I**
CAREER AND TECHNICAL EDUCATION ASSISTANCE TO THE STATES

PART A—ALLOTMENT AND ALLOCATION

SEC. 111. RESERVATIONS AND STATE ALLOTMENT.

(a) **Reservations and State Allotment.**—

   (1) **Reservations.**—From the sum appropriated under section 9 for each fiscal year, the Secretary shall reserve—
      (A) 0.13 percent to carry out section 115; and
      (B) 1.50 percent to carry out section 116, of which—
         (i) 1.25 percent of the sum shall be available to carry out section 116(b); and
         (ii) 0.25 percent of the sum shall be available to carry out section 116(h).

(2) **State Allotment Formula.**—Subject to paragraphs (3), (4), and (5), from the remainder of the sum appropriated under section 9 and not reserved under paragraph (1) for a fiscal year, the Secretary shall allot to a State for the fiscal year—

(A) an amount that bears the same ratio to 50 percent of the sum being allotted as the product of the population aged 15 to 19 inclusive, in the State in the fiscal year preceding the fiscal year for which the determination is made and the State's allotment ratio bears to the sum of the corresponding products for all the States;

(B) an amount that bears the same ratio to 20 percent of the sum being allotted as the product of the population aged 20 to 24, inclusive, in the State in the fiscal year preceding the fiscal year for which the determination is made and the State's allotment ratio bears to the sum of the corresponding products for all the States;

(C) an amount that bears the same ratio to 15 percent of the sum being allotted as the product of the population aged 25 to 65, inclusive, in the State in the fiscal year preceding the fiscal year for which the determination is made and the State's allotment ratio bears to the sum of the corresponding products for all the States; and

(D) an amount that bears the same ratio to 15 percent of the sum being allotted as the amounts allotted to the State under subparagraphs (A), (B), and (C) for such years bears to the sum of the amounts allotted to all the States under subparagraphs (A), (B), and (C) for such year.

(3) **Minimum Allotment for Years with No Additional Funds.**—

(A) **In General.**—Notwithstanding any other provision of law and subject to subparagraphs (B) and (C), and paragraph (5), for a fiscal year for which there are no additional funds (as such term is defined in paragraph (4)(D)), no State shall receive for such fiscal year under this subsection less than 1/2 of 1 percent of the amount appropriated under section 9 and not reserved under paragraph (1) for such fiscal year. Amounts necessary for increasing such payments to States to comply with the preceding sentence shall be obtained by ratably reducing the amounts to be paid to other States.

(B) **Requirement.**—No State, by reason of the application of subparagraph (A), shall receive for a fiscal year more than 150 percent of the amount the State received under this subsection for the preceding fiscal year.

(C) **Special Rule.**—

(i) **In General.**—Subject to paragraph (5), no State, by reason of the application of subparagraph (A), shall be allotted for a fiscal year more than the lesser of—

(I) 150 percent of the amount that the State received in the preceding fiscal year; and

(II) the amount calculated under clause (ii).

(ii) **Amount.**—The amount calculated under this clause shall be determined by multiplying—

(I) the number of individuals in the State counted under paragraph (2) in the preceding fiscal year; by

(II) 150 percent of the national average per pupil payment made with funds available under this section for that year.

(4) **Minimum Allotment for Years with Additional Funds.**—

(A) **In General.**—Subject to subparagraph (B) and paragraph (5), for a fiscal year for which there are additional funds, no State shall receive for such fiscal year under this subsection less than 1/2 of 1 percent of the amount appropriated under section 9 and not reserved under paragraph (1) for such fiscal year. Amounts necessary for increasing such payments to States to comply with the preceding sentence shall be obtained by ratably reducing the amounts to be paid to other States.

(B) **Special Rule.**—In the case of a qualifying State, the minimum allotment under subparagraph (A) for a fiscal year for the qualifying State shall be the lesser of—

    (i) 1/2 of 1 percent of the amount appropriated under section 9 and not reserved under paragraph (1) for such fiscal year; and

    (ii) the sum of—

        (I) the amount the qualifying State was allotted under paragraph (2) for fiscal year 2006 (as such paragraph was in effect on the day before the date of enactment of the Carl D. Perkins Career and Technical Education Improvement Act of 2006); and

        (II) the product of—

            (aa) 1/3 of the additional funds; multiplied by

            (bb) the quotient of—

                (AA) the qualifying State's ratio described in subparagraph (C) for the fiscal year for which the determination is made; divided by

                (BB) the sum of all such ratios for all qualifying States for the fiscal year for which the determination is made.

(C) **Ratio.**—For purposes of subparagraph (B)(ii)(II)(bb)(AA), the ratio for a qualifying State for a fiscal year shall be 1.00 less the quotient of—

    (i) the amount the qualifying State was allotted under paragraph (2) for fiscal year 2006 (as such paragraph was in effect on the day before the date of enactment of the Carl D. Perkins Career and Technical Education Improvement Act of 2006); divided by

    (ii) 1/2 of 1 percent of the amount appropriated under section 9 and not reserved under paragraph (1) for the fiscal year for which the determination is made.

(D) **Definitions.**—In this paragraph:

    (i) **Additional Funds.**—The term 'additional funds' means the amount by which—

        (I) the sum appropriated under section 9 and not reserved under paragraph (1) for a fiscal year; exceeds

        (II) the sum of—

            (aa) the amount allotted under paragraph (2) for fiscal year 2006 (as such paragraph (2) was in effect on the day before the date of enactment of the Carl D. Perkins Career and Technical Education Improvement Act of 2006);

            (bb) the amount reserved under paragraph (1)(C) for fiscal year 2006 (as such paragraph (1)(C) was so in effect); and

            (cc) $827,671.

    (ii) **Qualifying State.**—The term 'qualifying State' means a State (except the United States Virgin Islands) that, for the fiscal year for which a determination under this paragraph is made, would receive, under the allotment formula under paragraph (2) (without the application of this paragraph and paragraphs (3) and (5)), an amount that would be less than the amount the State would receive under subparagraph (A) for such fiscal year.

(5) **Hold Harmless.**—

    (A) **In General.**—No State shall receive an allotment under this section for a fiscal year that is less than the allotment the State received under part A of title I of the Carl D. Perkins Vocational and Applied Technology Education Act (20 U.S.C. 2311 et seq.) (as such part was in effect on the day before the date of enactment of the Carl D. Perkins Vocational and Applied Technology Education Amendments of 1998) for fiscal year 1998.

    (B) **Ratable Reduction.**—If for any fiscal year the amount appropriated for allotments

TEXT OF LAW

under this section is insufficient to satisfy the provisions of subparagraph (A), the payments to all States under such subparagraph shall be ratably reduced.

(b) **Reallotment.**—If the Secretary determines that any amount of any State's allotment under subsection (a) for any fiscal year will not be required for such fiscal year for carrying out the activities for which such amount has been allotted, the Secretary shall make such amount available for reallotment. Any such reallotment among other States shall occur on such dates during the same year as the Secretary shall fix, and shall be made on the basis of criteria established by regulation. No funds may be reallotted for any use other than the use for which the funds were appropriated. Any amount reallotted to a State under this subsection for any fiscal year shall remain available for obligation during the succeeding fiscal year and shall be deemed to be part of the State's allotment for the year in which the amount is obligated.

(c) **Allotment Ratio.**—

   (1) **In General.**—The allotment ratio for any State shall be 1.00 less the product of—

      (A) 0.50; and

      (B) the quotient obtained by dividing the per capita income for the State by the per capita income for all the States (exclusive of the Commonwealth of Puerto Rico and the United States Virgin Islands), except that—

         (i) the allotment ratio in no case shall be more than 0.60 or less than 0.40; and

         (ii) the allotment ratio for the Commonwealth of Puerto Rico and the United States Virgin Islands shall be 0.60.

   (2) **Promulgation.**—The allotment ratios shall be promulgated by the Secretary for each fiscal year between October 1 and December 31 of the fiscal year preceding the fiscal year for which the determination is made. Allotment ratios shall be computed on the basis of the average of the appropriate per capita incomes for the 3 most recent consecutive fiscal years for which satisfactory data are available.

   (3) **Definition of Per Capita Income.**—For the purpose of this section, the term 'per capita income' means, with respect to a fiscal year, the total personal income in the calendar year ending in such year, divided by the population of the area concerned in such year.

   (4) **Population Determination.**—For the purposes of this section, population shall be determined by the Secretary on the basis of the latest estimates available to the Department of Education.

(d) **Definition of State.**—For the purpose of this section, the term 'State' means each of the several States of the United States, the District of Columbia, the Commonwealth of Puerto Rico, and the United States Virgin Islands.

SEC. 112. WITHIN STATE ALLOCATION.

(a) **In General.**—From the amount allotted to each State under section 111 for a fiscal year, the eligible agency shall make available—

   (1) not less than 85 percent for distribution under section 131 or 132, of which not more than 10 percent of the 85 percent may be used in accordance with subsection (c);

   (2) not more than 10 percent to carry out State leadership activities described in section 124, of which—

      (A) an amount equal to not more than 1 percent of the amount allotted to the State under section 111 for the fiscal year shall be made available to serve individuals in

State institutions, such as State correctional institutions and institutions that serve individuals with disabilities; and

    (B) not less than $60,000 and not more than $150,000 shall be available for services that prepare individuals for non-traditional fields; and

(3) an amount equal to not more than 5 percent, or $250,000, whichever is greater, for administration of the State plan, which may be used for the costs of—

    (A) developing the State plan;

    (B) reviewing a local plan;

    (C) monitoring and evaluating program effectiveness;

    (D) assuring compliance with all applicable Federal laws;

    (E) providing technical assistance; and

    (F) supporting and developing State data systems relevant to the provisions of this Act.

(b) **Matching Requirement.**—Each eligible agency receiving funds made available under subsection (a)(3) shall match, from non-Federal sources and on a dollar-for-dollar basis, the funds received under subsection (a)(3).

(c) **Reserve.**—From amounts made available under subsection (a)(1) to carry out this subsection, an eligible agency may award grants to eligible recipients for career and technical education activities described in section 135 in—

(1) rural areas;

(2) areas with high percentages of career and technical education students; and

(3) areas with high numbers of career and technical education students.

SEC. 113. ACCOUNTABILITY.

(a) **Purpose.**—The purpose of this section is to establish and support State and local performance accountability systems, comprised of the activities described in this section, to assess the effectiveness of the State and the eligible recipients of the State in achieving statewide progress in career and technical education, and to optimize the return of investment of Federal funds in career and technical education activities.

(b) **State Performance Measures.**—

(1) **In General.**—Each eligible agency, with input from eligible recipients, shall establish performance measures for a State that consist of—

    (A) the core indicators of performance described in subparagraphs (A) and (B) of paragraph (2);

    (B) any additional indicators of performance (if any) identified by the eligible agency under paragraph (2)(C); and

    (C) a State adjusted level of performance described in paragraph (3)(A) for each core indicator of performance, and State levels of performance described in paragraph (3)(B) for each additional indicator of performance.

(2) **Indicators of Performance.**—

    (A) **Core Indicators of Performance for Career and Technical Education Students at the Secondary Level.**—Each eligible agency shall identify in the State plan core indicators of performance for career and technical education students at the secondary level that are valid and reliable, and that include, at a minimum, measures of each of the following:

        (i) Student attainment of challenging academic content standards and

TEXT OF LAW

student academic achievement standards, as adopted by a State in accordance with section 1111(b)(1) of the Elementary and Secondary Education Act of 1965 and measured by the State determined proficient levels on the academic assessments described in section 1111(b)(3) of such Act.

    (ii)   Student attainment of career and technical skill proficiencies, including student achievement on technical assessments, that are aligned with industry-recognized standards, if available and appropriate.

    (iii)   Student rates of attainment of each of the following:

        (I)   A secondary school diploma.

        (II)   A General Education Development (GED) credential, or other State-recognized equivalent (including recognized alternative standards for individuals with disabilities).

        (III)   A proficiency credential, certificate, or degree, in conjunction with a secondary school diploma (if such credential, certificate, or degree is offered by the State in conjunction with a secondary school diploma).

    (iv)   Student graduation rates (as described in section 1111(b)(2)(C)(vi) of the Elementary and Secondary Education Act of 1965).

    (v)   Student placement in postsecondary education or advanced training, in military service, or in employment.

    (vi)   Student participation in and completion of career and technical education programs that lead to non-traditional fields.

(B) **Core Indicators of Performance for Career and Technical Education Students at the Postsecondary Level.**—Each eligible agency shall identify in the State plan core indicators of performance for career and technical education students at the postsecondary level that are valid and reliable, and that include, at a minimum, measures of each of the following:

    (i)   Student attainment of challenging career and technical skill proficiencies, including student achievement on technical assessments, that are aligned with industry-recognized standards, if available and appropriate.

    (ii)   Student attainment of an industry-recognized credential, a certificate, or a degree.

    (iii)   Student retention in postsecondary education or transfer to a baccalaureate degree program.

    (iv)   Student placement in military service or apprenticeship programs or placement or retention in employment, including placement in high skill, high wage, or high demand occupations or professions.

    (v)   Student participation in, and completion of, career and technical education programs that lead to employment in non-traditional fields.

(C) **Additional Indicators of Performance.**—An eligible agency, with input from eligible recipients, may identify in the State plan additional indicators of performance for career and technical education activities authorized under this title, such as attainment of self-sufficiency.

(D) **Existing Indicators.**—If a State has developed, prior to the date of enactment of the Carl D. Perkins Career and Technical Education Improvement Act of 2006, State career and technical education performance measures that meet the requirements of this section (as amended by such Act), the State may use such performance measures to measure the progress of career and technical education students.

(E) **State Role.**—Indicators of performance described in this paragraph shall be established solely by each eligible agency with input from eligible recipients.

(F) **Alignment of Performance Indicators.**—In the course of developing core indicators of performance and additional indicators of performance, an eligible agency shall, to the greatest extent possible, align the indicators so that substantially similar information gathered for other State and Federal programs, or for any other purpose, is used to meet the requirements of this section.

(3) **State Levels of Performance.—**

(A) **State Adjusted Levels of Performance for Core Indicators of Performance.—**

(i) **In General.**—Each eligible agency, with input from eligible recipients, shall establish in the State plan submitted under section 122, levels of performance for each of the core indicators of performance described in subparagraphs (A) and (B) of paragraph (2) for career and technical education activities authorized under this title. The levels of performance established under this subparagraph shall, at a minimum—

(I) be expressed in a percentage or numerical form, so as to be objective, quantifiable, and measurable; and

(II) require the State to continually make progress toward improving the performance of career and technical education students.

(ii) **Identification in the State Plan.**—Subject to section 4, each eligible agency shall identify, in the State plan submitted under section 122, levels of performance for each of the core indicators of performance for the first 2 program years covered by the State plan.

(iii) **Agreement on State Adjusted Levels of Performance for First 2 Years.**—The Secretary and each eligible agency shall reach agreement on the levels of performance for each of the core indicators of performance, for the first 2 program years covered by the State plan, taking into account the levels identified in the State plan under clause (ii) and the factors described in clause (vi). The levels of performance agreed to under this clause shall be considered to be the State adjusted level of performance for the State for such years and shall be incorporated into the State plan prior to the approval of such plan.

(iv) **Role of the Secretary.**—The role of the Secretary in the agreement described in clauses (iii) and (v) is limited to reaching agreement on the percentage or number of students who attain the State adjusted levels of performance.

(v) **Agreement on State Adjusted Levels of Performance for Subsequent Years.**—Prior to the third and fifth program years covered by the State plan, the Secretary and each eligible agency shall reach agreement on the State adjusted levels of performance for each of the core indicators of performance for the corresponding subsequent program years covered by the State plan, taking into account the factors described in clause (vi). The State adjusted levels of performance agreed to under this clause shall be considered to be the State adjusted levels of performance for the State for such years and shall be incorporated into the State plan.

(vi) **Factors.**—The agreement described in clause (iii) or (v) shall take into account—

(I) how the levels of performance involved compare with the State adjusted levels of performance established for other States, taking into account factors including the characteristics of participants when the participants entered the program and the services or instruction to be provided; and

(II) the extent to which such levels of performance promote continuous improvement on the indicators of performance by such State.

(vii) **Revisions.**—If unanticipated circumstances arise in a State resulting in a significant change in the factors described in clause (vi), the eligible agency may request that the State adjusted levels of performance agreed to under clause (iii) or (v) be revised. The Secretary shall issue objective criteria and methods for making such revisions.

(B) **Levels of Performance for Additional Indicators.**—Each eligible agency shall identify in the State plan State levels of performance for each of the additional indicators of performance described in paragraph (2)(C). Such levels shall be considered to be the State levels of performance for purposes of this title.

(4) **Local Levels of Performance.—**

    (A) **Local Adjusted Levels of Performance for Core Indicators of Performance.—**

        (i) **In General.—**Each eligible recipient shall agree to accept the State adjusted levels of performance established under paragraph (3) as local adjusted levels of performances, or negotiate with the State to reach agreement on new local adjusted levels of performance, for each of the core indicators of performance described in subparagraphs (A) and (B) of paragraph (2) for career and technical education activities authorized under this title. The levels of performance established under this subparagraph shall, at a minimum—

            (I) be expressed in a percentage or numerical form, consistent with the State levels of performance established under paragraph (3), so as to be objective, quantifiable, and measurable; and

            (II) require the eligible recipient to continually make progress toward improving the performance of career and technical education students.

        (ii) **Identification in the Local Plan.—**Each eligible recipient shall identify, in the local plan submitted under section 134, levels of performance for each of the core indicators of performance for the first 2 program years covered by the local plan.

        (iii) **Agreement on Local Adjusted Levels of Performance for First 2 Years.—**The eligible agency and each eligible recipient shall reach agreement, as described in clause (i), on the eligible recipient's levels of performance for each of the core indicators of performance for the first 2 program years covered by the local plan, taking into account the levels identified in the local plan under clause (ii) and the factors described in clause (v). The levels of performance agreed to under this clause shall be considered to be the local adjusted levels of performance for the eligible recipient for such years and shall be incorporated into the local plan prior to the approval of such plan.

        (iv) **Agreement on Local Adjusted Levels of Performance for Subsequent Years.—**Prior to the third and fifth program years covered by the local plan, the eligible agency and each eligible recipient shall reach agreement on the local adjusted levels of performance for each of the core indicators of performance for the corresponding subsequent program years covered by the local plan, taking into account the factors described in clause (v). The local adjusted levels of performance agreed to under this clause shall be considered to be the local adjusted levels of performance for the eligible recipient for such years and shall be incorporated into the local plan.

        (v) **Factors.—**The agreement described in clause (iii) or (iv) shall take into account—

            (I) how the levels of performance involved compare with the local adjusted levels of performance established for other eligible recipients in the State, taking into account factors including the characteristics of participants when the participants entered the program and the services or instruction to be provided; and

            (II) the extent to which the local adjusted levels of performance promote continuous improvement on the core indicators of performance by the eligible recipient.

        (vi) **Revisions.—**If unanticipated circumstances arise with respect to an eligible recipient resulting in a significant change in the factors described in clause (v), the eligible recipient may request that the local adjusted levels of performance agreed to under clause (iii) or (iv) be revised. The eligible agency shall issue objective criteria and methods for making such revisions.

    (B) **Levels of Performance for Additional Indicators.—**Each eligible recipient may identify, in the local plan, local levels of performance for any additional indicators of performance described in paragraph (2)(C). Such levels shall be considered to be the local levels of performance for purposes of this title.

    (C)   **Local Report.**—

        (i)   **Content of Report.**—Each eligible recipient that receives an allocation described in section 112 shall annually prepare and submit to the eligible agency a report, which shall include the data described in clause (ii)(I), regarding the progress of such recipient in achieving the local adjusted levels of performance on the core indicators of performance.

        (ii)   **Data.**—Except as provided in clauses (iii) and (iv), each eligible recipient that receives an allocation described in section 112 shall—

            (I)   disaggregate data for each of the indicators of performance under paragraph (2) for the categories of students described in section 1111(h)(1)(C)(i) of the Elementary and Secondary Education Act of 1965 and section 3(29) that are served under this Act; and

            (II)   identify and quantify any disparities or gaps in performance between any such category of students and the performance of all students served by the eligible recipient under this Act.

        (iii)   **Nonduplication.**—The eligible agency shall ensure, in a manner that is consistent with the actions of the Secretary under subsection (c)(3), that each eligible recipient does not report duplicative information under this section.

        (iv)   **Rules for Reporting of Data.**—The disaggregation of data under clause (ii) shall not be required when the number of students in a category is insufficient to yield statistically reliable information or when the results would reveal personally identifiable information about an individual student.

        (v)   **Availability.**—The report described in clause (i) shall be made available to the public through a variety of formats, including electronically through the Internet.

(c)   **Report.**—

    (1)   **In General.**—Each eligible agency that receives an allotment under section 111 shall annually prepare and submit to the Secretary a report regarding—

        (A)   the progress of the State in achieving the State adjusted levels of performance on the core indicators of performance; and

        (B)   information on the levels of performance achieved by the State with respect to the additional indicators of performance, including the levels of performance for special populations.

    (2)   **Data.**—Except as provided in paragraphs (3) and (4), each eligible agency that receives an allotment under section 111 or 201 shall—

        (A)   disaggregate data for each of the indicators of performance under subsection (b)(2) for the categories of students described in section 1111(h)(1)(C)(i) of the Elementary and Secondary Education Act of 1965 and section 3(29) that are served under this Act; and

        (B)   identify and quantify any disparities or gaps in performance between any such category of students and the performance of all students served by the eligible agency under this Act, which shall include a quantifiable description of the progress each such category of students served by the eligible agency under this Act has made in meeting the State adjusted levels of performance.

    (3)   **Nonduplication.**—The Secretary shall ensure that each eligible agency does not report duplicative information under this section.

    (4)   **Rules for Reporting of Data.**—The disaggregation of data under paragraph (2) shall not

TEXT OF LAW

be required when the number of students in a category is insufficient to yield statistically reliable information or when the results would reveal personally identifiable information about an individual student.

    (5) **Information Dissemination.**—The Secretary—
- (A) shall make the information contained in such reports available to the general public through a variety of formats, including electronically through the Internet;
- (B) shall disseminate State-by-State comparisons of the information; and
- (C) shall provide the appropriate committees of Congress with copies of such reports.

SEC. 114. NATIONAL ACTIVITIES.

    (a) **Program Performance Information.**—

    (1) **In General.**—The Secretary shall collect performance information about, and report on, the condition of career and technical education and on the effectiveness of State and local programs, services, and activities carried out under this title in order to provide the Secretary and Congress, as well as Federal, State, local, and tribal agencies, with information relevant to improvement in the quality and effectiveness of career and technical education. The Secretary shall report annually to Congress on the Secretary's aggregate analysis of performance information collected each year pursuant to this title, including an analysis of performance data regarding special populations.

    (2) **Compatibility.**—The Secretary shall, to the extent feasible, ensure that the performance information system is compatible with other Federal information systems.

    (3) **Assessments.**—As a regular part of its assessments, the National Center for Education Statistics shall collect and report information on career and technical education for a nationally representative sample of students. Such assessment may include international comparisons in the aggregate.

    (b) **Miscellaneous Provisions.**—

    (1) **Collection of Information at Reasonable Cost.**— The Secretary shall take such action as may be necessary to secure at reasonable cost the information required by this title. To ensure reasonable cost, the Secretary, in consultation with the National Center for Education Statistics, the Office of Vocational and Adult Education, and an entity assisted under section 118 (if applicable), shall determine the methodology to be used and the frequency with which information is to be collected.

    (2) **Cooperation of States.**—All eligible agencies receiving assistance under this Act shall cooperate with the Secretary in implementing the information systems developed pursuant to this Act.

    (c) **Single Plan for Research, Development, Dissemination, Evaluation, and Assessment.**—

    (1) **In General.**—The Secretary may, directly or through grants, contracts, or cooperative agreements, carry out research, development, dissemination, evaluation and assessment, capacity building, and technical assistance with regard to the career and technical education programs under this Act. The Secretary shall develop a single plan for such activities.

    (2) **Plan.**—Such plan shall—
- (A) identify the career and technical education activities described in paragraph (1) that the Secretary will carry out under this section;

TEXT OF LAW

(B)   describe how the Secretary will evaluate such career and technical education activities in accordance with subsection (d)(2); and

(C)   include such other information as the Secretary determines to be appropriate.

(d)   **Advisory Panel; Evaluation; Reports.—**

(1)   **Independent Advisory Panel.—**

(A)   **In General.—**The Secretary shall appoint an independent advisory panel to advise the Secretary on the implementation of the assessment described in paragraph (2), including the issues to be addressed and the methodology of the studies involved to ensure that the assessment adheres to the highest standards of quality.

(B)   **Members.—**The advisory panel shall consist of—

(i)   educators, administrators, State directors of career and technical education, and chief executives, including those with expertise in the integration of academic and career and technical education;

(ii)   experts in evaluation, research, and assessment;

(iii)   representatives of labor organizations and businesses, including small businesses, economic development entities, and workforce investment entities;

(iv)   parents;

(v)   career guidance and academic counseling professionals; and

(vi)   other individuals and intermediaries with relevant expertise.

(C)   **Independent Analysis.—**The advisory panel shall transmit to the Secretary, the relevant committees of Congress, and the Library of Congress an independent analysis of the findings and recommendations resulting from the assessment described in paragraph (2).

(D)   **FACA.—**The Federal Advisory Committee Act (5 U.S.C. App.) shall not apply to the panel established under this paragraph.

(2)   **Evaluation and Assessment.—**

(A)   **In General.—**From amounts made available under subsection (e), the Secretary shall provide for the conduct of an independent evaluation and assessment of career and technical education programs under this Act, including the implementation of the Carl D. Perkins Career and Technical Education Improvement Act of 2006, to the extent practicable, through studies and analyses conducted independently through grants, contracts, and cooperative agreements that are awarded on a competitive basis.

(B)   **Contents.—**The assessment required under subparagraph (A) shall include descriptions and evaluations of—

(i)   the extent to which State, local, and tribal entities have developed, implemented, or improved State and local career and technical education programs assisted under this Act;

(ii)   the preparation and qualifications of teachers and faculty of career and technical education (such as meeting State established teacher certification or licensing requirements), as well as shortages of such teachers and faculty;

(iii)   academic and career and technical education achievement and employment outcomes of career and technical education, including analyses of—

(I)   the extent and success of the integration of rigorous and challenging academic and career and technical education for students participating in career and technical education programs, including a review of the effect of such integration on the academic and technical proficiency achievement of such students (including the number of such students receiving a secondary school diploma); and

(II)   the extent to which career and technical education programs prepare students, including special populations, for subsequent

TEXT OF LAW

employment in high skill, high wage occupations (including those in which mathematics and science skills are critical), or for participation in postsecondary education;

(iv) employer involvement in, and satisfaction with, career and technical education programs and career and technical education students' preparation for employment;

(v) the participation of students in career and technical education programs;

(vi) the use of educational technology and distance learning with respect to career and technical education and tech prep programs; and

(vii) the effect of State and local adjusted levels of performance and State and local levels of performance on the delivery of career and technical education services, including the percentage of career and technical education and tech prep students meeting the adjusted levels of performance described in section 113.

(C) **Reports.—**

(i) **In General.—**The Secretary shall submit to the relevant committees of Congress—

(I) an interim report regarding the assessment on or before January 1, 2010; and

(II) a final report, summarizing all studies and analyses that relate to the assessment and that are completed after the interim report, on or before July 1, 2011.

(ii) **Prohibition.—**Notwithstanding any other provision of law, the reports required by this subsection shall not be subject to any review outside the Department of Education before their transmittal to the relevant committees of Congress and the Secretary, but the President, the Secretary, and the independent advisory panel established under paragraph (1) may make such additional recommendations to Congress with respect to the assessment as the President, the Secretary, or the panel determine to be appropriate.

(3) **Collection of State Information and Report.—**

(A) **In General.—**The Secretary may collect and disseminate information from States regarding State efforts to meet State adjusted levels of performance described in section 113(b).

(B) **Report.—**The Secretary shall gather any information collected pursuant to subparagraph (A) and submit a report to the relevant committees in Congress.

(4) **Research.—**

(A) **In General.—**From amounts made available under subsection (e), the Secretary, after consulting with the States, shall award a grant, contract, or cooperative agreement, on a competitive basis, to an institution of higher education, a public or private nonprofit organization or agency, or a consortium of such institutions, organizations, or agencies to establish a national research center—

(i) to carry out scientifically based research and evaluation for the purpose of developing, improving, and identifying the most successful methods for addressing the education, employment, and training needs of participants, including special populations, in career and technical education programs, including research and evaluation in such activities as—

(I) the integration of—

(aa) career and technical instruction; and

(bb) academic, secondary and postsecondary instruction;

(II) education technology and distance learning approaches and strategies that are effective with respect to career and technical education;

(III) State adjusted levels of performance and State levels of performance that serve to improve career and technical education programs and student achievement;

(IV) academic knowledge and career and technical skills required for employment or participation in postsecondary education; and

(V) preparation for occupations in high skill, high wage, or high demand business and industry, including examination of—

(aa) collaboration between career and technical education programs and business and industry; and

(bb) academic and technical skills required for a regional or sectoral workforce, including small business;

(ii) to carry out scientifically based research and evaluation to increase the effectiveness and improve the implementation of career and technical education programs that are integrated with coherent and rigorous content aligned with challenging academic standards, including conducting research and development, and studies, that provide longitudinal information or formative evaluation with respect to career and technical education programs and student achievement;

(iii) to carry out scientifically based research and evaluation that can be used to improve the preparation and professional development of teachers, faculty, and administrators, and to improve student learning in the career and technical education classroom, including—

(I) effective in-service and preservice teacher and faculty education that assists career and technical education programs in—

(aa) integrating those programs with academic content standards and student academic achievement standards, as adopted by States under section 1111(b)(1) of the Elementary and Secondary Education Act of 1965; and

(bb) coordinating technical education with industry-recognized certification requirements;

(II) dissemination and training activities related to the applied research and demonstration activities described in this subsection, which may also include serving as a repository for information on career and technical skills, State academic standards, and related materials; and

(III) the recruitment and retention of career and technical education teachers, faculty, counselors, and administrators, including individuals in groups underrepresented in the teaching profession; and

(iv) to carry out such other research and evaluation, consistent with the purposes of this Act, as the Secretary determines appropriate to assist State and local recipients of funds under this Act.

(B) **Report.**—The center conducting the activities described in subparagraph (A) shall annually prepare a report of the key research findings of such center and shall submit copies of the report to the Secretary, the relevant committees of Congress, the Library of Congress, and each eligible agency.

(C) **Dissemination.**—The center shall conduct dissemination and training activities based upon the research described in subparagraph (A).

(5) **Demonstrations and Dissemination.**—The Secretary is authorized to carry out demonstration career and technical education programs, to replicate model career and technical education programs, to disseminate best practices information, and to provide technical assistance upon request of a State, for the purposes of developing, improving, and identifying the most successful methods and techniques for providing career and technical education programs assisted under this Act.

(e) **Authorization of Appropriations.**—There are authorized to be appropriated to carry out this section such sums as may be necessary for each of fiscal years 2007 through 2012.

TEXT OF LAW

SEC. 115. ASSISTANCE FOR THE OUTLYING AREAS.

(a) **Outlying Areas.**—From funds reserved pursuant to section 111(a)(1)(A), the Secretary shall—

    (1) make a grant in the amount of $660,000 to Guam;

    (2) make a grant in the amount of $350,000 to each of American Samoa and the Commonwealth of the Northern Mariana Islands; and

    (3) make a grant of $160,000 to the Republic of Palau, subject to subsection (d).

(b) **Remainder.**—

    (1) **First Year.**—Subject to subsection (a), for the first fiscal year following the date of enactment of the Carl D. Perkins Career and Technical Education Improvement Act of 2006, the Secretary shall make a grant of the remainder of funds reserved pursuant to section 111(a)(1)(A) to the Pacific Region Educational Laboratory in Honolulu, Hawaii, to make grants for career and technical education and training in Guam, American Samoa, and the Commonwealth of the Northern Mariana Islands, for the purpose of providing direct career and technical educational services, including—
        (A) teacher and counselor training and retraining;
        (B) curriculum development; and
        (C) the improvement of career and technical education and training programs in secondary schools and institutions of higher education, or improving cooperative education programs involving secondary schools and institutions of higher education.

    (2) **Subsequent Years.**—Subject to subsection (a), for the second fiscal year following the date of enactment of the Carl D. Perkins Career and Technical Education Improvement Act of 2006, and each subsequent year, the Secretary shall make a grant of the remainder of funds reserved pursuant to section 111(a)(1)(A) and subject to subsection (a), in equal proportion, to each of Guam, American Samoa, and the Commonwealth of the Northern Mariana Islands, to be used to provide direct career and technical educational services as described in subparagraphs (A) through (C) of paragraph (1).

(c) **Limitation.**—The Pacific Region Educational Laboratory may use not more than 5 percent of the funds received under subsection (b)(1) for administrative costs.

(d) **Restriction.**—The Republic of Palau shall cease to be eligible to receive funding under this section upon entering into an agreement for an extension of United States educational assistance under the Compact of Free Association, unless otherwise provided in such agreement.

SEC. 116. NATIVE AMERICAN PROGRAMS.

(a) **Definitions.**—In this section:

    (1) **Alaska Native.**—The term 'Alaska Native' means a Native as such term is defined in section 3 of the Alaska Native Claims Settlement Act (43 U.S.C. 1602).

    (2) **Bureau-Funded School.**—The term 'Bureau-funded school' has the meaning given the term in section 1141 of the Education Amendments of 1978 (25 U.S.C. 2021).

    (3) **Indian, Indian Tribe, and Tribal Organization.**—The terms 'Indian', 'Indian tribe', and 'tribal organization' have the meanings given the terms in section 4 of the Indian Self-Determination and Education Assistance Act (25 U.S.C. 450b).

TEXT OF LAW

(4) **Native Hawaiian.**—The term 'Native Hawaiian' means any individual any of whose ancestors were natives, prior to 1778, of the area which now comprises the State of Hawaii.

(5) **Native Hawaiian Organization.**—The term 'Native Hawaiian organization' has the meaning given the term in section 7207 of the Native Hawaiian Education Act (20 U.S.C. 7517).

(b) **Program Authorized.**—

(1) **Authority.**—From funds reserved under section 111(a)(1)(B)(i), the Secretary shall make grants to or enter into contracts with Indian tribes, tribal organizations, and Alaska Native entities to carry out the authorized programs described in subsection (c), except that such grants or contracts shall not be awarded to secondary school programs in Bureau-funded schools.

(2) **Indian Tribes and Tribal Organizations.**—The grants or contracts described in this section that are awarded to any Indian tribe or tribal organization shall be subject to the terms and conditions of section 102 of the Indian Self-Determination Act (25 U.S.C. 450f) and shall be conducted in accordance with the provisions of sections 4, 5, and 6 of the Act of April 16, 1934 (25 U.S.C. 455–457), which are relevant to the programs administered under this subsection.

(3) **Special Authority Relating to Secondary Schools Operated or Supported by the Bureau of Indian Affairs.**— An Indian tribe, a tribal organization, or an Alaska Native entity, that receives funds through a grant made or contract entered into under paragraph (1) may use the funds to provide assistance to a secondary school operated or supported by the Bureau of Indian Affairs to enable such school to carry out career and technical education programs.

(4) **Matching.**—If sufficient funding is available, the Bureau of Indian Affairs shall expend an amount equal to the amount made available under this subsection, relating to programs for Indians, to pay a part of the costs of programs funded under this subsection. During each fiscal year the Bureau of Indian Affairs shall expend not less than the amount expended during the prior fiscal year on career and technical education programs, services, and technical activities administered directly by, or under contract with, the Bureau of Indian Affairs, except that in no year shall funding for such programs, services, and activities be provided from accounts and programs that support other Indian education programs. The Secretary and the Assistant Secretary of the Interior for Indian Affairs shall prepare jointly a plan for the expenditure of funds made available and for the evaluation of programs assisted under this subsection. Upon the completion of a joint plan for the expenditure of the funds and the evaluation of the programs, the Secretary shall assume responsibility for the administration of the program, with the assistance and consultation of the Bureau of Indian Affairs.

(5) **Regulations.**—If the Secretary promulgates any regulations applicable to paragraph (2), the Secretary shall—
   (A) confer with, and allow for active participation by, representatives of Indian tribes, tribal organizations, and individual tribal members; and
   (B) promulgate the regulations under subchapter III of chapter 5 of title 5, United States Code, commonly known as the 'Negotiated Rulemaking Act of 1990'.

(6) **Application.**—Any Indian tribe, tribal organization, or Bureau-funded school eligible to receive assistance under this subsection may apply individually or as part of a consortium with another such Indian tribe, tribal organization, or Bureau-funded school.

TEXT OF LAW

(c) **Authorized Activities.—**

(1) **Authorized Programs.—**Funds made available under this section shall be used to carry out career and technical education programs consistent with the purpose of this Act.

(2) **Stipends.—**
  (A) **In General.—**Funds received pursuant to grants or contracts awarded under subsection (b) may be used to provide stipends to students who are enrolled in career and technical education programs and who have acute economic needs which cannot be met through work-study programs.
  (B) **Amount.—**Stipends described in subparagraph (A) shall not exceed reasonable amounts as prescribed by the Secretary.

(d) **Grant or Contract Application.—**In order to receive a grant or contract under this section, an organization, tribe, or entity described in subsection (b) shall submit an application to the Secretary that shall include an assurance that such organization, tribe, or entity shall comply with the requirements of this section.

(e) **Restrictions and Special Considerations.—**The Secretary may not place upon grants awarded or contracts entered into under subsection (b) any restrictions relating to programs other than restrictions that apply to grants made to or contracts entered into with States pursuant to allotments under section 111(a). The Secretary, in awarding grants and entering into contracts under this section, shall ensure that the grants and contracts will improve career and technical education programs, and shall give special consideration to—

(1) programs that involve, coordinate with, or encourage tribal economic development plans; and

(2) applications from tribally controlled colleges or universities that—
  (A) are accredited or are candidates for accreditation by a nationally recognized accreditation organization as an institution of postsecondary career and technical education; or
  (B) operate career and technical education programs that are accredited or are candidates for accreditation by a nationally recognized accreditation organization, and issue certificates for completion of career and technical education programs.

(f) **Consolidation of Funds.—**Each organization, tribe, or entity receiving assistance under this section may consolidate such assistance with assistance received from related programs in accordance with the provisions of the Indian Employment, Training and Related Services Demonstration Act of 1992 (25 U.S.C. 3401 et seq.).

(g) **Nonduplicative and Nonexclusive Services.—**Nothing in this section shall be construed—

(1) to limit the eligibility of any organization, tribe, or entity described in subsection (b) to participate in any activity offered by an eligible agency or eligible recipient under this title; or

(2) to preclude or discourage any agreement, between any organization, tribe, or entity described in subsection (b) and any eligible agency or eligible recipient, to facilitate the provision of services by such eligible agency or eligible recipient to the population served by such eligible agency or eligible recipient.

(h) **Native Hawaiian Programs.—**From the funds reserved pursuant to section 111(a)(1)(B)(ii), the Secretary shall award grants to or enter into contracts with community-based organizations primarily serving and representing Native Hawaiians to plan, conduct, and administer programs, or portions thereof, which are authorized by and consistent with the provisions of this section for the benefit of Native Hawaiians.

SEC. 117. TRIBALLY CONTROLLED POSTSECONDARY CAREER AND TECHNICAL INSTITUTIONS.

(a) **Grants Authorized.**—The Secretary shall, subject to the availability of appropriations, make grants pursuant to this section to tribally controlled postsecondary career and technical institutions that are not receiving Federal support under the Tribally Controlled College or University Assistance Act of 1978 (25 U.S.C. 1801 et seq.) or the Navajo Community College Act (25 U.S.C. 640a et seq.) to provide basic support for the education and training of Indian students.

(b) **Uses of Grants.**—Amounts made available under this section shall be used for career and technical education programs for Indian students and for the institutional support costs of the grant, including the expenses described in subsection (e).

(c) **Amount of Grants.**—

    (1) **In General.**—If the sums appropriated for any fiscal year for grants under this section are not sufficient to pay in full the total amount which approved applicants are eligible to receive under this section for such fiscal year, the Secretary shall first allocate to each such applicant who received funds under this part for the preceding fiscal year an amount equal to 100 percent of the product of the per capita payment for the preceding fiscal year and such applicant's Indian student count for the current program year, plus an amount equal to the actual cost of any increase to the per capita figure resulting from inflationary increases to necessary costs beyond the institution's control.

    (2) **Per Capita Determination.**—For the purposes of paragraph (1), the per capita payment for any fiscal year shall be determined by dividing the amount available for grants to tribally controlled postsecondary career and technical institutions under this section for such program year by the sum of the Indian student counts of such institutions for such program year. The Secretary shall, on the basis of the most accurate data available from the institutions, compute the Indian student count for any fiscal year for which such count was not used for the purpose of making allocations under this section.

    (3) **Indirect Costs.**—Notwithstanding any other provision of law or regulation, the Secretary shall not require the use of a restricted indirect cost rate for grants issued under this section.

(d) **Applications.**—Any tribally controlled postsecondary career and technical institution that is not receiving Federal support under the Tribally Controlled College or University Assistance Act of 1978 (25 U.S.C. 1801 et seq.) or the Navajo Community College Act (25 U.S.C. 640a et seq.) that desires to receive a grant under this section shall submit an application to the Secretary in such manner and form as the Secretary may require.

(e) **Expenses.**—

    (1) **In General.**—The Secretary shall, subject to the availability of appropriations, provide for each program year to each tribally controlled postsecondary career and technical institution having an application approved by the Secretary, an amount necessary to pay expenses associated with—

        (A) the maintenance and operation of the program, including development costs, costs of basic and special instruction (including special programs for individuals with disabilities and academic instruction), materials, student costs, administrative expenses, boarding costs, transportation, student services, daycare and family support programs for students and their families (including contributions to the costs of education for dependents), and student stipends;

(B) capital expenditures, including operations and maintenance, and minor improvements and repair, and physical plant maintenance costs, for the conduct of programs funded under this section;

(C) costs associated with repair, upkeep, replacement, and upgrading of the instructional equipment; and

(D) institutional support of career and technical education.

(2) **Accounting.**—Each institution receiving a grant under this section shall provide annually to the Secretary an accurate and detailed accounting of the institution's operating and maintenance expenses and such other information concerning costs as the Secretary may reasonably require.

(f) **Other Programs.**—

(1) **In General.**—Except as specifically provided in this Act, eligibility for assistance under this section shall not preclude any tribally controlled postsecondary career and technical institution from receiving Federal financial assistance under any program authorized under the Higher Education Act of 1965, or under any other applicable program for the benefit of institutions of higher education or career and technical education.

(2) **Prohibition on Alteration of Grant Amount.**—The amount of any grant for which tribally controlled postsecondary career and technical institutions are eligible under this section shall not be altered because of funds allocated to any such institution from funds appropriated under the Act of November 2, 1921 (commonly known as the 'Snyder Act') (25 U.S.C. 13).

(3) **Prohibition on Contract Denial.**—No tribally controlled postsecondary career and technical institution for which an Indian tribe has designated a portion of the funds appropriated for the tribe from funds appropriated under the Act of November 2, 1921 (25 U.S.C. 13), may be denied a contract for such portion under the Indian Self-Determination and Education Assistance Act (except as provided in that Act), or denied appropriate contract support to administer such portion of the appropriated funds.

(g) **Complaint Resolution Procedure.**—The Secretary shall establish (after consultation with tribally controlled postsecondary career and technical institutions) a complaint resolution procedure for grant determinations and calculations under this section for tribally controlled postsecondary career and technical institutions.

(h) **Definitions.**—In this section:

(1) **Indian; Indian Tribe.**—The terms 'Indian' and 'Indian tribe' have the meanings given the terms in section 2 of the Tribally Controlled College or University Assistance Act of 1978 (25 U.S.C. 1801).

(2) **Indian Student Count.**—

(A) **In General.**—The term 'Indian student count' means a number equal to the total number of Indian students enrolled in each tribally controlled postsecondary career and technical institution, as determined in accordance with subparagraph (B).

(B) **Determination.**—

(i) **Enrollment.**—For each academic year, the Indian student count shall be determined on the basis of the enrollments of Indian students as in effect at the conclusion of—

(I) in the case of the fall term, the third week of the fall term; and

TEXT OF LAW

         (II)   in the case of the spring term, the third week of the spring term.

    (ii)   **Calculation.**—For each academic year, the Indian student count for a tribally controlled postsecondary career and technical institution shall be the quotient obtained by dividing—

         (I)   the sum of the credit hours of all Indian students enrolled in the tribally controlled postsecondary career and technical institution (as determined under clause (i)); by

         (II)   12.

    (iii) **Summer Term.**—Any credit earned in a class offered during a summer term shall be counted in the determination of the Indian student count for the succeeding fall term.

    (iv) **Students without Secondary School Degrees.**—

         (I)   **In General.**—A credit earned at a tribally controlled postsecondary career and technical institution by any Indian student that has not obtained a secondary school degree (or the recognized equivalent of such a degree) shall be counted toward the determination of the Indian student count if the institution at which the student is enrolled has established criteria for the admission of the student on the basis of the ability of the student to benefit from the education or training of the institution.

         (II)   **Presumption.**—The institution shall be presumed to have established the criteria described in subclause (I) if the admission procedures for the institution include counseling or testing that measures the aptitude of a student to successfully complete a course in which the student is enrolled.

         (III) **Credits toward Secondary School Degree.**—No credit earned by an Indian student for the purpose of obtaining a secondary school degree (or the recognized equivalent of such a degree) shall be counted toward the determination of the Indian student count under this clause.

    (v)   **Continuing Education Programs.**—Any credit earned by an Indian student in a continuing education program of a tribally controlled postsecondary career and technical institution shall be included in the determination of the sum of all credit hours of the student if the credit is converted to a credit hour basis in accordance with the system of the institution for providing credit for participation in the program.

(i)   **Authorization of Appropriations.**—There are authorized to be appropriated to carry out this section such sums as may be necessary for each of fiscal years 2007 through 2012.

SEC. 118. OCCUPATIONAL AND EMPLOYMENT INFORMATION.

(a)   **National Activities.**—From funds appropriated under subsection (g), the Secretary, in consultation with appropriate Federal agencies, is authorized—

   (1)   to provide assistance to an entity to enable the entity—

      (A)   to provide technical assistance to State entities designated under subsection (c) to enable the State entities to carry out the activities described in such subsection;

      (B)   to disseminate information that promotes the replication of high quality practices described in subsection (c); and

      (C)   to develop and disseminate products and services related to the activities described in subsection (c); and

   (2)   to award grants to States that designate State entities in accordance with subsection (c)

to enable the State entities to carry out the State level activities described in such subsection.

(b) **State Application.**—

(1) **In General.**—A jointly designated State entity described in subsection (c) that desires to receive a grant under this section shall submit an application to the Secretary at the same time the State submits its State plan under section 122, in such manner, and accompanied by such additional information, as the Secretary may reasonably require.

(2) **Contents.**—Each application submitted under paragraph (1) shall include a description of how the jointly designated State entity described in subsection (c) will provide information based on trends provided pursuant to section 15 of the Wagner-Peyser Act to inform program development.

(c) **State Level Activities.**—In order for a State to receive a grant under this section, the eligible agency and the Governor of the State shall jointly designate an entity in the State—

(1) to provide support for career guidance and academic counseling programs designed to promote improved career and education decision making by students (and parents, as appropriate) regarding education (including postsecondary education) and training options and preparations for high skill, high wage, or high demand occupations and non-traditional fields;

(2) to make available to students, parents, teachers, administrators, faculty, and career guidance and academic counselors, and to improve accessibility with respect to, information and planning resources that relate academic and career and technical educational preparation to career goals and expectations;

(3) to provide academic and career and technical education teachers, faculty, administrators, and career guidance and academic counselors with the knowledge, skills, and occupational information needed to assist parents and students, especially special populations, with career exploration, educational opportunities, education financing, and exposure to high skill, high wage, or high demand occupations and non-traditional fields, including occupations and fields requiring a baccalaureate degree;

(4) to assist appropriate State entities in tailoring career related educational resources and training for use by such entities, including information on high skill, high wage, or high demand occupations in current or emerging professions and on career ladder information;

(5) to improve coordination and communication among administrators and planners of programs authorized by this Act and by section 15 of the Wagner-Peyser Act at the Federal, State, and local levels to ensure nonduplication of efforts and the appropriate use of shared information and data;

(6) to provide ongoing means for customers, such as students and parents, to provide comments and feedback on products and services and to update resources, as appropriate, to better meet customer requirements; and

(7) to provide readily available occupational information such as—
(A) information relative to employment sectors;
(B) information on occupation supply and demand; and
(C) other information provided pursuant to section 15 of the Wagner-Peyser Act as the jointly designated State entity considers relevant.

(d) **Nonduplication.—**

  (1) **Wagner-Peyser Act.—**The jointly designated State entity described under subsection (c) may use funds provided under subsection (a)(2) to supplement activities under section 15 of the Wagner-Peyser Act to the extent such activities do not duplicate activities assisted under such section.

  (2) **Public Law 105–220.—**None of the functions and activities assisted under this section shall duplicate the functions and activities carried out under Public Law 105–220.

(e) **Funding Rule.—**Of the amounts appropriated to carry out this section, the Federal entity designated under subsection (a) shall use—

  (1) not less than 85 percent to carry out subsection (c); and

  (2) not more than 15 percent to carry out subsection (a).

(f) **Report.—**The Secretary, in consultation with appropriate Federal agencies, shall prepare and submit to the appropriate committees of Congress, an annual report that includes—

  (1) a description of activities assisted under this section during the prior program year;

  (2) a description of the specific products and services assisted under this section that were delivered in the prior program year; and

  (3) an assessment of the extent to which States have effectively coordinated activities assisted under this section with activities authorized under section 15 of the Wagner-Peyser Act.

(g) **Authorization of Appropriations.—**There are authorized to be appropriated to carry out this section such sums as may be necessary for each of the fiscal years 2007 through 2012.

PART B—STATE PROVISIONS

SEC. 121. STATE ADMINISTRATION.

(a) **Eligible Agency Responsibilities.—**The responsibilities of an eligible agency under this title shall include—

  (1) coordination of the development, submission, and implementation of the State plan, and the evaluation of the program, services, and activities assisted under this title, including preparation for non-traditional fields;

  (2) consultation with the Governor and appropriate agencies, groups, and individuals including parents, students, teachers, teacher and faculty preparation programs, representatives of businesses (including small businesses), labor organizations, eligible recipients, State and local officials, and local program administrators, involved in the planning, administration, evaluation, and coordination of programs funded under this title;

  (3) convening and meeting as an eligible agency (consistent with State law and procedure for the conduct of such meetings) at such time as the eligible agency determines neces-

TEXT OF LAW

sary to carry out the eligible agency's responsibilities under this title, but not less than 4 times annually; and

    (4)   the adoption of such procedures as the eligible agency considers necessary to—

        (A)   implement State level coordination with the activities undertaken by the State boards under section 111 of Public Law 105–220; and

        (B)   make available to the service delivery system under section 121 of Public Law 105–220 within the State a listing of all school dropout, postsecondary education, and adult programs assisted under this title.

(b)   **Exception.**—Except with respect to the responsibilities set forth in subsection (a), the eligible agency may delegate any of the other responsibilities of the eligible agency that involve the administration, operation, or supervision of activities assisted under this title, in whole or in part, to 1 or more appropriate State agencies.

SEC. 122. STATE PLAN.

(a)   **State Plan.**—

    (1)   **In General.**—Each eligible agency desiring assistance under this title for any fiscal year shall prepare and submit to the Secretary a State plan for a 6-year period, together with such annual revisions as the eligible agency determines to be necessary, except that, during the period described in section 4, each eligible agency may submit a transition plan that shall fulfill the eligible agency's obligation to submit a State plan under this section for the first fiscal year following the date of enactment of the Carl D. Perkins Career and Technical Education Improvement Act of 2006.

    (2)   **Revisions.**—Each eligible agency—

        (A)   may submit such annual revisions of the State plan to the Secretary as the eligible agency determines to be necessary; and

        (B)   shall, after the second year of the 6-year period, conduct a review of activities assisted under this title and submit any revisions of the State plan that the eligible agency determines necessary to the Secretary.

    (3)   **Hearing Process.**—The eligible agency shall conduct public hearings in the State, after appropriate and sufficient notice, for the purpose of affording all segments of the public and interested organizations and groups (including charter school authorizers and organizers consistent with State law, employers, labor organizations, parents, students, and community organizations), an opportunity to present their views and make recommendations regarding the State plan. A summary of such recommendations and the eligible agency's response to such recommendations shall be included in the State plan.

(b)   **Plan Development.**—

    (1)   **In General.**—The eligible agency shall—

        (A)   develop the State plan in consultation with—

            (i)   academic and career and technical education teachers, faculty, and administrators;

            (ii)   career guidance and academic counselors;

            (iii)   eligible recipients;

            (iv)   charter school authorizers and organizers consistent with State law;

            (v)   parents and students;

            (vi)   institutions of higher education;

            (vii)   the State tech prep coordinator and representatives of tech prep consortia (if applicable);

TEXT OF LAW

(viii) entities participating in activities described in section 111 of Public Law 105–220;

(ix) interested community members (including parent and community organizations);

(x) representatives of special populations;

(xi) representatives of business and industry (including representatives of small business); and

(xii) representatives of labor organizations in the State; and

(B) consult the Governor of the State with respect to such development.

(2) **Activities and Procedures.**—The eligible agency shall develop effective activities and procedures, including access to information needed to use such procedures, to allow the individuals and entities described in paragraph (1) to participate in State and local decisions that relate to development of the State plan.

(c) **Plan contents.**—The State plan shall include information that—

(1) describes the career and technical education activities to be assisted that are designed to meet or exceed the State adjusted levels of performance, including a description of—

(A) the career and technical programs of study, which may be adopted by local educational agencies and postsecondary institutions to be offered as an option to students (and their parents as appropriate) when planning for and completing future coursework, for career and technical content areas that—

(i) incorporate secondary education and postsecondary education elements;

(ii) include coherent and rigorous content aligned with challenging academic standards and relevant career and technical content in a coordinated, non-duplicative progression of courses that align secondary education with postsecondary education to adequately prepare students to succeed in postsecondary education;

(iii) may include the opportunity for secondary education students to participate in dual or concurrent enrollment programs or other ways to acquire postsecondary education credits; and

(iv) lead to an industry-recognized credential or certificate at the postsecondary level, or an associate or baccalaureate degree;

(B) how the eligible agency, in consultation with eligible recipients, will develop and implement the career and technical programs of study described in subparagraph (A);

(C) how the eligible agency will support eligible recipients in developing and implementing articulation agreements between secondary education and postsecondary education institutions;

(D) how the eligible agency will make available information about career and technical programs of study offered by eligible recipients;

(E) the secondary and postsecondary career and technical education programs to be carried out, including programs that will be carried out by the eligible agency to develop, improve, and expand access to appropriate technology in career and technical education programs;

(F) the criteria that will be used by the eligible agency to approve eligible recipients for funds under this Act, including criteria to assess the extent to which the local plan will—

(i) promote continuous improvement in academic achievement;

(ii) promote continuous improvement of technical skill attainment; and

(iii) identify and address current or emerging occupational opportunities;

(G) how programs at the secondary level will prepare career and technical education students, including special populations, to graduate from secondary school with a diploma;

(H) how such programs will prepare career and technical education students, including special populations, academically and technically for opportunities in postsecondary education or entry into high skill, high wage, or high demand occupations in current or emerging occupations, and how participating students will be made aware of such opportunities;

(I) how funds will be used to improve or develop new career and technical education courses—

    (i) at the secondary level that are aligned with rigorous and challenging academic content standards and student academic achievement standards adopted by the State under section 1111 (b)(1) of the Elementary and Secondary Education Act of 1965;

    (ii) at the postsecondary level that are relevant and challenging; and

    (iii) that lead to employment in high skill, high wage, or high demand occupations;

(J) how the eligible agency will facilitate and coordinate communication on best practices among successful recipients of tech prep program grants under title II and eligible recipients to improve program quality and student achievement;

(K) how funds will be used effectively to link academic and career and technical education at the secondary level and at the postsecondary level in a manner that increases student academic and career and technical achievement; and

(L) how the eligible agency will report on the integration of coherent and rigorous content aligned with challenging academic standards in career and technical education programs in order to adequately evaluate the extent of such integration;

(2) describes how comprehensive professional development (including initial teacher preparation and activities that support recruitment) for career and technical education teachers, faculty, administrators, and career guidance and academic counselors will be provided, especially professional development that—

(A) promotes the integration of coherent and rigorous academic content standards and career and technical education curricula, including through opportunities for the appropriate academic and career and technical education teachers to jointly develop and implement curricula and pedagogical strategies, as appropriate;

(B) increases the percentage of teachers that meet teacher certification or licensing requirements;

(C) is high quality, sustained, intensive, and focused on instruction, and increases the academic knowledge and understanding of industry standards, as appropriate, of career and technical education teachers;

(D) encourages applied learning that contributes to the academic and career and technical knowledge of the student;

(E) provides the knowledge and skills needed to work with and improve instruction for special populations;

(F) assists in accessing and utilizing data, including data provided under section 118, student achievement data, and data from assessments; and

(G) promotes integration with professional development activities that the State carries out under title II of the Elementary and Secondary Education Act of 1965 and title II of the Higher Education Act of 1965;

(3) describes efforts to improve—

(A) the recruitment and retention of career and technical education teachers, faculty, and career guidance and academic counselors, including individuals in groups underrepresented in the teaching profession; and

(B) the transition to teaching from business and industry, including small business;

(4) describes efforts to facilitate the transition of subbaccalaureate career and technical education students into baccalaureate degree programs at institutions of higher education;

(5) describes how the eligible agency will actively involve parents, academic and career and technical education teachers, administrators, faculty, career guidance and academic counselors, local business (including small businesses), and labor organizations in the planning, development, implementation, and evaluation of such career and technical education programs;

(6) describes how funds received by the eligible agency through the allotment made under section 111 will be allocated—

    (A) among career and technical education at the secondary level, or career and technical education at the postsecondary and adult level, or both, including the rationale for such allocation; and

    (B) among any consortia that will be formed among secondary schools and eligible institutions, and how funds will be allocated among the members of the consortia, including the rationale for such allocation;

(7) describes how the eligible agency will—

    (A) improve the academic and technical skills of students participating in career and technical education programs, including strengthening the academic and career and technical components of career and technical education programs through the integration of academics with career and technical education to ensure learning in—

        (i) the core academic subjects (as defined in section 9101 of the Elementary and Secondary Education Act of 1965); and

        (ii) career and technical education subjects;

    (B) provide students with strong experience in, and understanding of, all aspects of an industry; and

    (C) ensure that students who participate in such career and technical education programs are taught to the same challenging academic proficiencies as are taught to all other students;

(8) describes how the eligible agency will annually evaluate the effectiveness of such career and technical education programs, and describe, to the extent practicable, how the eligible agency is coordinating such programs to ensure nonduplication with other Federal programs;

(9) describes the eligible agency's program strategies for special populations, including a description of how individuals who are members of the special populations—

    (A) will be provided with equal access to activities assisted under this Act;

    (B) will not be discriminated against on the basis of their status as members of the special populations; and

    (C) will be provided with programs designed to enable the special populations to meet or exceed State adjusted levels of performance, and prepare special populations for further learning and for high skill, high wage, or high demand occupations;

(10) describes—

    (A) the eligible agency's efforts to ensure that eligible recipients are given the opportunity to provide input in determining the State adjusted levels of performance described in section 113; and

    (B) how the eligible agency, in consultation with eligible recipients, will develop a process for the negotiation of local adjusted levels of performance under section 113(b)(4) if an eligible recipient does not accept the State adjusted levels of performance under section 113(b)(3);

(11) provides assurances that the eligible agency will comply with the requirements of this Act and the provisions of the State plan, including the provision of a financial audit of funds received under this Act which may be included as part of an audit of other Federal or State programs;

(12) provides assurances that none of the funds expended under this Act will be used to acquire equipment (including computer software) in any instance in which such acquisition results in a direct financial benefit to any organization representing the interests of the acquiring entity or the employees of the acquiring entity, or any affiliate of such an organization;

(13) describes how the eligible agency will report data relating to students participating in career and technical education in order to adequately measure the progress of the students, including special populations, and how the eligible agency will ensure that the data reported to the eligible agency from local educational agencies and eligible institutions under this title and the data the eligible agency reports to the Secretary are complete, accurate, and reliable;

(14) describes how the eligible agency will adequately address the needs of students in alternative education programs, if appropriate;

(15) describes how the eligible agency will provide local educational agencies, area career and technical education schools, and eligible institutions in the State with technical assistance;

(16) describes how career and technical education relates to State and regional occupational opportunities;

(17) describes the methods proposed for the joint planning and coordination of programs carried out under this title with other Federal education programs;

(18) describes how funds will be used to promote preparation for high skill, high wage, or high demand occupations and non-traditional fields;

(19) describes how funds will be used to serve individuals in State correctional institutions; and

(20) contains the description and information specified in sections 112(b)(8) and 121(c) of Public Law 105–220 concerning the provision of services only for postsecondary students and school dropouts.

(d) **Plan Options.—**

(1) **Single Plan.—**An eligible agency not choosing to consolidate funds under section 202 shall fulfill the plan or application submission requirements of this section, and section 201(c), by submitting a single State plan. In such plan, the eligible agency may allow recipients to fulfill the plan or application submission requirements of section 134 and subsections (a) and (b) of section 204 by submitting a single local plan.

(2) **Plan Submitted as Part of 501 Plan.—**The eligible agency may submit the plan required under this section as part of the plan submitted under section 501 of Public Law 105–220, if the plan submitted pursuant to the requirement of this section meets the requirements of this Act.

(e) **Plan Approval.—**

(1) **In General.—**The Secretary shall approve a State plan, or a revision to an approved State plan, unless the Secretary determines that—

(A)　the State plan, or revision, respectively, does not meet the requirements of this Act; or

(B)　the State's levels of performance on the core indicators of performance consistent with section 113 are not sufficiently rigorous to meet the purpose of this Act.

(2)　**Disapproval.**—The Secretary shall not finally disapprove a State plan, except after giving the eligible agency notice and an opportunity for a hearing.

(3)　**Consultation.**—The eligible agency shall develop the portion of each State plan relating to the amount and uses of any funds proposed to be reserved for adult career and technical education, postsecondary career and technical education, tech prep education, and secondary career and technical education after consultation with the State agency responsible for supervision of community colleges, technical institutes, or other 2-year postsecondary institutions primarily engaged in providing postsecondary career and technical education, and the State agency responsible for secondary education. If a State agency finds that a portion of the final State plan is objectionable, the State agency shall file such objections with the eligible agency. The eligible agency shall respond to any objections of the State agency in the State plan submitted to the Secretary.

(4)　**Timeframe.**—A State plan shall be deemed approved by the Secretary if the Secretary has not responded to the eligible agency regarding the State plan within 90 days of the date the Secretary receives the State plan.

SEC. 123. IMPROVEMENT PLANS.

(a)　**State Program Improvement.**—

(1)　**Plan.**—If a State fails to meet at least 90 percent of an agreed upon State adjusted level of performance for any of the core indicators of performance described in section 113(b)(3), the eligible agency shall develop and implement a program improvement plan (with special consideration to performance gaps identified under section 113(c)(2)) in consultation with the appropriate agencies, individuals, and organizations during the first program year succeeding the program year for which the eligible agency failed to so meet the State adjusted level of performance for any of the core indicators of performance.

(2)　**Technical Assistance.**—If the Secretary determines that an eligible agency is not properly implementing the eligible agency's responsibilities under section 122, or is not making substantial progress in meeting the purposes of this Act, based on the State's adjusted levels of performance, the Secretary shall work with the eligible agency to implement the improvement activities consistent with the requirements of this Act.

(3)　**Subsequent Action.**—

(A)　**In General.**—The Secretary may, after notice and opportunity for a hearing, withhold from an eligible agency all, or a portion, of the eligible agency's allotment under paragraphs (2) and (3) of section 112(a) if the eligible agency—

(i)　fails to implement an improvement plan as described in paragraph (1);

(ii)　fails to make any improvement in meeting any of the State adjusted levels of performance for the core indicators of performance identified under paragraph (1) within the first program year of implementation of its improvement plan described in paragraph (1); or

(iii)　fails to meet at least 90 percent of an agreed upon State adjusted level of performance for the same core indicator of performance for 3 consecutive years.

(B)　**Waiver for Exceptional Circumstances.**—The Secretary may waive the sanction in subparagraph (A) due to exceptional or uncontrollable circumstances, such as a

TEXT OF LAW

natural disaster or a precipitous and unforeseen decline in the financial resources of the State.

(4) **Funds Resulting from Reduced Allotments.**—The Secretary shall use funds withheld under paragraph (3) for a State served by an eligible agency to provide technical assistance, to assist in the development of an improved State improvement plan, or for other improvement activities consistent with the requirements of this Act for such State.

(b) **Local Program Improvement.**—

(1) **Local Evaluation.**—Each eligible agency shall evaluate annually, using the local adjusted levels of performance described in section 113(b)(4), the career and technical education activities of each eligible recipient receiving funds under this title.

(2) **Plan.**—If, after reviewing the evaluation in paragraph (1), the eligible agency determines that an eligible recipient failed to meet at least 90 percent of an agreed upon local adjusted level of performance for any of the core indicators of performance described in section 113(b)(4), the eligible recipient shall develop and implement a program improvement plan (with special consideration to performance gaps identified under section 113(b)(4)(C)(ii)(II)) in consultation with the eligible agency, appropriate agencies, individuals, and organizations during the first program year succeeding the program year for which the eligible recipient failed to so meet any of the local adjusted levels of performance for any of the core indicators of performance.

(3) **Technical Assistance.**—If the eligible agency determines that an eligible recipient is not properly implementing the eligible recipient's responsibilities under section 134, or is not making substantial progress in meeting the purposes of this Act, based on the local adjusted levels of performance, the eligible agency shall work with the eligible recipient to implement improvement activities consistent with the requirements of this Act.

(4) **Subsequent Action.**—
  (A) **In General.**—The eligible agency may, after notice and opportunity for a hearing, withhold from the eligible recipient all, or a portion, of the eligible recipient's allotment under this title if the eligible recipient—
    (i) fails to implement an improvement plan as described in paragraph (2);
    (ii) fails to make any improvement in meeting any of the local adjusted levels of performance for the core indicators of performance identified under paragraph (2) within the first program year of implementation of its improvement plan described in paragraph (2); or
    (iii) fails to meet at least 90 percent of an agreed upon local adjusted level of performance for the same core indicator of performance for 3 consecutive years.
  (B) **Waiver for Exceptional Circumstances.**—In determining whether to impose sanctions under subparagraph (A), the eligible agency may waive imposing sanctions—
    (i) due to exceptional or uncontrollable circumstances, such as a natural disaster or a precipitous and unforeseen decline in the financial resources of the eligible recipient; or
    (ii) based on the impact on the eligible recipient's reported performance of the small size of the career and technical education program operated by the eligible recipient.

(5) **Funds Resulting from Reduced Allotments.**—The eligible agency shall use funds withheld under paragraph (4) from an eligible recipient to provide (through alternative arrangements) services and activities to students within the area served by such recipient to meet the purposes of this Act.

TEXT OF LAW

SEC. 124. STATE LEADERSHIP ACTIVITIES.

(a) General Authority.—From amounts reserved under section 112(a)(2), each eligible agency shall conduct State leadership activities.

(b) **Required Uses of Funds.**—The State leadership activities described in subsection (a) shall include—

(1) an assessment of the career and technical education programs carried out with funds under this title, including an assessment of how the needs of special populations are being met and how the career and technical education programs are designed to enable special populations to meet State adjusted levels of performance and prepare the special populations for further education, further training, or for high skill, high wage, or high demand occupations;

(2) developing, improving, or expanding the use of technology in career and technical education that may include—
  (A) training of career and technical education teachers, faculty, career guidance and academic counselors, and administrators to use technology, including distance learning;
  (B) providing career and technical education students with the academic and career and technical skills (including the mathematics and science knowledge that provides a strong basis for such skills) that lead to entry into technology fields, including non-traditional fields; or
  (C) encouraging schools to collaborate with technology industries to offer voluntary internships and mentoring programs;

(3) professional development programs, including providing comprehensive professional development (including initial teacher preparation) for career and technical education teachers, faculty, administrators, and career guidance and academic counselors at the secondary and postsecondary levels, that support activities described in section 122 and—
  (A) provide in-service and preservice training in career and technical education programs—
    (i) on effective integration and use of challenging academic and career and technical education provided jointly with academic teachers to the extent practicable;
    (ii) on effective teaching skills based on research that includes promising practices;
    (iii) on effective practices to improve parental and community involvement; and
    (iv) on effective use of scientifically based research and data to improve instruction;
  (B) are high quality, sustained, intensive, and classroom-focused in order to have a positive and lasting impact on classroom instruction and the teacher's performance in the classroom, and are not 1-day or short-term workshops or conferences;
  (C) will help teachers and personnel to improve student achievement in order to meet the State adjusted levels of performance established under section 113;
  (D) will support education programs for teachers of career and technical education in public schools and other public school personnel who are involved in the direct delivery of educational services to career and technical education students to ensure that teachers and personnel—
    (i) stay current with the needs, expectations, and methods of industry;
    (ii) can effectively develop rigorous and challenging, integrated academic and career and technical education curricula jointly with academic teachers, to the extent practicable;

(iii) develop a higher level of academic and industry knowledge and skills in career and technical education; and

(iv) effectively use applied learning that contributes to the academic and career and technical knowledge of the student; and

(E) are coordinated with the teacher certification or licensing and professional development activities that the State carries out under title II of the Elementary and Secondary Education Act of 1965 and title II of the Higher Education Act of 1965;

(4) supporting career and technical education programs that improve the academic and career and technical skills of students participating in career and technical education programs by strengthening the academic and career and technical components of such career and technical education programs, through the integration of coherent and relevant content aligned with challenging academic standards and relevant career and technical education, to ensure achievement in—

(A) the core academic subjects (as defined in section 9101 of the Elementary and Secondary Education Act of 1965); and

(B) career and technical education subjects;

(5) providing preparation for non-traditional fields in current and emerging professions, and other activities that expose students, including special populations, to high skill, high wage occupations;

(6) supporting partnerships among local educational agencies, institutions of higher education, adult education providers, and, as appropriate, other entities, such as employers, labor organizations, intermediaries, parents, and local partnerships, to enable students to achieve State academic standards, and career and technical skills, or complete career and technical programs of study, as described in section 122(c)(1)(A);

(7) serving individuals in State institutions, such as State correctional institutions and institutions that serve individuals with disabilities;

(8) support for programs for special populations that lead to high skill, high wage, or high demand occupations; and

(9) technical assistance for eligible recipients.

(c) **Permissible Uses of Funds.**—The leadership activities described in subsection (a) may include—

(1) improvement of career guidance and academic counseling programs that assist students in making informed academic and career and technical education decisions, including—

(A) encouraging secondary and postsecondary students to graduate with a diploma or degree; and

(B) exposing students to high skill, high wage occupations and non-traditional fields;

(2) establishment of agreements, including articulation agreements, between secondary school and postsecondary career and technical education programs in order to provide postsecondary education and training opportunities for students participating in such career and technical education programs, such as tech prep programs;

(3) support for initiatives to facilitate the transition of sub-baccalaureate career and technical education students into baccalaureate degree programs, including—

(A) statewide articulation agreements between associate degree granting career and technical postsecondary educational institutions and baccalaureate degree granting postsecondary educational institutions;

TEXT OF LAW

(B) postsecondary dual and concurrent enrollment programs;

(C) academic and financial aid counseling; and

(D) other initiatives—

    (i) to encourage the pursuit of a baccalaureate degree; and

    (ii) to overcome barriers to participation in baccalaureate degree programs, including geographic and other barriers affecting rural students and special populations;

(4) support for career and technical student organizations, especially with respect to efforts to increase the participation of students who are members of special populations;

(5) support for public charter schools operating career and technical education programs;

(6) support for career and technical education programs that offer experience in, and understanding of, all aspects of an industry for which students are preparing to enter;

(7) support for family and consumer sciences programs;

(8) support for partnerships between education and business or business intermediaries, including cooperative education and adjunct faculty arrangements at the secondary and postsecondary levels;

(9) support to improve or develop new career and technical education courses and initiatives, including career clusters, career academies, and distance education, that prepare individuals academically and technically for high skill, high wage, or high demand occupations;

(10) awarding incentive grants to eligible recipients—

(A) for exemplary performance in carrying out programs under this Act, which awards shall be based on—

    (i) eligible recipients exceeding the local adjusted levels of performance established under section 113(b) in a manner that reflects sustained or significant improvement;

    (ii) eligible recipients effectively developing connections between secondary education and postsecondary education and training;

    (iii) the adoption and integration of coherent and rigorous content aligned with challenging academic standards and technical coursework;

    (iv) eligible recipients' progress in having special populations who participate in career and technical education programs meet local adjusted levels of performance; or

    (v) other factors relating to the performance of eligible recipients under this Act as the eligible agency determines are appropriate; or

(B) if an eligible recipient elects to use funds as permitted under section 135(c)(19);

(11) providing for activities to support entrepreneurship education and training;

(12) providing career and technical education programs for adults and school dropouts to complete their secondary school education, in coordination, to the extent practicable, with activities authorized under the Adult Education and Family Literacy Act;

(13) providing assistance to individuals, who have participated in services and activities under this title, in continuing the individuals' education or training or finding appropriate jobs, such as through referral to the system established under section 121 of Public Law 105–220;

TEXT OF LAW

(14) developing valid and reliable assessments of technical skills;

(15) developing and enhancing data systems to collect and analyze data on secondary and postsecondary academic and employment outcomes;

(16) improving—
   (A) the recruitment and retention of career and technical education teachers, faculty, administrators, and career guidance and academic counselors, including individuals in groups underrepresented in the teaching profession; and
   (B) the transition to teaching from business and industry, including small business; and

(17) support for occupational and employment information resources, such as those described in section 118.

(d) **Restriction on Uses Of Funds.**—An eligible agency that receives funds under section 112(a)(2) may not use any of such funds for administrative costs.

PART C—LOCAL PROVISIONS

SEC. 131. DISTRIBUTION OF FUNDS TO SECONDARY EDUCATION PROGRAMS.

(a) **Distribution Rules.**—Except as provided in section 133 and as otherwise provided in this section, each eligible agency shall distribute the portion of funds made available under section 112(a)(1) to carry out this section to local educational agencies within the State as follows:

(1) **Thirty Percent.**—Thirty percent shall be allocated to such local educational agencies in proportion to the number of individuals aged 5 through 17, inclusive, who reside in the school district served by such local educational agency for the preceding fiscal year compared to the total number of such individuals who reside in the school districts served by all local educational agencies in the State for such preceding fiscal year, as determined on the basis of the most recent satisfactory—
   (A) data provided to the Secretary by the Bureau of the Census for the purpose of determining eligibility under title I of the Elementary and Secondary Education Act of 1965; or
   (B) student membership data collected by the National Center for Education Statistics through the Common Core of Data survey system.

(2) **Seventy Percent.**—Seventy percent shall be allocated to such local educational agencies in proportion to the number of individuals aged 5 through 17, inclusive, who reside in the school district served by such local educational agency and are from families below the poverty level for the preceding fiscal year, as determined on the basis of the most recent satisfactory data used under section 1124(c)(1)(A) of the Elementary and Secondary Education Act of 1965, compared to the total number of such individuals who reside in the school districts served by all the local educational agencies in the State for such preceding fiscal year.

(3) **Adjustments.**—Each eligible agency, in making the allocations under paragraphs (1) and (2), shall adjust the data used to make the allocations to—
   (A) reflect any change in school district boundaries that may have occurred since the data were collected; and
   (B) include local educational agencies without geographical boundaries, such as charter schools and secondary schools funded by the Bureau of Indian Affairs.

(b) **Waiver for More Equitable Distribution.**—The Secretary may waive the application of subsection (a) in the case of any eligible agency that submits to the Secretary an application for such a waiver that—

(1) demonstrates that a proposed alternative formula more effectively targets funds on the basis of poverty (as defined by the Office of Management and Budget and revised annually in accordance with section 673(2) of the Community Services Block Grant Act (42 U.S.C. 9902(2))) to local educational agencies within the State than the formula described in subsection (a); and

(2) includes a proposal for such an alternative formula.

(c) **Minimum Allocation.**—

(1) **In General.**—Except as provided in paragraph (2), a local educational agency shall not receive an allocation under subsection (a) unless the amount allocated to such agency under subsection (a) is greater than $15,000. A local educational agency may enter into a consortium with other local educational agencies for purposes of meeting the minimum allocation requirement of this paragraph.

(2) **Waiver.**—The eligible agency shall waive the application of paragraph (1) in any case in which the local educational agency—
(A) **(i)** is located in a rural, sparsely populated area; or
(ii) is a public charter school operating secondary school career and technical education programs; and
(B) demonstrates that the local educational agency is unable to enter into a consortium for purposes of providing activities under this part.

(3) **Redistribution.**—Any amounts that are not allocated by reason of paragraph (1) or paragraph (2) shall be redistributed to local educational agencies that meet the requirements of paragraph (1) or (2) in accordance with the provisions of this section.

(d) **Limited Jurisdiction Agencies.**—

(1) **In General.**—In applying the provisions of subsection (a), no eligible agency receiving assistance under this title shall allocate funds to a local educational agency that serves only elementary schools, but shall distribute such funds to the local educational agency or regional educational agency that provides secondary school services to secondary school students in the same attendance area.

(2) **Special Rule.**—The amount to be allocated under paragraph (1) to a local educational agency that has jurisdiction only over secondary schools shall be determined based on the number of students that entered such secondary schools in the previous year from the elementary schools involved.

(e) **Allocations to Area Career and Technical Education Schools and Educational Service Agencies.**—

(1) **In General.**—Each eligible agency shall distribute the portion of funds made available under section 112(a)(1) for any fiscal year by such eligible agency for career and technical education activities at the secondary level under this section to the appropriate area career and technical education school or educational service agency in any case in which the area career and technical education school or educational service agency, and the local educational agency concerned—

TEXT OF LAW

(A) have formed or will form a consortium for the purpose of receiving funds under this section; or

(B) have entered into or will enter into a cooperative arrangement for such purpose.

(2) **Allocation Basis.**—If an area career and technical education school or educational service agency meets the requirements of paragraph (1), then the amount that would otherwise be distributed to the local educational agency shall be allocated to the area career and technical education school, the educational service agency, and the local educational agency based on each school, agency or entity's relative share of students who are attending career and technical education programs (based, if practicable, on the average enrollment for the preceding 3 years).

(3) **Appeals Procedure.**—The eligible agency shall establish an appeals procedure for resolution of any dispute arising between a local educational agency and an area career and technical education school or an educational service agency with respect to the allocation procedures described in this section, including the decision of a local educational agency to leave a consortium or terminate a cooperative arrangement.

(f) **Consortium Requirements.**—

(1) **Alliance.**—Any local educational agency receiving an allocation that is not sufficient to conduct a program which meets the requirements of section 135 is encouraged to—

(A) form a consortium or enter into a cooperative agreement with an area career and technical education school or educational service agency offering programs that meet the requirements of section 135;

(B) transfer such allocation to the area career and technical education school or educational service agency; and

(C) operate programs that are of sufficient size, scope, and quality to be effective.

(2) **Funds to Consortium.**—Funds allocated to a consortium formed to meet the requirements of this subsection shall be used only for purposes and programs that are mutually beneficial to all members of the consortium and can be used only for programs authorized under this title. Such funds may not be reallocated to individual members of the consortium for purposes or programs benefitting only 1 member of the consortium.

(g) **Data.**—The Secretary shall collect information from eligible agencies regarding the specific dollar allocations made available by the eligible agency for career and technical education programs under subsections (a), (b), (c), (d), and (e) and how these allocations are distributed to local educational agencies, area career and technical education schools, and educational service agencies, within the State in accordance with this section.

(h) **Special Rule.**—Each eligible agency distributing funds under this section shall treat a secondary school funded by the Bureau of Indian Affairs within the State as if such school were a local educational agency within the State for the purpose of receiving a distribution under this section.

SEC. 132. DISTRIBUTION OF FUNDS FOR POSTSECONDARY EDUCATION PROGRAMS.

(a) **Allocation.**—

(1) **In General.**—Except as provided in subsections (b) and (c) and section 133, each eligible agency shall distribute the portion of the funds made available under section 112(a)(1) to carry out this section for any fiscal year to eligible institutions or consortia of eligible institutions within the State.

(2) **Formula.**—Each eligible institution or consortium of eligible institutions shall be allo-

TEXT OF LAW

cated an amount that bears the same relationship to the portion of funds made available under section 112(a)(1) to carry out this section for any fiscal year as the sum of the number of individuals who are Federal Pell Grant recipients and recipients of assistance from the Bureau of Indian Affairs enrolled in programs meeting the requirements of section 135 offered by such institution or consortium in the preceding fiscal year bears to the sum of the number of such recipients enrolled in such programs within the State for such year.

(3) **Consortium Requirements.—**

    (A) **In General.—**In order for a consortium of eligible institutions described in paragraph (2) to receive assistance pursuant to such paragraph, such consortium shall operate joint projects that—

        (i) provide services to all postsecondary institutions participating in the consortium; and

        (ii) are of sufficient size, scope, and quality to be effective.

    (B) **Funds To Consortium.—**Funds allocated to a consortium formed to meet the requirements of this section shall be used only for purposes and programs that are mutually beneficial to all members of the consortium and shall be used only for programs authorized under this title. Such funds may not be reallocated to individual members of the consortium for purposes or programs benefitting only 1 member of the consortium.

(4) **Waiver.—**The eligible agency may waive the application of paragraph (3)(A)(i) in any case in which the eligible institution is located in a rural, sparsely populated area.

(b) **Waiver for More Equitable Distribution.—**The Secretary may waive the application of subsection (a) if an eligible agency submits to the Secretary an application for such a waiver that—

(1) demonstrates that the formula described in subsection (a) does not result in a distribution of funds to the eligible institutions or consortia within the State that have the highest numbers of economically disadvantaged individuals and that an alternative formula will result in such a distribution; and

(2) includes a proposal for such an alternative formula.

(c) **Minimum Grant Amount.—**

(1) **In General.—**No institution or consortium shall receive an allocation under this section in an amount that is less than $50,000.

(2) **Redistribution.—**Any amounts that are not distributed by reason of paragraph (1) shall be redistributed to eligible institutions or consortia in accordance with this section.

SEC. 133. SPECIAL RULES FOR CAREER AND TECHNICAL EDUCATION.

(a) **Special Rule for Minimal Allocation.—**

(1) **General Authority.—**Notwithstanding the provisions of sections 131 and 132 and in order to make a more equitable distribution of funds for programs serving the areas of greatest economic need, for any program year for which a minimal amount is made available by an eligible agency for distribution under section 131 or 132, such eligible agency may distribute such minimal amount for such year—

    (A) on a competitive basis; or

    (B) through any alternative method determined by the eligible agency.

TEXT OF LAW

(2) **Minimal Amount.**—For purposes of this section, the term 'minimal amount' means not more than 15 percent of the total amount made available for distribution under section 112(a)(1).

(b) **Redistribution.**—

(1) **In General.**—In any academic year that an eligible recipient does not expend all of the amounts the eligible recipient is allocated for such year under section 131 or 132, such eligible recipient shall return any unexpended amounts to the eligible agency to be real-located under section 131 or 132, as appropriate.

(2) **Redistribution of Amounts Returned Late in an Academic Year.**—In any academic year in which amounts are returned to the eligible agency under section 131 or 132 and the eligible agency is unable to reallocate such amounts according to such sections in time for such amounts to be expended in such academic year, the eligible agency shall retain such amounts for distribution in combination with amounts provided under section 112(a)(1) for the following academic year.

(c) **Construction.**—Nothing in section 131 or 132 shall be construed—

(1) to prohibit a local educational agency or a consortium thereof that receives assistance under section 131, from working with an eligible institution or consortium thereof that receives assistance under section 132, to carry out career and technical education pro-grams at the secondary level in accordance with this title;

(2) to prohibit an eligible institution or consortium thereof that receives assistance under section 132, from working with a local educational agency or consortium thereof that receives assistance under section 131, to carry out postsecondary and adult career and technical education programs in accordance with this title; or

(3) to require a charter school, that provides career and technical education programs and is considered a local educational agency under State law, to jointly establish the charter school's eligibility for assistance under this title unless the charter school is explicitly permitted to do so under the State's charter school statute.

(d) **Consistent Application.**—For purposes of this section, the eligible agency shall provide funds to charter schools offering career and technical education programs in the same manner as the eligible agency provides those funds to other schools. Such career and technical education programs within a charter school shall be of sufficient size, scope, and quality to be effective.

SEC. 134. LOCAL PLAN FOR CAREER AND TECHNICAL EDUCATION PROGRAMS.

(a) **Local Plan Required.**—Any eligible recipient desiring financial assistance under this part shall, in accordance with requirements established by the eligible agency (in consultation with such other educational training entities as the eligible agency determines to be appropriate) submit a local plan to the eligible agency. Such local plan shall cover the same period of time as the period of time applicable to the State plan submitted under section 122.

(b) **Contents.**—The eligible agency shall determine the requirements for local plans, except that each local plan shall—

(1) describe how the career and technical education programs required under section 135(b) will be carried out with funds received under this title;

(2) describe how the career and technical education activities will be carried out with

respect to meeting State and local adjusted levels of performance established under section 113;

(3) describe how the eligible recipient will—

   (A) offer the appropriate courses of not less than 1 of the career and technical programs of study described in section 122(c)(1)(A);

   (B) improve the academic and technical skills of students participating in career and technical education programs by strengthening the academic and career and technical education components of such programs through the integration of coherent and rigorous content aligned with challenging academic standards and relevant career and technical education programs to ensure learning in—

      (i) the core academic subjects (as defined in section 9101 of the Elementary and Secondary Education Act of 1965); and

      (ii) career and technical education subjects;

   (C) provide students with strong experience in, and understanding of, all aspects of an industry;

   (D) ensure that students who participate in such career and technical education programs are taught to the same coherent and rigorous content aligned with challenging academic standards as are taught to all other students; and

   (E) encourage career and technical education students at the secondary level to enroll in rigorous and challenging courses in core academic subjects (as defined in section 9101 of the Elementary and Secondary Education Act of 1965);

(4) describe how comprehensive professional development (including initial teacher preparation) for career and technical education, academic, guidance, and administrative personnel will be provided that promotes the integration of coherent and rigorous content aligned with challenging academic standards and relevant career and technical education (including curriculum development);

(5) describe how parents, students, academic and career and technical education teachers, faculty, administrators, career guidance and academic counselors, representatives of tech prep consortia (if applicable), representatives of the entities participating in activities described in section 117 of Public Law 105–220 (if applicable), representatives of business (including small business) and industry, labor organizations, representatives of special populations, and other interested individuals are involved in the development, implementation, and evaluation of career and technical education programs assisted under this title, and how such individuals and entities are effectively informed about, and assisted in understanding, the requirements of this title, including career and technical programs of study;

(6) provide assurances that the eligible recipient will provide a career and technical education program that is of such size, scope, and quality to bring about improvement in the quality of career and technical education programs;

(7) describe the process that will be used to evaluate and continuously improve the performance of the eligible recipient;

(8) describe how the eligible recipient will—

   (A) review career and technical education programs, and identify and adopt strategies to overcome barriers that result in lowering rates of access to or lowering success in the programs, for special populations;

   (B) provide programs that are designed to enable the special populations to meet the local adjusted levels of performance; and

   (C) provide activities to prepare special populations, including single parents and dis-

TEXT OF LAW

placed homemakers, for high skill, high wage, or high demand occupations that will lead to self-sufficiency;

(9) describe how individuals who are members of special populations will not be discriminated against on the basis of their status as members of the special populations;

(10) describe how funds will be used to promote preparation for non-traditional fields;

(11) describe how career guidance and academic counseling will be provided to career and technical education students, including linkages to future education and training opportunities; and

(12) describe efforts to improve—

    (A) the recruitment and retention of career and technical education teachers, faculty, and career guidance and academic counselors, including individuals in groups underrepresented in the teaching profession; and

    (B) the transition to teaching from business and industry.

SEC. 135. LOCAL USES OF FUNDS.

(a) **General Authority.**—Each eligible recipient that receives funds under this part shall use such funds to improve career and technical education programs.

(b) **Requirements for Uses of Funds.**—Funds made available to eligible recipients under this part shall be used to support career and technical education programs that—

(1) strengthen the academic and career and technical skills of students participating in career and technical education programs, by strengthening the academic and career and technical education components of such programs through the integration of academics with career and technical education programs through a coherent sequence of courses, such as career and technical programs of study described in section 122(c)(1)(A), to ensure learning in—

    (A) the core academic subjects (as defined in section 9101 of the Elementary and Secondary Education Act of 1965); and

    (B) career and technical education subjects;

(2) link career and technical education at the secondary level and career and technical education at the postsecondary level, including by offering the relevant elements of not less than 1 career and technical program of study described in section 122(c)(1)(A);

(3) provide students with strong experience in and understanding of all aspects of an industry, which may include work-based learning experiences;

(4) develop, improve, or expand the use of technology in career and technical education, which may include—

    (A) training of career and technical education teachers, faculty, and administrators to use technology, which may include distance learning;

    (B) providing career and technical education students with the academic and career and technical skills (including the mathematics and science knowledge that provides a strong basis for such skills) that lead to entry into the technology fields; or

    (C) encouraging schools to collaborate with technology industries to offer voluntary internships and mentoring programs, including programs that improve the mathematics and science knowledge of students;

(5) provide professional development programs that are consistent with section 122 to

secondary and postsecondary teachers, faculty, administrators, and career guidance and academic counselors who are involved in integrated career and technical education programs, including—

(A)   in-service and preservice training on—

(i)   effective integration and use of challenging academic and career and technical education provided jointly with academic teachers to the extent practicable;

(ii)   effective teaching skills based on research that includes promising practices;

(iii)   effective practices to improve parental and community involvement; and

(iv)   effective use of scientifically based research and data to improve instruction;

(B)   support of education programs for teachers of career and technical education in public schools and other public school personnel who are involved in the direct delivery of educational services to career and technical education students, to ensure that such teachers and personnel stay current with all aspects of an industry;

(C)   internship programs that provide relevant business experience; and

(D)   programs designed to train teachers specifically in the effective use and application of technology to improve instruction;

(6)   develop and implement evaluations of the career and technical education programs carried out with funds under this title, including an assessment of how the needs of special populations are being met;

(7)   initiate, improve, expand, and modernize quality career and technical education programs, including relevant technology;

(8)   provide services and activities that are of sufficient size, scope, and quality to be effective; and

(9)   provide activities to prepare special populations, including single parents and displaced homemakers who are enrolled in career and technical education programs, for high skill, high wage, or high demand occupations that will lead to self-sufficiency.

(c)   **Permissive.**—Funds made available to an eligible recipient under this title may be used—

(1)   to involve parents, businesses, and labor organizations as appropriate, in the design, implementation, and evaluation of career and technical education programs authorized under this title, including establishing effective programs and procedures to enable informed and effective participation in such programs;

(2)   to provide career guidance and academic counseling, which may include information described in section 118, for students participating in career and technical education programs, that—

(A)   improves graduation rates and provides information on postsecondary and career options, including baccalaureate degree programs, for secondary students, which activities may include the use of graduation and career plans; and

(B)   provides assistance for postsecondary students, including for adult students who are changing careers or updating skills;

(3)   for local education and business (including small business) partnerships, including for—

(A)   work-related experiences for students, such as internships, cooperative education, school-based enterprises, entrepreneurship, and job shadowing that are related to career and technical education programs;

(B)   adjunct faculty arrangements for qualified industry professionals; and

(C)   industry experience for teachers and faculty;

(4)   to provide programs for special populations;

(5)   to assist career and technical student organizations;

(6)   for mentoring and support services;

(7)   for leasing, purchasing, upgrading or adapting equipment, including instructional aids and publications (including support for library resources) designed to strengthen and support academic and technical skill achievement;

(8)   for teacher preparation programs that address the integration of academic and career and technical education and that assist individuals who are interested in becoming career and technical education teachers and faculty, including individuals with experience in business and industry;

(9)   to develop and expand postsecondary program offerings at times and in formats that are accessible for students, including working students, including through the use of distance education;

(10) to develop initiatives that facilitate the transition of subbaccalaureate career and technical education students into baccalaureate degree programs, including—

(A)   articulation agreements between sub-baccalaureate degree granting career and technical education postsecondary educational institutions and baccalaureate degree granting postsecondary educational institutions;

(B)   postsecondary dual and concurrent enrollment programs;

(C)   academic and financial aid counseling for sub-baccalaureate career and technical education students that informs the students of the opportunities for pursuing a baccalaureate degree and advises the students on how to meet any transfer requirements; and

(D)   other initiatives—

(i)   to encourage the pursuit of a baccalaureate degree; and

(ii) to overcome barriers to enrollment in and completion of baccalaureate degree programs, including geographic and other barriers affecting rural students and special populations;

(11) to provide activities to support entrepreneurship education and training;

(12) for improving or developing new career and technical education courses, including the development of new proposed career and technical programs of study for consideration by the eligible agency and courses that prepare individuals academically and technically for high skill, high wage, or high demand occupations and dual or concurrent enrollment opportunities by which career and technical education students at the secondary level could obtain postsecondary credit to count towards an associate or baccalaureate degree;

(13) to develop and support small, personalized career-themed learning communities;

(14) to provide support for family and consumer sciences programs;

(15) to provide career and technical education programs for adults and school dropouts to complete the secondary school education, or upgrade the technical skills, of the adults and school dropouts;

(16) to provide assistance to individuals who have participated in services and activities under this Act in continuing their education or training or finding an appropriate job, such

as through referral to the system established under section 121 of Public Law 105–220 (29 U.S.C. 2801 et seq.);

(17) to support training and activities (such as mentoring and outreach) in non-traditional fields;

(18) to provide support for training programs in automotive technologies;

(19) to pool a portion of such funds with a portion of funds available to not less than 1 other eligible recipient for innovative initiatives, which may include—

(A) improving the initial preparation and professional development of career and technical education teachers, faculty, administrators, and counselors;

(B) establishing, enhancing, or supporting systems for—

(i) accountability data collection under this Act; or

(ii) reporting data under this Act;

(C) implementing career and technical programs of study described in section 122(c)(1)(A); or

(D) implementing technical assessments; and

(20) to support other career and technical education activities that are consistent with the purpose of this Act.

(d) **Administrative Costs.**—Each eligible recipient receiving funds under this part shall not use more than 5 percent of the funds for administrative costs associated with the administration of activities assisted under this section.

TITLE II
TECH PREP EDUCATION

SEC. 201. STATE ALLOTMENT AND APPLICATION.

(a) **In General.**—For any fiscal year, the Secretary shall allot the amount made available under section 206 among the States in the same manner as funds are allotted to States under paragraph (2) of section 111(a).

(b) **Payments to Eligible Agencies.**—The Secretary shall make a payment in the amount of a State's allotment under subsection (a) to the eligible agency that serves the State and has an application approved under subsection (c).

(c) **State Application.**—Each eligible agency desiring an allotment under this title shall submit, as part of its State plan under section 122, an application that—

(1) describes how activities under this title will be coordinated, to the extent practicable, with activities described in the State plan submitted under section 122; and

(2) contains such information as the Secretary may require.

SEC. 202. CONSOLIDATION OF FUNDS.

(a) **In General.**—An eligible agency receiving an allotment under sections 111 and 201 may choose to consolidate all, or a portion of, funds received under section 201 with funds received

TEXT OF LAW

under section 111 in order to carry out the activities described in the State plan submitted under section 122.

(b) Notification Requirement.—Each eligible agency that chooses to consolidate funds under this section shall notify the Secretary, in the State plan submitted under section 122, of the eligible agency's decision to consolidate funds under this section.

(c) Treatment of Consolidated Funds.—Funds consolidated under this section shall be considered as funds allotted under section 111 and shall be distributed in accordance with section 112.

SEC. 203. TECH PREP PROGRAM.

(a) Grant Program Authorized.—

    (1) In General.—From amounts made available to each eligible agency under section 201, the eligible agency, in accordance with the provisions of this title, shall award grants, on a competitive basis or on the basis of a formula determined by the eligible agency, for tech prep programs described in subsection (c). The grants shall be awarded to consortia between or among—

        (A) a local educational agency, an intermediate educational agency, educational service agency, or area career and technical education school, serving secondary school students, or a secondary school funded by the Bureau of Indian Affairs; and

        (B)   **(i)** a nonprofit institution of higher education that—

            (I)   **(aa)** offers a 2-year associate degree program or a 2-year certificate program; and

                (bb) is qualified as an institution of higher education pursuant to section 102 of the Higher Education Act of 1965, including—

                    (AA) an institution receiving assistance under the Tribally Controlled College or University Assistance Act of 1978 (25 U.S.C. 1801 et seq.); and

                    (BB) a tribally controlled postsecondary career and technical institution; or

            (II) offers a 2-year apprenticeship program that follows secondary education instruction, if such nonprofit institution of higher education is not prohibited from receiving assistance under part B of title IV of the Higher Education Act of 1965 pursuant to the provisions of section 435(a)(2) of such Act; or

        (ii) a proprietary institution of higher education that offers a 2-year associate degree program and is qualified as an institution of higher education pursuant to section 102 of the Higher Education Act of 1965, if such proprietary institution of higher education is not subject to a default management plan required by the Secretary.

    (2) Special Rule.—In addition, a consortium described in paragraph (1) may include 1 or more—

        (A) institutions of higher education that award a baccalaureate degree; and

        (B) employers (including small businesses), business intermediaries, or labor organizations.

(b) Duration.—Each consortium receiving a grant under this title shall use amounts provided under the grant to develop and operate a 4- or 6-year tech prep program described in subsection (c).

(c) Contents of Tech Prep Program.—Each tech prep program shall—

(1)   be carried out under an articulation agreement between the participants in the consortium;

(2)   consist of a program of study that—
       (A)   combines—
              (i)   a minimum of 2 years of secondary education (as determined under State law); with
              (ii)   (I)   a minimum of 2 years of postsecondary education in a nonduplicative, sequential course of study; or
                     (II)   an apprenticeship program of not less than 2 years following secondary education instruction; and
       (B)   integrates academic and career and technical education instruction, and utilizes work-based and worksite learning experiences where appropriate and available;
       (C)   provides technical preparation in a career field, including high skill, high wage, or high demand occupations;
       (D)   builds student competence in technical skills and in core academic subjects (as defined in section 9101 of the Elementary and Secondary Education Act of 1965), as appropriate, through applied, contextual, and integrated instruction, in a coherent sequence of courses;
       (E)   leads to technical skill proficiency, an industry-recognized credential, a certificate, or a degree, in a specific career field;
       (F)   leads to placement in high skill or high wage employment, or to further education; and
       (G)   utilizes career and technical education programs of study, to the extent practicable;

(3)   include the development of tech prep programs for secondary education and postsecondary education that—
       (A)   meet academic standards developed by the State;
       (B)   link secondary schools and 2-year postsecondary institutions, and if possible and practicable, 4-year institutions of higher education, through—
              (i)   nonduplicative sequences of courses in career fields;
              (ii)   the use of articulation agreements; and
              (iii)   the investigation of opportunities for tech prep secondary education students to enroll concurrently in secondary education and postsecondary education coursework;
       (C)   use, if appropriate and available, work-based or worksite learning experiences in conjunction with business and all aspects of an industry; and
       (D)   use educational technology and distance learning, as appropriate, to involve all the participants in the consortium more fully in the development and operation of programs;

(4)   include in-service professional development for teachers, faculty, and administrators that—
       (A)   supports effective implementation of tech prep programs;
       (B)   supports joint training in the tech prep consortium;
       (C)   supports the needs, expectations, and methods of business and all aspects of an industry;
       (D)   supports the use of contextual and applied curricula, instruction, and assessment;
       (E)   supports the use and application of technology; and
       (F)   assists in accessing and utilizing data, information available pursuant to section 118, and information on student achievement, including assessments;

(5)   include professional development programs for counselors designed to enable counselors to more effectively—
       (A)   provide information to students regarding tech prep programs;

TEXT OF LAW

    (B)   support student progress in completing tech prep programs, which may include the use of graduation and career plans;

    (C)   provide information on related employment opportunities;

    (D)   ensure that students are placed in appropriate employment or further postsecondary education;

    (E)   stay current with the needs, expectations, and methods of business and all aspects of an industry; and

    (F)   provide comprehensive career guidance and academic counseling to participating students, including special populations;

(6)   provide equal access, to the full range of technical preparation programs (including preapprenticeship programs), to individuals who are members of special populations, including the development of tech prep program services appropriate to the needs of special populations;

(7)   provide for preparatory services that assist participants in tech prep programs; and

(8)   coordinate with activities conducted under title I.

(d)   **Additional Authorized Activities.**—Each tech prep program may—

(1)   provide for the acquisition of tech prep program equipment;

(2)   acquire technical assistance from State or local entities that have designed, established, and operated tech prep programs that have effectively used educational technology and distance learning in the delivery of curricula and services;

(3)   establish articulation agreements with institutions of higher education, labor organizations, or businesses located inside or outside the State and served by the consortium, especially with regard to using distance learning and educational technology to provide for the delivery of services and programs;

(4)   improve career guidance and academic counseling for participating students through the development and implementation of graduation and career plans; and

(5)   develop curriculum that supports effective transitions between secondary and postsecondary career and technical education programs.

(e)   **Indicators of Performance and Accountability.**—

(1)   **In General.**—Each consortium shall establish and report to the eligible agency indicators of performance for each tech prep program for which the consortium receives a grant under this title. The indicators of performance shall include the following:

    (A)   The number of secondary education tech prep students and postsecondary education tech prep students served.

    (B)   The number and percent of secondary education tech prep students enrolled in the tech prep program who—

        (i)   enroll in postsecondary education;

        (ii)   enroll in postsecondary education in the same field or major as the secondary education tech prep students were enrolled at the secondary level;

        (iii)   complete a State or industry-recognized certification or licensure;

        (iv)   successfully complete, as a secondary school student, courses that award postsecondary credit at the secondary level; and

        (v)   enroll in remedial mathematics, writing, or reading courses upon entering postsecondary education.

TEXT OF LAW

(C) The number and percent of postsecondary education tech prep students who—

    (i) are placed in a related field of employment not later than 12 months after graduation from the tech prep program;

    (ii) complete a State or industry-recognized certification or licensure;

    (iii) complete a 2-year degree or certificate program within the normal time for completion of such program; and

    (iv) complete a baccalaureate degree program within the normal time for completion of such program.

(2) **Number and Percent.**—For purposes of subparagraphs (B) and (C) of paragraph (1), the numbers and percentages shall be determined separately with respect to each clause of each such subparagraph.

SEC. 204. CONSORTIUM APPLICATIONS.

(a) **In General.**—Each consortium that desires to receive a grant under this title shall submit an application to the eligible agency at such time and in such manner as the eligible agency shall require.

(b) **Plan.**—Each application submitted under this section shall contain a 6-year plan for the development and implementation of tech prep programs under this title, which plan shall be reviewed after the second year of the plan.

(c) **Approval.**—The eligible agency shall approve applications under this title based on the potential of the activities described in the application to create an effective tech prep program.

(d) **Special Consideration.**—The eligible agency, as appropriate, shall give special consideration to applications that—

(1) provide for effective employment placement activities or the transfer of students to baccalaureate or advanced degree programs;

(2) are developed in consultation with business, industry, institutions of higher education, and labor organizations;

(3) address effectively the issues of school dropout prevention and reentry, and the needs of special populations;

(4) provide education and training in an area or skill, including an emerging technology, in which there is a significant workforce shortage based on the data provided by the eligible entity in the State under section 118;

(5) demonstrate how tech prep programs will help students meet high academic and employability competencies; and

(6) demonstrate success in, or provide assurances of, coordination and integration with eligible recipients described in part C of title I.

(e) **Performance Levels.**—

(1) **In General.**—Each consortium receiving a grant under this title shall enter into an agreement with the eligible agency to meet a minimum level of performance for each of the performance indicators described in sections 113(b) and 203(e).

(2) **Resubmission of Application; Termination of Funds.**—An eligible agency—

    (A) shall require consortia that do not meet the performance levels described in para-

TEXT OF LAW

graph (1) for 3 consecutive years to resubmit an application to the eligible agency for a tech prep program grant; and

    (B)   may choose to terminate the funding for the tech prep program for a consortium that does not meet the performance levels described in paragraph (1) for 3 consecutive years, including when the grants are made on the basis of a formula determined by the eligible agency.

(f)   **Equitable Distribution of Assistance.**—In awarding grants under this title, the eligible agency shall ensure an equitable distribution of assistance between or among urban and rural participants in the consortium.

SEC. 205. REPORT.

Each eligible agency that receives an allotment under this title annually shall prepare and submit to the Secretary a report on the effectiveness of the tech prep programs assisted under this title, including a description of how grants were awarded within the State.

SEC. 206. AUTHORIZATION OF APPROPRIATIONS.

There are authorized to be appropriated to carry out this title such sums as may be necessary for fiscal year 2007 and each of the 5 succeeding fiscal years.

TITLE III
GENERAL PROVISIONS

PART A—FEDERAL ADMINISTRATIVE PROVISIONS

SEC. 311. FISCAL REQUIREMENTS.

(a)   **Supplement not Supplant.**—Funds made available under this Act for career and technical education activities shall supplement, and shall not supplant, non-Federal funds expended to carry out career and technical education activities and tech prep program activities.

(b)   **Maintenance of Effort.**—

    (1)   **Determination.**—

        (A)   **In General.**—Except as provided in subparagraphs (B) and (C), no payments shall be made under this Act for any fiscal year to a State for career and technical education programs or tech prep programs unless the Secretary determines that the fiscal effort per student or the aggregate expenditures of such State for career and technical education programs for the fiscal year preceding the fiscal year for which the determination is made, equaled or exceeded such effort or expenditures for career and technical education programs for the second fiscal year preceding the fiscal year for which the determination is made.

        (B)   **Computation.**—In computing the fiscal effort or aggregate expenditures pursuant to subparagraph (A), the Secretary shall exclude capital expenditures, special 1-time project costs, and the cost of pilot programs.

        (C)   **Decrease in Federal Support.**—If the amount made available for career and technical education programs under this Act for a fiscal year is less than the amount made available for career and technical education programs under this Act for the preceding fiscal year, then the fiscal effort per student or the aggregate expenditures of a State required by subparagraph (A) for the preceding fiscal year shall be decreased by the same percentage as the percentage decrease in the amount so made available.

(2) **Waiver.**—The Secretary may waive the requirements of this section, with respect to not more than 5 percent of expenditures by any eligible agency for 1 fiscal year only, on making a determination that such waiver would be equitable due to exceptional or uncontrollable circumstances affecting the ability of the eligible agency to meet such requirements, such as a natural disaster or an unforeseen and precipitous decline in financial resources. No level of funding permitted under such a waiver may be used as the basis for computing the fiscal effort or aggregate expenditures required under this section for years subsequent to the year covered by such waiver. The fiscal effort or aggregate expenditures for the subsequent years shall be computed on the basis of the level of funding that would, but for such waiver, have been required.

SEC. 312. AUTHORITY TO MAKE PAYMENTS.

Any authority to make payments or to enter into contracts under this Act shall be available only to such extent or in such amounts as are provided in advance in appropriation Acts.

SEC. 313. CONSTRUCTION.

Nothing in this Act shall be construed to permit, allow, encourage, or authorize any Federal control over any aspect of a private, religious, or home school, regardless of whether a home school is treated as a private school or home school under State law. This section shall not be construed to bar students attending private, religious, or home schools from participation in programs or services under this Act.

SEC. 314. VOLUNTARY SELECTION AND PARTICIPATION.

No funds made available under this Act shall be used—

(1) to require any secondary school student to choose or pursue a specific career path or major; or

(2) to mandate that any individual participate in a career and technical education program, including a career and technical education program that requires the attainment of a federally funded skill level, standard, or certificate of mastery.

SEC. 315. LIMITATION FOR CERTAIN STUDENTS.

No funds received under this Act may be used to provide career and technical education programs to students prior to the seventh grade, except that equipment and facilities purchased with funds under this Act may be used by such students.

SEC. 316. FEDERAL LAWS GUARANTEEING CIVIL RIGHTS.

Nothing in this Act shall be construed to be inconsistent with applicable Federal law prohibiting discrimination on the basis of race, color, sex, national origin, age, or disability in the provision of Federal programs or services.

SEC. 317. PARTICIPATION OF PRIVATE SCHOOL PERSONNEL AND CHILDREN.

(a) **Personnel.**—An eligible agency or eligible recipient that uses funds under this Act for

TEXT OF LAW

in-service and preservice career and technical education professional development programs for career and technical education teachers, administrators, and other personnel shall, to the extent practicable, upon written request, permit the participation in such programs of career and technical education secondary school teachers, administrators, and other personnel in nonprofit private schools offering career and technical secondary education programs located in the geographical area served by such eligible agency or eligible recipient.

(b) **Student Participation.**—

(1) **Student Participation.**—Except as prohibited by State or local law, an eligible recipient may, upon written request, use funds made available under this Act to provide for the meaningful participation, in career and technical education programs and activities receiving funding under this Act, of secondary school students attending nonprofit private schools who reside in the geographical area served by the eligible recipient.

(2) **Consultation.**—An eligible recipient shall consult, upon written request, in a timely and meaningful manner with representatives of nonprofit private schools in the geographical area served by the eligible recipient described in paragraph (1) regarding the meaningful participation, in career and technical education programs and activities receiving funding under this Act, of secondary school students attending nonprofit private schools.

SEC. 318. LIMITATION ON FEDERAL REGULATIONS.

The Secretary may issue regulations under this Act only to the extent necessary to administer and ensure compliance with the specific requirements of this Act.

_____

PART B—STATE ADMINISTRATIVE PROVISIONS

SEC. 321. JOINT FUNDING.

(a) **General Authority.**—Funds made available to eligible agencies under this Act may be used to provide additional funds under an applicable program if—

(1) such program otherwise meets the requirements of this Act and the requirements of the applicable program;

(2) such program serves the same individuals that are served under this Act;

(3) such program provides services in a coordinated manner with services provided under this Act; and

(4) such funds are used to supplement, and not supplant, funds provided from non-Federal sources.

(b) **Applicable Program.**—For the purposes of this section, the term 'applicable program' means any program under any of the following provisions of law:

(1) Chapters 4 and 5 of subtitle B of title I of Public Law 105–220.

(2) The Wagner-Peyser Act.

(c)   **Use of Funds as Matching Funds.**—For the purposes of this section, the term 'additional funds' does not include funds used as matching funds.

SEC. 322. PROHIBITION ON USE OF FUNDS TO INDUCE OUT-OF-STATE RELOCATION OF BUSINESSES.

No funds provided under this Act shall be used for the purpose of directly providing incentives or inducements to an employer to relocate a business enterprise from one State to another State if such relocation will result in a reduction in the number of jobs available in the State where the business enterprise is located before such incentives or inducements are offered.

SEC. 323. STATE ADMINISTRATIVE COSTS.

(a)   **General Rule.**—Except as provided in subsection (b), for each fiscal year for which an eligible agency receives assistance under this Act, the eligible agency shall provide, from non-Federal sources for the costs the eligible agency incurs for the administration of programs under this Act, an amount that is not less than the amount provided by the eligible agency from non-Federal sources for such costs for the preceding fiscal year.

(b)   **Exception.**—If the amount made available from Federal sources for the administration of programs under this Act for a fiscal year (referred to in this section as the 'determination year') is less than the amount made available from Federal sources for the administration of programs under this Act for the preceding fiscal year, then the amount the eligible agency is required to provide from non-Federal sources for costs the eligible agency incurs for the administration of programs under this Act for the determination year under subsection (a) shall bear the same ratio to the amount the eligible agency provided from non-Federal sources for such costs for the preceding fiscal year, as the amount made available from Federal sources for the administration of programs under this Act for the determination year bears to the amount made available from Federal sources for the administration of programs under this Act for the preceding fiscal year.

SEC. 324. STUDENT ASSISTANCE AND OTHER FEDERAL PROGRAMS.

(a)   **Attendance Costs not Treated as Income or Resources.**—The portion of any student financial assistance received under this Act that is made available for attendance costs described in subsection (b) shall not be considered as income or resources in determining eligibility for assistance under any other program funded in whole or in part with Federal funds.

(b)   **Attendance Costs.**—The attendance costs described in this subsection are—

(1)   tuition and fees normally assessed a student carrying an academic workload as determined by the institution, and including costs for rental or purchase of any equipment, materials, or supplies required of all students in that course of study; and

(2)   an allowance for books, supplies, transportation, dependent care, and miscellaneous personal expenses for a student attending the institution on at least a half-time basis, as determined by the institution.

(c)   **Costs of Career and Technical Education Services.**— Funds made available under this Act may be used to pay for the costs of career and technical education services required in an individualized education program developed pursuant to section 614(d) of the Individuals with Disabilities Education Act and services necessary to meet the requirements of section 504 of the Rehabilitation Act of 1973 with respect to ensuring equal access to career and technical education.

TEXT OF LAW

SEC. 2. TECHNICAL AMENDMENTS TO OTHER LAWS.

(a) **Immigration and Nationality Act.**—Section 245A(h)(4)(C) of the Immigration and Nationality Act (8 U.S.C. 1255a(h)(4)(C)) is amended by striking "Carl D. Perkins Vocational and Technical Education Act of 1998" and inserting "The Carl D. Perkins Career and Technical Education Act of 2006".

(b) **Trade Act of 1974.**—The Trade Act of 1974 (19 U.S.C. 2101 et seq.) is amended—

    (1) in section 231(c)(1)(F) (19 U.S.C. 2291(c)(1)(F))—

        (A) by striking "area vocational education schools" and inserting "area career and technical education schools"; and

        (B) by striking "Carl D. Perkins Vocational and Technical Education Act of 1998" and inserting "Carl D. Perkins Career and Technical Education Act of 2006"; and

    (2) in section 236(a)(1)(D) (19 U.S.C. 2296(a)(1)(D)), by striking "area vocational" and all that follows through "Act of 1963" and inserting "area career and technical education schools, as defined in section 3 of the Carl D. Perkins Career and Technical Education Act of 2006".

(c) **Higher Education Act of 1965.**—The Higher Education Act of 1965 (20 U.S.C. 1001 et seq.) is amended—

    (1) in section 102(a)(3)(A) (20 U.S.C. 1002(a)(3)(A))—

        (A) by striking "section 521(4)(C)" and inserting "section 3(3)(C)"; and

        (B) by striking "Carl D. Perkins Vocational and Applied Technology Education Act" and inserting "Carl D. Perkins Career and Technical Education Act of 2006"; and

    (2) in section 484(l)(1)(B)(i) (20 U.S.C. 1091(l)(1)(B)(i)), by striking "section 521(4)(C) of the Carl D. Perkins Vocational and Technical Education Act of 1998" and inserting "section 3(C) of the Carl D. Perkins Career and Technical Education Act of 2006".

(d) **Education for Economic Security Act.**—Section 3(1) of the Education for Economic Security Act (20 U.S.C. 3902(1)) is amended—

    (1) by striking "area vocational education school" and inserting "area career and technical education school"; and

    (2) by striking "section 521(3) of the Carl D. Perkins Vocational Educational Act.." and inserting "section 3(3) of the Carl D. Perkins Career and Technical Education Act of 2006.".

(e) **Education Flexibility Partnership Act of 1999.**—Section 4(b)(2) of the Education Flexibility Partnership Act of 1999 (20 U.S.C. 5891b(b)(2)) is amended by striking "Carl D. Perkins Vocational and Technical Education Act of 1998" and inserting "Carl D. Perkins Career and Technical Education Act of 2006".

(f) **Elementary and Secondary Education Act of 1965.**—The Elementary and Secondary Education Act of 1965 (20 U.S.C. 6301 et seq.) is amended—

    (1) in section 1111(a)(1) (20 U.S.C. 6311(a)(1)), by striking "Carl D. Perkins Vocational and Technical Education Act of 1998" and inserting "Carl D. Perkins Career and Technical Education Act of 2006";

    (2) in section 1112(a)(1) (20 U.S.C. 6312(a)(1)), by striking "Carl D. Perkins Vocational and Technical Education Act of 1998" and inserting "Carl D. Perkins Career and Technical Education Act of 2006";

(3)   in section 1114(b)(2)(B)(v) (20 U.S.C. 6314(b)(2)(B)(v)), by striking "Carl D. Perkins Vocational and Technical Education Act of 1998" and inserting "the Carl D. Perkins Career and Technical Education Act of 2006"; and

(4)   in section 7115(b)(5) (20 U.S.C. 7425(b)(5)), by striking "Carl D. Perkins Vocational and Technical Education Act of 1998" and inserting "Carl D. Perkins Career and Technical Education Act of 2006".

(g)   **Wagner-Peyser Act.**—Section 15(f) of the Wagner-Peyser Act (29 U.S.C. 49l–2(f)) is amended by striking "Carl D. Perkins Vocational and Applied Technology Education Act" and inserting "Carl D. Perkins Career and Technical Education Act of 2006".

(h)   **Public Law 105–220.**—Public Law 105–220 is amended—

(1)   in section 101(3) (29 U.S.C. 2801(3))—

    (A)   by striking "given the term" and inserting "given the term 'area career and technical education school'"; and

    (B)   by striking "Carl D. Perkins Vocational and Technical Education Act of 1998" and inserting "Carl D. Perkins Career and Technical Education Act of 2006";

(2)   in section 101(50) (29 U.S.C. 2801(50)), by striking "given" and all that follows through the period at the end and inserting "given the term 'career and technical education' in section 3 of the Carl D. Perkins Career and Technical Education Act of 2006.";

(3)   in section 111(d)(3) (29 U.S.C. 2821(d)(3)), by striking "section 113(b)(14) of the Carl D. Perkins Vocational and Applied Technology Education Act" and inserting "section 113(b)(3) of the Carl D. Perkins Career and Technical Education Act of 2006";

(4)   in section 112(b)(8)(A)(iii) (29 U.S.C. 2822(b)(8)(A)(iii))—

    (A)   by striking "postsecondary vocational education activities" and inserting "career and technical education activities at the postsecondary level"; and

    (B)   by striking "Carl D. Perkins Vocational and Applied Technology Education Act" and inserting "Carl D. Perkins Career and Technical Education Act of 2006";

(5)   in section 121(b)(1)(B)(vii) (29 U.S.C. 2841(b)(1)(B)(vii))—

    (A)   by striking "postsecondary vocational education activities" and inserting "career and technical education activities at the postsecondary level"; and

    (B)   by striking "Carl D. Perkins Vocational and Applied Technology Education Act" and inserting "Carl D. Perkins Career and Technical Education Act of 2006";

(6)   in section 134(d)(2)(F) (29 U.S.C. 2864(d)(2)(F)), by striking "postsecondary vocational" and all that follows through "Education Act" and inserting "career and technical education activities at the postsecondary level, and career and technical education activities available to school dropouts, under the Carl D. Perkins Career and Technical Education Act of 2006";

(7)   in section 501(b)(2)(A) (20 U.S.C. 9271(b)(2)(A))—

    (A)   by striking "secondary vocational education programs" and inserting "career and technical education programs at the secondary level"; and

    (B)   by striking "Carl D. Perkins Vocational and Applied Technology Education Act" and inserting "Carl D. Perkins Career and Technical Education Act of 2006";

(8)   in section 501(b)(2)(B) (20 U.S.C. 9271(b)(2)(B))—

    (A)   by striking "postsecondary vocational education programs" and inserting "career and technical education programs at the postsecondary level"; and

TEXT OF LAW

(B)   by striking "Carl D. Perkins Vocational and Applied Technology Education Act" and inserting "Carl D. Perkins Career and Technical Education Act of 2006"; and

(9)   in section 501(d)(2)(B) (20 U.S.C. 9271(d)(2)(B)), by striking "Carl D. Perkins Vocational and Applied Technology Education Act" and inserting "Carl D. Perkins Career and Technical Education Act of 2006".

(i)   **Title 31.**—Section 6703(a)(12) of title 31, United States Code, is amended by striking "Carl D. Perkins Vocational and Applied Technology Education Act" and inserting "Carl D. Perkins Career and Technical Education Act of 2006".

(j)   **Title 40.**—Section 14507(a)(1)(A)(iv) of title 40, United States Code, is amended by striking "Carl D. Perkins Vocational and Technical Education Act of 1998" and inserting "Carl D. Perkins Career and Technical Education Act of 2006".

(k)   **Older Americans Act of 1965.**—The Older Americans Act of 1965 (42 U.S.C. 3001 et seq.) is amended—

(1)   in section 502(b)(1)(N)(i) (42 U.S.C. 3056(b)(1)(N)(i)), by striking "Carl D. Perkins Vocational and Technical Education Act of 1998" and inserting "Carl D. Perkins Career and Technical Education Act of 2006";

(2)   in section 503(b)(2) (42 U.S.C. 3056a(b)(2)), by striking "Carl D. Perkins Vocational and Technical Education Act of 1998" each place that term appears and inserting "Carl D. Perkins Career and Technical Education Act of 2006"; and

(3)   in section 505(c)(2) (42 U.S.C. 3056c(c)(2)), by striking "Vocational and Technical Education Act of 1998" and inserting "Career and Technical Education Act of 2006".

(l)   **Compact of Free Association Amendments Act of 2003.**—Section 105(f)(1)(B)(iii) of the Compact of Free Association Amendments Act of 2003 (48 U.S.C. 1921d(f)(1)(B)(iii)) is amended by striking "Carl D. Perkins Vocational and Technical Education Act of 1998" and inserting "Carl D. Perkins Career and Technical Education Act of 2006".

TEXT OF LAW

COORDINATION WITH NO CHILD LEFT BEHIND

As has been mentioned throughout this Guide, one of the themes of the new Perkins Act is increased focus on the integration of academic and career and technical education. This is especially evident in increased linkages throughout the Act to the Elementary and Secondary Education Act of 1965 (ESEA), last reauthorized in 2002 as the No Child Left Behind Act (NCLB). ESEA is referenced 21 times throughout the text of the 2006 Perkins Act, up from only six times in the 1998 Act. Congress made it clear that the new Perkins Act must be closely aligned with NCLB. Significantly, the statement issued by Secretary Spellings after the congressional passage of the 2006 Perkins Act emphasizes this alignment with NCLB: "success will be determined through valid and reliable tests, including No Child Left Behind assessments in reading, math and science."

Below is a summary of where these linkages take place, and the corresponding text from the Elementary and Secondary Education Act.

Definitions

Four terms from Section 3 (Definitions) of the 2006 Perkins Act are defined as they are in Section 5210 and Section 9101 of the ESEA. These terms include:

- Charter School
- Educational Service Agency
- Local Educational Agency
- Secondary School

Coherent and Rigorous Content

Throughout the law, the term "coherent and rigorous content" is used in reference to academic content. Section 8 (Prohibitions) of the 2006 Perkins Act states that "For the purposes of this Act, coherent and rigorous content shall be determined by the state consistent with Section 1111(b)(1)(D) of the Elementary and Secondary Education Act of 1965." The emphasis is on the role of the state, not the Secretary of Education. The law limits the role of the Secretary to reaching agreement on adjusted levels of performance.

Secondary Indicators of Performance

Two new references to the ESEA are added to Section 113 (Accountability) of the 2006 Perkins Act. These references are contained within the following core indicators of performance for career and technical education students at the secondary level:

- Student attainment of challenging academic content standards and student academic achievement standards, as adopted by a state in accordance with Section 1111(b)(1) of the Elementary and Secondary Education Act of 1965 and measured by the state determined proficient levels on the academic assessments described in Section 1111(b)(3) of such Act.
- Student graduation rates (as described in Section 1111(b)(2)(C)(vi) of the Elementary and Secondary Education Act of 1965).

Both of these indicators are important components of the NCLB accountability system. Under NCLB, states, local educational agencies, and schools are required to make "adequate yearly progress" (AYP). Part of AYP is determined by the number of students scoring proficient or higher on state academic assessments developed under NCLB. States are required to establish annual measurable objectives for student achievement on such assessments—how many students will score at the proficient level. While the first indicator references the "proficient" achievement levels on state approved assessments under NCLB, there are no references to the annual measurable objectives established under NCLB in this indicator. Presumably, this provides states and local school districts with flexibility in establishing different adjusted levels of performance under the 2006 Perkins Act based on their unique situations.

Similarly, graduation rates are another component of AYP. Graduation rate is defined as the percentage of students, measured from the beginning of high school, who graduate from high school with a "regular diploma" in the standard number of years, unless the Department of Education approved another definition developed by the state. A "regular diploma" must be fully aligned with the state's academic standards, and does not include alternatives such as a certificate or a GED.

Disaggregation of Data

Section 113 (Accountability) of the Act also calls for a local and state report that includes disaggregated data for each of the performance indicators (unless personally identifiable information would be exposed because of small subgroups). This data must be disaggregated by the categories of special populations listed in the 2006 Perkins Act, as well as the categories of students described in Section 1111(h)(1)(C)(i) of the Elementary and Secondary Education Act of 1965 that are served under this Act.

The groups of "special populations" have been slightly revised to include (1) individuals with disabilities, (2) individuals from economically disadvantaged families (including foster children), (3) individuals preparing for nontraditional fields, (4) single parents, including single pregnant women, (5) displaced homemakers, and (6) individuals with limited English proficiency. The ESEA categories include race, ethnicity, gender, disability status, migrant status, English proficiency, and status as economically disadvantaged. Under NCLB, this information must be reported annually in state and local report cards, and thus should be readily available from state and local Title I offices, although some deficiencies may exist.

Professional Development

Under the new Act, professional development activities carried out by the state should be coordinated with efforts under Title II of ESEA (as well as Title II of the Higher Education Act).

This is specified in Section 122 (State Plan), which states that the plan should describe how professional development will be provided that "promotes integration with professional development activities that the state carries out under Title II of the Elementary and Secondary Education Act of 1965" and in Section 124 (State Leadership Activities), which states that leadership activities shall include professional development programs that, "are coordinated with the teacher certification or licensing and professional development activities that the state carries out under Title II of the Elementary and Secondary Education Act of 1965."

Professional development under the 2006 Perkins Act must be high-quality, sustained, intensive and focused on instruction. This is consistent with the definition of professional development in Section 9101(34) of ESEA, which prohibits one-day or short-term workshops or conferences (unless such workshops and conferences are part of a larger series of professional development activities).

Core Academic Subjects

The 2006 Perkins Act includes ensuring learning in "core academic subjects" six times. Each time, "core academic subjects" are defined as in Section 9101 of the Elementary and Secondary Education Act of 1965. These core academic subjects include English, reading or language arts, mathematics, science, foreign languages, civics and government, economics, arts, history, and geography.

References include:

- In Section 122 (State Plan), states must describe how they will "improve the academic and technical skills of students participating in career and technical education programs, including strengthening the academic and career and technical components of career and technical education programs through the integration of academics with career and technical education to ensure learning in the core academic subjects (as defined in Section 9101 of the Elementary and Secondary Education Act of 1965); and career and technical education subjects."
- In Section 134 (Local Plan), local recipients must describe how they will "improve the academic and technical skills of students participating in career and technical education programs by strengthening the academic and career and technical education components of such programs through the integration of coherent and rigorous content aligned with challenging academic standards and relevant career and technical education programs to ensure learning in the core academic subjects (as defined in Section 9101 of the Elementary and Secondary Education Act of 1965); and career and technical education subjects."
- In Section 124 (State Leadership Activities), states are required to support CTE programs "that improve the academic and career and technical skills of students participating in career and technical education programs by strengthening the academic and career and technical components of such career and technical education programs, through the integration of coherent and relevant content aligned with challenging academic standards and relevant career and technical education, to ensure achievement in the core academic subjects (as defined in Section 9101 of the Elementary and Secondary Education Act of 1965); and career and technical education subjects."
- In Section 134 (Local Plan), local recipients must describe how they will "encourage career and technical education students at the secondary level to enroll in rigorous and challenging courses in core academic subjects (as defined in Section 9101 of the Elementary and Secondary Education Act of 1965)."
- In Section 135 (Local Uses of Funds), local recipients are required to support CTE programs that "strengthen the academic and career and technical skills of students participating in career and technical education programs, by strengthening the academic and career and technical education components of such programs through the integration of academics with career and technical education programs through a coherent sequence of

courses, such as career and technical programs of study described in Section 122(c)(1)(A), to ensure learning in the core academic subjects (as defined in Section 9101 of the Elementary and Secondary Education Act of 1965); and career and technical education subjects."

- In Title II, Section 203 (Tech Prep Program), Each Tech Prep program shall consist of a program of study that "builds student competence in technical skills and in core academic subjects (as defined in Section 9101 of the Elementary and Secondary Education Act of 1965), as appropriate, through applied, contextual and integrated instruction, in a coherent sequence of courses."

Academic Content Standards and Student Academic Achievement Standards

In addition to being included in the secondary academic attainment indicator, references to "academic content standards and student academic achievement standards" are included in two other locations. These references refer to the standards adopted by states under Section 1111(b)(1) of the Elementary and Secondary Education Act of 1965.

- In Section 114 (National Activities), research should be conducted that includes "effective inservice and preservice teacher and faculty education that assists career and technical education programs in integrating those programs with academic content standards and student academic achievement standards, as adopted by states under Section 1111(b)(1) of the Elementary and Secondary Education Act of 1965."

- In Section 122 (State Plan), states must describe "how funds will be used to improve or develop new career and technical education courses at the secondary level that are aligned with rigorous and challenging academic content standards and student academic achievement standards adopted by the state under Section 1111(b)(1) of the Elementary and Secondary Education Act of 1965."

Distribution of Funds

The population factor (students aged 5–17 who reside in the school district) in the formula for distributing funds to local secondary programs must be based on data provided under Title I, Part A of ESEA or on student membership data from the National Center for Education Statistics. The poverty factor (the number of these students from families below the poverty level) must be determined on the basis of the most recent data used under Section 1124(c)(1)(A) of ESEA.

RELEVANT TEXT OF NO CHILD LEFT BEHIND*

Section 5210 of the Elementary and Secondary Education Act of 1965
[Perkins Section 3(8)]

(1) **Charter School.**—The term 'charter school' means a public school that—

(A) in accordance with a specific State statute authorizing the granting of charters to schools, is exempt from significant State or local rules that inhibit the flexible operation and management of public schools, but not from any rules relating to the other requirements of this paragraph;

(B) is created by a developer as a public school, or is adapted by a developer from an existing public school, and is operated under public supervision and direction;

(C) operates in pursuit of a specific set of educational objectives determined by the school's developer and agreed to by the authorized public chartering agency;

(D) provides a program of elementary or secondary education, or both;

(E) is nonsectarian in its programs, admissions policies, employment practices, and all other operations, and is not affiliated with a sectarian school or religious institution;

(F) does not charge tuition;

(G) complies with the Age Discrimination Act of 1975, title VI of the Civil Rights Act of 1964, title IX of the Education Amendments of 1972, section 504 of the Rehabilitation Act of 1973, and part B of the Individuals with Disabilities Education Act;

(H) is a school to which parents choose to send their children, and that admits students on the basis of a lottery, if more students apply for admission than can be accommodated;

(I) agrees to comply with the same Federal and State audit requirements as do other elementary schools and secondary schools in the State, unless such requirements are specifically waived for the purpose of this program;

(J) meets all applicable Federal, State, and local health and safety requirements;

(K) operates in accordance with State law; and

(L) has a written performance contract with the authorized public chartering agency in the State that includes a description of how student performance will be measured in charter schools pursuant to State assessments that are required of other schools and pursuant to any other assessments mutually agreeable to the authorized public chartering agency and the charter school.

Section 9101 of the Elementary and Secondary Education Act of 1965
[Perkins Section 3(11), (19), (27), Section 122(c)(7)(A)(i), Section 124(b)(4)(A), Section 134(b)(3)(B)(i), Section 134(b)(3)(E), Section 135(b)(1)(A), & Section 203(c)(2)(D)]

(11) **Core Academic Subjects.**—The term 'core academic subjects' means English, reading or language arts, mathematics, science, foreign languages, civics and government, economics, arts, history, and geography.

(17) **Educational Service Agency.**—The term 'educational service agency' means a regional public multi-service agency authorized by State statute to develop, manage, and provide services or programs to local educational agencies.

(26) **Local Educational Agency.**—

(A) **In General.**—The term 'local educational agency' means a public board of education or other public authority legally constituted within a State for either administrative control or direction of, or to perform a service function for, public elementary schools or secondary schools in a city, county, township, school district, or other political subdivision of a State, or of or for a combination of school districts or counties that is recognized in a State as an administrative agency for its public elementary schools or secondary schools.

(B) **Administrative Control and Direction.**—The term includes any other public institution or agency having administrative control and direction of a public elementary school or secondary school.

(C) **BIA Schools.**—The term includes an elementary school or secondary school funded by the Bureau of Indian Affairs but only to the extent that including the school makes the school eligible for programs for which specific eligibility is not provided to the school in another provision of law and the school does not have a student population that is smaller than the student population of the local educational agency receiving assistance under this Act with the smallest student population, except that the school shall not be subject to the jurisdiction of any State educational agency other than the Bureau of Indian Affairs.

(38) **Secondary School.**—The term 'secondary school' means a nonprofit institutional day or residential school, including a public secondary charter school, that provides secondary education, as determined under State law, except that the term does not include any education beyond grade 12.

Section 1111(b)(1) of the Elementary and Secondary Education Act of 1965
[Perkins Section 113(b)(2)(A)(i), Section 114(d)(4)(A)(iii)(I)(aa), & Section 122(c)(1)(I)(i)]

(b) **Academic Standards, Academic Assessments, and Accountability.**—

(1) **Challenging Academic Standards.**—

(A) **In General.**—Each State plan shall demonstrate that the State has adopted challenging academic content standards and challenging student academic achievement standards that will be used by the State, its local educational agencies, and its schools to carry out this part, except that a State shall not be required to submit such standards to the Secretary.

(B) **Same Standards.**—The academic standards required by subparagraph (A) shall be the same academic standards that the State applies to all schools and children in the State.

(C) **Subjects.**—The State shall have such academic standards for all public elementary school and secondary school children, including children served under this part, in subjects determined by the State, but including at least mathematics, reading or language arts, and (beginning in the 2005–2006 school year) science, which shall include the same knowledge, skills, and levels of achievement expected of all children.

(D) **Challenging Academic Standards.**—Standards under this paragraph shall include—

(i) challenging academic content standards in academic subjects that—

(I) specify what children are expected to know and be able to do;

(II) contain coherent and rigorous content; and

(III) encourage the teaching of advanced skills; and

(ii) challenging student academic achievement standards that—

(I) are aligned with the State's academic content standards;

(II) describe two levels of high achievement (proficient and advanced) that determine how well children are mastering the material in the State academic content standards; and

(III) describe a third level of achievement (basic) to provide complete information about the progress of the lower-achieving children toward mastering the proficient and advanced levels of achievement.

(E) **Information.**—For the subjects in which students will be served under this part, but for which a State is not required by subparagraphs (A), (B), and (C) to develop, and has not otherwise developed, such academic standards, the State plan shall describe a strategy for ensuring that students are taught the same knowledge and skills in such subjects and held to the same expectations as are all children.

(F) **Existing Standards.**—Nothing in this part shall prohibit a State from revising, consistent with this section, any standard adopted under this part before or after the date of enactment of the No Child Left Behind Act of 2001.

Section 1111(b)(3) of the Elementary and Secondary Education Act of 1965.
[Perkins Section 113(b)(2)(A)(i)]

(3) **Academic Assessments.**—

(A) **In General.**—Each State plan shall demonstrate that the State educational agency, in consultation with local educational agencies, has implemented a set of high-quality, yearly student academic assessments that include, at a minimum, academic assessments in mathematics, reading or language arts, and science that will be used as the primary means of determining the yearly performance of the State and of each local educational agency and school in the State in enabling all children to meet the State's challenging student academic achievement standards, except that no State shall be required to meet the requirements of this part relating to science assessments until the beginning of the 2007–2008 school year.

(B) **Use of Assessments.**—Each State educational agency may incorporate the data from the assessments under this paragraph into a State-developed longitudinal data system that links student test scores, length of enrollment, and graduation records over time.

(C) **Requirements.**—Such assessments shall—

(i) be the same academic assessments used to measure the achievement of all children;

(ii) be aligned with the State's challenging academic content and student academic achievement standards, and provide coherent information about student attainment of such standards;

(iii) be used for purposes for which such assessments are valid and reliable, and be consistent with relevant, nationally recognized professional and technical standards;

(iv) be used only if the State educational agency provides to the Secretary evidence from the test publisher or other relevant sources that the assessments used are of adequate technical quality for each purpose required under this Act and are consistent with the requirements of this section, and such evidence is made public by the Secretary upon request;

(v) (I) except as otherwise provided for grades 3 through 8 under clause vii, measure the proficiency of students in, at a minimum, mathematics and reading or language arts, and be administered not less than once during—

(aa) grades 3 through 5;

(bb) grades 6 through 9; and

(cc) grades 10 through 12;

(II) beginning not later than school year 2007–2008, measure the proficiency of all students in science and be administered not less than one time during—

(aa) grades 3 through 5;

(bb) grades 6 through 9; and

(cc) grades 10 through 12;

(vi) involve multiple up-to-date measures of student academic achievement, including measures that assess higher-order thinking skills and understanding;

(vii) beginning not later than school year 2005–2006, measure the achievement of students against the challenging State academic content and student academic achievement standards in each of grades 3 through 8 in, at a minimum, mathematics, and reading or language arts, except that the Secretary may provide the State 1 additional year if the State demonstrates that exceptional or uncontrollable circumstances, such as a natural disaster or a precipitous and unforeseen decline in the financial resources of the State, prevented full implementation of the academic assessments by that deadline and that the State will complete implementation within the additional 1-year period;

(viii) at the discretion of the State, measure the proficiency of students in academic subjects not described in clauses (v), (vi), (vii) in which the State has adopted challenging academic content and academic achievement standards;

(ix) provide for—

(I) the participation in such assessments of all students;

(II) he reasonable adaptations and accommodations for students with disabilities (as defined under section 602(3) of the Individuals with Disabilities Education Act) necessary to measure the academic achievement of such students relative to State academic content and State student academic achievement standards; and

(III) the inclusion of limited English proficient students, who shall be assessed in a valid and reliable manner and provided reasonable accommodations on assessments administered to such students under this paragraph, including, to the extent practicable, assessments in the language and form most likely to yield accurate data on what such students know and can do in academic content areas, until such students have achieved English language proficiency as determined under paragraph (7);

(x) notwithstanding subclause (III), the academic assessment (using tests written in English) of reading or language arts of any student who has attended school in the United States (not including Puerto Rico) for three or more consecutive school years, except that if the local educational agency determines, on a case-by-case individual basis, that academic assessments in another language or form would likely yield more accurate and reliable information on what such student knows and can do, the local educational agency may make a determination to assess such student in the appropriate language other than English for a period that does not exceed two additional consecutive years, provided that such student has not yet reached a level of English language proficiency sufficient to yield valid and reliable information on what such student knows and can do on tests (written in English) of reading or language arts;

(xi) include students who have attended schools in a local educational agency for a full academic year but have not attended a single school for a full academic year, except that the performance of students who have attended more than 1 school in the local educational agency in any academic year shall be used only in determining the progress of the local educational agency;

(xii) produce individual student interpretive, descriptive, and diagnostic reports, consistent with clause (iii) that allow parents, teachers, and principals to understand and address the specific academic needs of students, and include information regarding achievement on academic assessments aligned with State academic achievement standards, and that are provided to parents, teachers, and principals, as soon as is practicably possible after the assessment is given, in an understandable and uniform format, and to the extent practicable, in a language that parents can understand;

(xiii) enable results to be disaggregated within each State, local educational agency, and school by gender, by each major racial and ethnic group, by English proficiency status, by migrant status, by students with disabilities as compared to nondisabled students, and by economically disadvantaged students as compared to students who are not economically disadvantaged, except that, in the case of a local educational agency or a school, such disaggregation shall not be required in a case in which the number of students in a category is insufficient to yield statistically reliable information or the results would reveal personally identifiable information about an individual student;

(xiv) be consistent with widely accepted professional testing standards, objectively measure academic achievement, knowledge, and skills, and be tests that do not evaluate or assess personal or family beliefs and attitudes, or publicly disclose personally identifiable information; and

(xv) enable itemized score analyses to be produced and reported, consistent with clause (iii), to local educational agencies and schools, so that parents, teachers, principals, and administrators can interpret and address the specific academic needs of students as indicated by the students' achievement on assessment items.

(D) **Deferral.**—A State may defer the commencement, or suspend the administration, but not cease the development, of the assessments described in this paragraph, that were not required prior to the date of enactment of the No Child Left Behind Act of 2001, for 1 year for each year for which the amount appropriated for grants under section 6113(a)(2) is less than—

(i) $370,000,000 for fiscal year 2002;

(ii) $380,000,000 for fiscal year 2003;

(iii) $390,000,000 for fiscal year 2004; and

(iv) $400,000,000 for fiscal years 2005 through 2007.

Section 1111(b)(2)(C)(vi) of the Elementary and Secondary Education Act of 1965
[Perkins Section 113(b)(2)(A)(iv)]

(vi) in accordance with subparagraph (D), includes graduation rates for public secondary school students (defined as the percentage of students who graduate from secondary school with a regular diploma in the standard number of years) and at least one other academic indicator, as determined by the State for all public elementary school students; and

Section 1111(h)(1)(C)(i) of the Elementary and Secondary Education Act of 1965
[Perkins Section 113(b)(4)(C)(ii)(I) & Section 113(c)(2)(A)]

(i) information, in the aggregate, on student achievement at each proficiency level on the State academic assessments described in subsection (b)(3) (disaggregated by race, ethnicity, gender, disability status, migrant status, English proficiency, and status as economically disadvantaged, except that such disaggregation shall not be required in a case in which the number of students in a category is insufficient to yield statistically reliable information or the results would reveal personally identifiable information about an individual student);

Title II of the Elementary and Secondary Education Act of 1965
[Perkins Section 122(c)(2)(G) & Section 124(b)(3)(E)]

Refers to "**Preparing, Training, and Recruiting High Quality Teachers and Principals**"

Title I of the Elementary and Secondary Education Act of 1965
[Perkins Section 131(a)(1)(A)]

Refers to "**Improving the Academic Achievement of the Disadvantaged**"

Section 1124(c)(1)(A) of the Elementary and Secondary Education Act of 1965
[Perkins Section 131(a)(2)]

(c) **Children to be Counted.**—

(1) **Categories of Children.**—The number of children to be counted for purposes of this section is the aggregate of—

(A) the number of children aged 5 to 17, inclusive, in the school district of the local educational agency from families below the poverty level as determined under paragraph (2);

(B) the number of children (determined under paragraph (4) for either the preceding year as described in that paragraph, or for the second preceding year, as the Secretary finds appropriate) aged 5 to 17, inclusive, in the school district of such agency in institutions for neglected and delinquent children (other than such institutions operated by the United States), but not counted pursuant to subpart 1 of part D for the purposes of a grant to a State agency, or being supported in foster homes with public funds; and

(C) the number of children aged 5 to 17, inclusive, in the school district of such agency from families above the poverty level as determined under paragraph (4).

(2) **Determination of Number of Children.**—For the purposes of this section, the Secretary shall determine the number of children aged 5 to 17, inclusive, from families below the pov-

erty level on the basis of the most recent satisfactory data, described in paragraph (3), available from the Department of Commerce. The District of Columbia and the Commonwealth of Puerto Rico shall be treated as individual local educational agencies. If a local educational agency contains two or more counties in their entirety, then each county will be treated as if such county were a separate local educational agency for purposes of calculating grants under this part. The total of grants for such counties shall be allocated to such a local educational agency, which local educational agency shall distribute to schools in each county within such agency a share of the local educational agency's total grant that is no less than the county's share of the population counts used to calculate the local educational agency's grant.

COORDINATION WITH THE WORKFORCE INVESTMENT ACT

Two months prior to the enactment of the 1998 Perkins Act, Congress enacted the Workforce Investment Act (WIA). This Act was designed to streamline the patchwork of federal job training programs through a one-stop approach, strengthen accountability, and enhance the role of business and industry in the workforce development system. One of the federal job training programs included in this newly created one-stop system was Perkins. Both WIA and the 1998 Perkins Act required coordination at the state and local level.

In addition to the numerous planning coordination requirements in both the state and local Perkins plans and WIA plans, local workforce boards are required to use WIA "Youth" funds for occupational skills training and for strong linkages between academic and occupational learning for in-school and out-of-school youth. Postsecondary educational institutions receiving Perkins funds are also required to use a portion of those funds to support the establishment of the one-stop centers, and to support "core services" (informational services) at the one-stop centers.

Congress was expected to reauthorize the WIA in tandem with the reauthorization of Perkins. However, final action on the WIA legislation is not expected in 2006. Accordingly, this chapter addresses the references in the 2006 Perkins Act to the existing WIA.

While many of the references to WIA in the 2006 Perkins Act remain the same as in the 1998 Act, there are a few notable additions—and deletions. Especially in the Senate, one of the priorities of this reauthorization was to increase coordination between these two federal programs. This was accomplished primarily through adding requirements for the involvement of entities participating in workforce investment boards to the Perkins planning process.

However, one key change was made to the relationship between Perkins and WIA. The incentive grant program from the 1998 Perkins Act was eliminated in the new law. The previous incentive grant required states to meet performance measures under Perkins, WIA, and the Adult Education Act to be eligible for incentive funding. When reauthorizing Perkins, Congress found that the incentive grant was not necessarily working as intended to provide coordinated activities under the three programs, and that the funding that had been reserved from the Perkins allocation would be better utilized in the federal-to-state formula. Without this national activity, it seems as if most of the coordination between Perkins and WIA will fall to the state and local levels.

Below is a summary of where linkages take place within the 2006 Perkins Act, and the corresponding text from the Workforce Investment Act of 1998.

Section 118

As in the previous Perkins Act, there remains a non-duplication clause within Section 118 (Occupational and Employment Information) of the Perkins Act, specifying that activities carried out under the Perkins Occupational and Employment Information program must not duplicate activities carried out under the WIA. Effective July 1, 2006, Congress has not funded the Perkins Occupational and Employment Information program. This could have a negative impact on coordination between Perkins and WIA.

Eligible Agency Responsibilities

As in the previous Perkins Act, one of the four key responsibilities of the Perkins eligible agency is the adoption of such procedures as the eligible agency considers necessary to implement state level coordination with the activities undertaken by the state workforce investment board, and make available to the state's one-stop delivery system a listing of all school dropout, postsecondary education, and adult programs assisted under Perkins.

State and Local Plan Development

Entities participating in the activities of state workforce investment boards are added to the list of groups that the state should consult with on the development of the Perkins state plan. Similarly, in the local plan, Perkins recipients must now describe how representatives of local workforce investment boards will be involved in the development, implementation and evaluation of career and technical education programs, and informed about, and assisted in understanding, the requirements of this Perkins Act, including career and technical programs of study.

Joint Perkins and WIA Plan

The 2006 Perkins Act maintains the option for states to submit their Perkins state plans as part of their state plans submitted under WIA, as long as the plan meets all other Perkins requirements.

State Plan Contents

As in the 1998 Perkins Act, the state plan must include a description of how the state will assure coordination of and avoid duplication among federal programs serving postsecondary students and school dropouts, and how common data collection and reporting processes will be used. Also, the plan must continue to provide information related to local memoranda of understanding between Perkins postsecondary providers and the one-stop delivery system.

State and Local Uses of Funds

Permissive uses of state and local Perkins funds now reference providing referral to the one-stop system as a way of providing assistance to individuals who have participated in CTE services and activities in continuing their education or training or finding appropriate jobs.

Joint Funding

The provision in the 1998 Perkins Act that allowed Perkins funds to be used to provide additional funds to WIA youth, adult and dislocated worker programs (as long as the program met the requirements of Perkins, served the same individuals, was provided in a coordinated manner with other Perkins programs, and funds were used to supplement, not supplant) is maintained.

RELEVANT TEXT OF THE WORKFORCE INVESTMENT ACT*

Public Law 105–220
[Perkins Section 118(d)(2)]

Refers to the **"Workforce Investment Act of 1998"**

Section 111 of Public Law 105–220
[Perkins Section 121(a)(4)(A)
& Section 122(b)(1)(viii)]

SEC. 111. STATE WORKFORCE INVESTMENT BOARDS.

(a) **In General.**—The Governor of a State shall establish a State workforce investment board to assist in the development Establishment. of the State plan described in section 112 and to carry out the other functions described in subsection (d).

(b) **Membership.—**

  (1) **In General.**—The State Board shall include—

    (A) the Governor;

    (B) 2 members of each chamber of the State legislature, appointed by the appropriate presiding officers of each such chamber; and

    (C) representatives appointed by the Governor, who are—

      (i) representatives of business in the State, who—

        (I) are owners of businesses, chief executives or operating officers of businesses, and other business executives or employers with optimum policymaking or hiring authority, including members of local boards described in section 117(b)(2)(A)(i);

        (II) represent businesses with employment opportunities that reflect the employment opportunities of the State; and (III) are appointed from among individuals nominated by State business organizations and business trade associations;

      (ii) chief elected officials (representing both cities and counties, where appropriate);

      (iii) representatives of labor organizations, who have been nominated by State labor federations;

      (iv) representatives of individuals and organizations that have experience with respect to youth activities;

      (v) representatives of individuals and organizations that have experience and expertise in the delivery of workforce investment activities, including chief executive officers of community colleges and community- based organizations within the State;

      (vi) (I) the lead State agency officials with responsibility for the programs and activities that are described in section 121(b) and carried out by onestop partners; and

        (II) in any case in which no lead State agency official has responsibility for such a program, service, or activity, a representative in the State with expertise relating to such program, service, or activity; and

      (vii) such other representatives and State agency officials as the Governor may designate, such as the State agency officials responsible for economic development and juvenile justice programs in the State.

(2) **Authority and Regional Representation of Board Members.**—Members of the board that represent organizations, agencies, or other entities shall be individuals with optimum policymaking authority within the organizations, agencies, or entities. The members of the board shall represent diverse regions of the State, including urban, rural, and suburban areas.

(3) **Majority.**—A majority of the members of the State Board shall be representatives described in paragraph (1)(C)(i).

(c) **Chairman.**—The Governor shall select a chairperson for the State Board from among the representatives described in subsection (b)(1)(C)(i).

(d) **Functions.**—The State Board shall assist the Governor in—

(1) development of the State plan;

(2) development and continuous improvement of a statewide system of activities that are funded under this subtitle or carried out through a one-stop delivery system described in section 134(c) that receives funds under this subtitle (referred to in this title as a "statewide workforce investment system"), including—

  (A) development of linkages in order to assure coordination and nonduplication among the programs and activities described in section 121(b); and

  (B) review of local plans;

(3) commenting at least once annually on the measures taken pursuant to section 113(b)(14) of the Carl D. Perkins Vocational and Applied Technology Education Act (20 U.S.C 2323(b)(14));

(4) designation of local areas as required in section 116;

(5) development of allocation formulas for the distribution of funds for adult employment and training activities and youth activities to local areas as permitted under sections 128(b)(3)(B) and 133(b)(3)(B);

(6) development and continuous improvement of comprehensive State performance measures, including State adjusted levels of performance, to assess the effectiveness of the workforce investment activities in the State as required under section 136(b);

(7) preparation of the annual report to the Secretary described in section 136(d);

(8) development of the statewide employment statistics system described in section 15(e) of the Wagner-Peyser Act; and

(9) development of an application for an incentive grant under section 503.

(e) **Alternative Entity.**—

(1) **In General.**—For purposes of complying with subsections (a), (b), and (c), a State may use any State entity (including a State council, State workforce development board, combination of regional workforce development boards, or similar entity) that—

  (A) was in existence on December 31, 1997;

  (B) (i) was established pursuant to section 122 or title VII of the Job Training Partnership Act, as in effect on December 31, 1997; or

    (ii) is substantially similar to the State board described in subsections (a), (b), and (c); and (C)

includes representatives of business in the State and representatives of labor organizations in the State.

(2) **References.**—References in this Act to a State board shall be considered to include such an entity.

(f) **Conflict of Interest.**—A member of a State board may not—

(1) vote on a matter under consideration by the State board—

  (A) regarding the provision of services by such member (or by an entity that such member represents); or

  (B) that would provide direct financial benefit to such member or the immediate family of such member; or

(2) engage in any other activity determined by the Governor to constitute a conflict of interest as specified in the State plan.

(g) **Sunshine Provision.**—The State board shall make available to the public, on a regular basis through open meetings, information regarding the activities of the State board, including information regarding the State plan prior to submission of the plan, information regarding membership, and, on request, minutes of formal meetings of the State board.

Section 112(b)(8) of Public Law 105–220
[Perkins Section 122(c)(20)]

(8) (A) a description of the procedures that will be taken by the State to assure coordination of and avoid duplication among—

  (i) workforce investment activities authorized under this title;

  (ii) other activities authorized under this title;

  (iii) programs authorized under the Wagner-Peyser Act (29 U.S.C. 49 et seq.), title II of this Act, title I of the Rehabilitation Act of 1973 (29 U.S.C. 720 et seq.), part A of title IV of the Social Security Act (42 U.S.C. 601 et seq.), and section 6(d)(4) of the Food Stamp Act of 1977 (7 U.S.C. 2015(d)(4)), activities authorized under title V of the Older Americans Act of 1965 (42 U.S.C. 3056 et seq.), and postsecondary vocational education activities authorized under the Carl D. Perkins Vocational and Applied Technology Education Act (20 U.S.C. 2301 et seq.);

  (iv) work programs authorized under section 6(o) of the Food Stamp Act of 1977 (7 U.S.C. 2015(o));

  (v) activities authorized under chapter 2 of title II of the Trade Act of 1974 (19 U.S.C. 2271 et seq.);

  (vi) activities authorized under chapter 41 of title 38, United States Code;

  (vii) employment and training activities carried out under the Community Services Block Grant Act (42 U.S.C. 9901 et seq.);

  (viii) activities authorized under the National and Community Service Act of 1990 (42 U.S.C. 12501 et seq.);

  (ix) employment and training activities carried out by the Department of Housing and Urban Development; and

  (x) programs authorized under State unemployment compensation laws (in accordance with applicable Federal law); and

(B) a description of thte common data collection and reporting processes used for the programs and activities described in subparagraph (A);

Section 117 of Public Law 105–220
[Perkins Section 134(b)(5)]

Refers to "Local Workforce Investement Boards"

Section 121 of Public Law 105–220
[Perkins Section 121(a)(4)(B), Section 122(c)(20), Section 124(c)(13), & Section 135(c)(16)]

SEC. 121. ESTABLISHMENT OF ONE-STOP DELIVERY SYSTEMS.

(a) **In General.**—Consistent with the State plan, the local board for a local area, with the agreement of the chief elected official for the local area, shall—

(1) develop and enter into the memorandum of understanding described in subsection (c) with one-stop partners;

(2) designate or certify one-stop operators under subsection (d); and

(3) conduct oversight with respect to the one-stop delivery system in the local area.

(b) **One-stop Partners.**—

(1) **Required Partners.**—

(A) **In General.**—Each entity that carries out a program or activities described in subparagraph (B) shall—

(i) make available to participants, through a onestop delivery system, the services described in section 134(d)(2) that are applicable to such program or activities; and

(ii) participate in the operation of such system consistent with the terms of the memorandum described in subsection (c), and with the requirements of the Federal law in which the program or activities are authorized.

(B) **Programs and Activities.**—The programs and activities referred to in subparagraph (A) consist of—

(i) programs authorized under this title;

(ii) programs authorized under the Wagner-Peyser Act (29 U.S.C. 49 et seq.);

(iii) adult education and literacy activities authorized under title II;

(iv) programs authorized under title I of the Rehabilitation Act of 1973 (29 U.S.C. 720 et seq.);

(v) programs authorized under section 403(a)(5) of the Social Security Act (42 U.S.C. 603(a)(5) (as added by section 5001 of the Balanced Budget Act of 1997);

(vi) activities authorized under title V of the Older Americans Act of 1965 (42 U.S.C. 3056 et seq.);

(vii) postsecondary vocational education activities authorized under the Carl D. Perkins Vocational and Applied Technology Education Act (20 U.S.C. 2301 et seq.);

(viii) activities authorized under chapter 2 of title II of the Trade Act of 1974 (19 U.S.C. 2271 et seq.);

(ix) activities authorized under chapter 41 of title 38, United States Code;

(x) employment and training activities carried out under the Community Services Block Grant Act (42 U.S.C. 9901 et seq.);

(xi) employment and training activities carried out by the Department of Housing and Urban Development; and

(xii) programs authorized under State unemployment compensation laws (in accordance with applicable Federal law).

(2) **Additional Partners.**—

(A) **In General.**—In addition to the entities described in paragraph (1), other entities that carry out a human resource program described in subparagraph (B) may—

(i) make available to participants, through the onestop delivery system, the services described in section 134(d)(2) that are applicable to such program; and

(ii) participate in the operation of such system consistent with the terms of the memorandum described in subsection (c), and with the requirements of the Federal law in which the program is authorized; if the local board and chief elected official involved approve such participation.

(B) **Programs.**—The programs referred to in subparagraph (A) may include—

(i) programs authorized under part A of title IV of the Social Security Act (42 U.S.C. 601 et seq.);

(ii) programs authorized under section 6(d)(4) of the Food Stamp Act of 1977 (7 U.S.C. 2015(d)(4));

(iii) work programs authorized under section 6(o) of the Food Stamp Act of 1977 (7 U.S.C. 2015(o));

(iv) programs authorized under the National and Community Service Act of 1990 (42 U.S.C. 12501 et seq.); and

(v) other appropriate Federal, State, or local programs, including programs in the private sector.

(c) **Memorandum of Understanding.**—

(1) **Development.**—The local board, with the agreement of the chief elected official, shall develop and enter into a memorandum of understanding (between the local board and the one-stop partners), consistent with paragraph (2), concerning the operation of the one-stop delivery system in the local area.

(2) **Contents.**—Each memorandum of understanding shall contain—

(A) provisions describing—

(i) the services to be provided through the onestop delivery system;

    (ii) how the costs of such services and the operating costs of the system will be funded;

    (iii) methods for referral of individuals between the one-stop operator and the one-stop partners, for the appropriate services and activities; and

    (iv) the duration of the memorandum and the procedures for amending the memorandum during the term of the memorandum; and

  (B) such other provisions, consistent with the requirements of this title, as the parties to the agreement determine to be appropriate.

(d) **One-stop Operators.**—

  (1) **Designation and Certification.**—Consistent with paragraphs (2) and (3), the local board, with the agreement of the chief elected official, is authorized to designate or certify one-stop operators and to terminate for cause the eligibility of such operators.

  (2) **Eligibility.**—To be eligible to receive funds made available under this subtitle to operate a one-stop center referred to in section 134(c), an entity (which may be a consortium of entities)—

    (A) shall be designated or certified as a one-stop operator—

      (i) through a competitive process; or

      (ii) in accordance with an agreement reached between the local board and a consortium of entities that, at a minimum, includes 3 or more of the onestop partners described in subsection (b)(1); and

    (B) may be a public or private entity, or consortium of entities, of demonstrated effectiveness, located in the local area, which may include—

      (i) a postsecondary educational institution;

      (ii) an employment service agency established under the Wagner-Peyser Act (29 U.S.C. 49 et seq.), on behalf of the local office of the agency;

      (iii) a private, nonprofit organization (including a community-based organization);

      (iv) a private for-profit entity;

      (v) a government agency; and

      (vi) another interested organization or entity, which may include a local chamber of commerce or other business organization.

  (3) **Exception.**—Elementary schools and secondary schools shall not be eligible for designation or certification as onestop operators, except that nontraditional public secondary schools and area vocational education schools shall be eligible for such designation or certification.

(e) **Established One-stop Delivery System.**—If a one-stop delivery system has been established in a local area prior to the date of enactment of this Act, the local board, the chief elected official, and the Governor involved may agree to certify an entity carrying out activities through the system as a one-stop operator for purposes of subsection (d), consistent with the requirements of subsection (b), of the memorandum of understanding, and of section 134(c).

SEC. 501. STATE UNIFIED PLAN.

(a) **Definition of Appropriate Secretary.**—In this section, the term "appropriate Secretary" means the head of the Federal agency who exercises administrative authority over an activity or program described in subsection (b).

(b) **State Unified Plan.**—

  (1) **In General.**—A State may develop and submit to the appropriate Secretaries a State unified plan for 2 or more of the activities or programs set forth in paragraph (2), except that the State may include in the plan the activities described in paragraph (2)(A) only with the prior approval of the legislature of the State. The State unified plan shall cover one or more of the activities set forth in subparagraphs (A) through (D) of paragraph (2) and may cover one or more of the activities set forth in subparagraphs (E) through (O) of paragraph (2).

  (2) **Activities.**—The activities and programs referred to in paragraph (1) are as follows:

    (A) Secondary vocational education programs authorized under the Carl D. Perkins Vocational and Applied Technology Education Act (20 U.S.C. 2301 et seq.).

    (B) Postsecondary vocational education programs authorized under the Carl D. Perkins Vocational and Applied Technology Education Act (20 U.S.C. 2301 et seq.).

    (C) Activities authorized under title I.

    (D) Activities authorized under title II.

    (E) Programs authorized under section 6(d) of the Food Stamp Act of 1977 (7 U.S.C. 2015(d)).

    (F) Work programs authorized under section 6(o) of the Food Stamp Act of 1977 (7 U.S.C. 2015(o)).

    (G) Activities authorized under chapter 2 of title II of the Trade Act of 1974 (19 U.S.C. 2271 et seq.).

    (H) Programs authorized under the Wagner-Peyser Act (29 U.S.C. 49 et seq.).

    (I) Programs authorized under title I of the Rehabilitation Act of 1973 (29 U.S.C. 720 et seq.), other than section 112 of such Act (29 U.S.C. 732).

    (J) Activities authorized under chapter 41 of title 38, United States Code.

    (K) Programs authorized under State unemployment compensation laws (in accordance with applicable Federal law).

    (L) Programs authorized under part A of title IV of the Social Security Act (42 U.S.C. 601 et seq.).

    (M) Programs authorized under title V of the Older Americans Act of 1965 (42 U.S.C. 3056 et seq.).

    (N) Training activities carried out by the Department of Housing and Urban Development.

    (O) Programs authorized under the Community Services Block Grant Act (42 U.S.C. 9901 et seq.).

(c) **Requirements.**—

  (1) **In General.**—The portion of a State unified plan covering an activity or program described in subsection (b) shall be subject to the requirements, if any, applicable to a plan or application for assistance under the Federal statute authorizing the activity or program.

  (2) **Additional Submission not Required.**—A State that submits a

State unified plan covering an activity or program described in subsection (b) that is approved under subsection (d) shall not be required to submit any other plan or application in order to receive Federal funds to carry out the activity or program.

(3) **Coordination.**—A State unified plan shall include—

(A) a description of the methods used for joint planning and coordination of the programs and activities included in the unified plan; and

(B) an assurance that the methods included an opportunity for the entities responsible for planning or administering such programs and activities to review and comment on all portions of the unified plan.

(d) **Approval by the Appropriate Secretaries.**—

(1) **Jurisdiction.**—The appropriate Secretary shall have the authority to approve the portion of the State unified plan relating to the activity or program over which the appropriate Secretary exercises administrative authority. On the approval of the appropriate Secretary, the portion of the plan relating to the activity or program shall be implemented by the State pursuant to the applicable portion of the State unified plan.

(2) **Approval.**—

(A) **In General.**—A portion of the State unified plan covering an activity or program described in subsection (b) that is submitted to the appropriate Secretary under this section shall be considered to be approved by the appropriate Secretary at the end of the 90-day period beginning on the day the appropriate Secretary receives the portion, unless the appropriate Secretary makes a written determination, during the 90-day period, that the portion is not consistent with the requirements of the Federal statute authorizing the activity or program including the criteria for approval of a plan or application, if any, under such statute or the plan is not consistent with the requirements of subsection (c)(3).

(B) **Special Rule.**—In subparagraph (A), the term "criteria for approval of a State plan", relating to activities carried out under title I or II or under the Carl D. Perkins Vocational and Applied Technology Education Act (20 U.S.C. 2301 et seq.), includes a requirement for agreement between the State and the appropriate Secretary regarding State performance measures, including levels of performance.

Chapters 4 and 5 of subtitle B of title I of Public Law 105–220
[Perkins Section 321(b)(1)]

Refers to **"Youth Activities"** and **"Adult and Dislocated Worker Employment and Training Activities"**

APPENDIX C
OTHER LEGISLATIVE REFERENCES

In this appendix are pertinent sections of other laws referred to in the 2006 Perkins Act. When you encounter such citations in the text of the 2006 Act or in other parts of this Guide, match the name of the law cited with the titles below, then go to that title in the pages that follow for the text of the

section(s) cites. Noted in the brackets under the title and number of each law is the section number of the 2006 Perkins Act that refers to that law. References to the Elementary and Secondary Education Act of 1965 and Public Law 105–220 (Workforce Investment Act) are included in *Appendix A* and *Appendix B*.

RELEVANT TEXT OF OTHER LEGISLATION*

Adult Education and Family Literacy Act
20 U.S.C. 9223
[Perkins Section 24 (c)(12)]

(a) **In General.**—Each eligible agency shall use funds made available under section 222(a)(2) of this title for one or more of the following adult education and literacy activities:

(1) The establishment or operation of professional development programs to improve the quality of instruction provided pursuant to local activities required under section 9241(b) of this title, including instruction incorporating phonemic awareness, systematic phonics, fluency, and reading comprehension, and instruction provided by volunteers or by personnel of a State or outlying area.

(2) The provision of technical assistance to eligible providers of adult education and literacy activities.

(3) The provision of technology assistance, including staff training, to eligible providers of adult education and literacy activities to enable the eligible providers to improve the quality of such activities.

(4) The support of State or regional networks of literacy resource centers.

(5) The monitoring and evaluation of the quality of, and the improvement in, adult education and literacy activities.

(6) Incentives for—

(A) program coordination and integration; and

(B) performance awards.

(7) Developing and disseminating curricula, including curricula incorporating phonemic awareness, systematic phonics, fluency, and reading comprehension.

(8) Other activities of statewide significance that promote the purpose of this subchapter.

(9) Coordination with existing support services, such as transportation, child care, and other assistance designed to increase rates of enrollment in, and successful completion of, adult education and literacy activities, to adults enrolled in such activities.

(10) Integration of literacy instruction and occupational skill training, and promoting linkages with employers.

(11) Linkages with postsecondary educational institutions.

(b) **Collaboration.**—In carrying out this section, eligible agencies shall collaborate where possible, and avoid duplicating efforts, in order to maximize the impact of the activities described in subsection (a) of this section.

(c) **State-imposed Requirements.**—Whenever a State or outlying area implements any rule or policy relating to the administration or operation of a program authorized under this part that has the effect of imposing a requirement that is not imposed under Federal law (including any rule or policy based on a State or outlying area interpretation of a Federal statute, regulation, or guideline), the State or outlying area shall identify, to eligible providers, the rule or policy as being State— or outlying area—imposed.

Section 3 of the Alaska Native Claims Settlement Act
43 U.S.C. 1602
[Perkins Section 116(a)(1)]

(b) "Native" means a citizen of the United States who is a person of one-fourth degree or more Alaska Indian (including Tsimshian Indians not enrolled in the Metlaktla (FOOTNOTE 1) Indian Community) Eskimo, or Aleut blood, or combination thereof. The term includes any Native as so defined either or both of whose adoptive parents are not Natives. It also includes, in the absence of proof of a minimum blood quantum, any citizen of the United States who is regarded as an Alaska Native by the Native village or Na-

APPENDICES

tive group of which he claims to be a member and whose father or mother is (or, if deceased, was) regarded as Native by any village or group. Any decision of the Secretary regarding eligibility for enrollment shall be final; (FOOTNOTE 1) So in original. Probably should be "Metlakatla".

Section 3 of the Americans with Disabilities Act of 1990
42 U.S.C. 12102
[Perkins Section 3(17)(A)]

(2) **Disability.**—The term "disability" means, with respect to an individual—

   (A) a physical or mental impairment that substantially limits one or more of the major life activities of such individual;

   (B) a record of such an impairment; or

   (C) being regarded as having such an impairment.

Section 673(2) of the Community Services Block Grant Act
42 U.S.C. 9902(2)
[Perkins Section 131(b)(1)]

(2) **Poverty line.**—The term "poverty line" means the official poverty line defined by the Office of Management and Budget based on the most recent data available from the Bureau of the Census. The Secretary shall revise annually (or at any shorter interval the Secretary determines to be feasible and desirable) the poverty line, which shall be used as a criterion of eligibility in the community services block grant program established under this chapter. The required revision shall be accomplished by multiplying the official poverty line by the percentage change in the Consumer Price Index for All Urban Consumers during the annual or other interval immediately preceding the time at which the revision is made. Whenever a State determines that it serves the objectives of the block grant program established under this chapter, the State may revise the poverty line to not to exceed 125 percent of the official poverty line otherwise applicable under this paragraph.

Section 1141 of the Education Amendments of 1978
42 U.S.C. 2021
[Perkins Section 116(a)(2)]

(3) The term "Bureau-funded school" means—

   (A) a Bureau school;

   (B) a contract or grant school; or

   (C) a school for which assistance is provided under the Tribally Controlled Schools Act of 1988 [25 U.S.C. 2501 et seq.].

The Appendix of the Federal Advisory Committee Act
5 U.S.C. App.
[Perkins Section 114(d)(1)(D)]

SEC. 14. TERMINATION OF ADVISORY COMMITTEES; RENEWAL; CONTINUATION

(a) (1) Each advisory committee which is in existence on the effective date of this Act shall terminate not later than the expiration of the two-year period following such effective date unless—

   (A) in the case of an advisory committee established by the President or an officer of the Federal Government, such advisory committee is renewed by the President or that officer by appropriate action prior to the expiration of such two-year period; or

   (B) in the case of an advisory committee established by an Act of Congress, its duration is otherwise provided for by law.

(2) Each advisory committee established after such effective date shall terminate not later than the expiration of the two-year period beginning on the date of its establishment unless—

   (A) in the case of an advisory committee established by the President or an officer of the Federal Government such advisory committee is renewed by the President or such officer by appropriate action prior to the end of such period; or

   (B) in the case of an advisory committee established by an Act of Congress, its duration is otherwise provided for by law.

(b) (1) Upon the renewal of any advisory committee, such advisory committee shall file a charter in accordance with section 9(c).

(2) Any advisory committee established by an Act of Congress shall file a charter in accordance with such section upon the expiration of each successive two-year period following the date of enactment of the Act establishing such advisory committee.

(3) No advisory committee required under this subsection to file a charter shall take any action (other than preparation and filing of such charter) prior to the date on which such charter is filed.

(c) Any advisory committee which is renewed by the President or any officer of the Federal Government may be continued only for successive two-year periods by appropriate action taken by the President or such officer prior to the date on which such advisory committee would otherwise terminate.

Section 102 of the Education Sciences Reform Act of 2002
20 U.S.C. 9501
[Perkins Section 3(25)]

(18) **Scientifically based research standards.**—

   (A) The term "scientifically based research standards" means research standards that—

   (i) apply rigorous, systematic, and objective methodology to obtain reliable and valid knowledge relevant to education activities and programs; and

(ii) present findings and make claims that are appropriate to and supported by the methods that have been employed.

(B) The term includes, appropriate to the research being conducted—

(i) employing systematic, empirical methods that draw on observation or experiment;

(ii) involving data analyses that are adequate to support the general findings;

(iii) relying on measurements or observational methods that provide reliable data;

(iv) making claims of causal relationships only in random assignment experiments or other designs (to the extent such designs substantially eliminate plausible competing explanations for the obtained results);

(v) ensuring that studies and methods are presented in sufficient detail and clarity to allow for replication or, at a minimum, to offer the opportunity to build systematically on the findings of the research;

(vi) obtaining acceptance by a peer-reviewed journal or approval by a panel of independent experts through a comparably rigorous, objective, and scientific review; and

(vii) using research designs and methods appropriate to the research question posed.

Section 444 of the General Education Provisions Act
20 U.S.C. 1232g
[Perkins Section 5(a)]

SEC. 1232G. FAMILY EDUCATIONAL AND PRIVACY RIGHTS.—

(a) **Conditions for availability of funds to educational agencies or institutions; inspection and review of education records; specific information to be made available; procedure for access to education records; reasonableness of time for such access; hearings; written explanations by parents; definitions.—**

(1) (A) No funds shall be made available under any applicable program to any educational agency or institution which has a policy of denying, or which effectively prevents, the parents of students who are or have been in attendance at a school of such agency or at such institution, as the case may be, the right to inspect and review the education records of their children. If any material or document in the education record of a student includes information on more than one student, the parents of one of such students shall have the right to inspect and review only such part of such material or document as relates to such student or to be informed of the specific information contained in such part of such material. Each educational agency or institution shall establish appropriate procedures for the granting of a request by parents for access to the education records of their children within a reasonable period of time, but in no case more than forty-five days after the request has been made.

(B) No funds under any applicable program shall be made

available to any State educational agency (whether or not that agency is an educational agency or institution under this section) that has a policy of denying, or effectively prevents, the parents of students the right to inspect and review the education records maintained by the State educational agency on their children who are or have been in attendance at any school of an educational agency or institution that is subject to the provisions of this section.

(C) The first sentence of subparagraph (A) shall not operate to make available to students in institutions of postsecondary education the following materials:

(i) financial records of the parents of the student or any information contained therein;

(ii) confidential letters and statements of recommendation, which were placed in the education records prior to January 1, 1975, if such letters or statements are not used for purposes other than those for which they were specifically intended;

(iii) if the student has signed a waiver of the student's right of access under this subsection in accordance with subparagraph (D), confidential recommendations—

(I) respecting admission to any educational agency or institution,

(II) respecting an application for employment, and

(III) respecting the receipt of an honor or honorary recognition.

(D) A student or a person applying for admission may waive his right of access to confidential statements described in clause (iii) of subparagraph (C), except that such waiver shall apply to recommendations only if (i) the student is, upon request, notified of the names of all persons making confidential recommendations and (ii) such recommendations are used solely for the purpose for which they were specifically intended. Such waivers may not be required as a condition for admission to, receipt of financial aid from, or receipt of any other services or benefits from such agency or institution.

(2) No funds shall be made available under any applicable program to any educational agency or institution unless the parents of students who are or have been in attendance at a school of such agency or at such institution are provided an opportunity for a hearing by such agency or institution, in accordance with regulations of the Secretary, to challenge the content of such student's education records, in order to insure that the records are not inaccurate, misleading, or otherwise in violation of the privacy rights of students, and to provide an opportunity for the correction or deletion of any such inaccurate, misleading or otherwise inappropriate data contained therein and to insert into such records a written explanation of the parents respecting the content of such records.

(3) For the purposes of this section the term "educational agency or institution" means any public or private agency or institution which is the recipient of funds under any applicable program.

(4) (A) For the purposes of this section, the term "education records" means, except as may be provided otherwise in subparagraph (B), those records, files, documents, and other materials which—

(i) contain information directly related to a student; and

(ii) are maintained by an educational agency or institution or by a person acting for such agency or institution.

(B) The term "education records" does not include—

(i) records of instructional, supervisory, and administrative personnel and educational personnel ancillary thereto which are in the sole possession of the maker thereof and which are not accessible or revealed to any other person except a substitute;

(ii) records maintained by a law enforcement unit of the educational agency or institution that were created by that law enforcement unit for the purpose of law enforcement;

(iii) in the case of persons who are employed by an educational agency or institution but who are not in attendance at such agency or institution, records made and maintained in the normal course of business which relate exclusively to such person in that person's capacity as an employee and are not available for use for any other purpose; or

(iv) records on a student who is eighteen years of age or older, or is attending an institution of postsecondary education, which are made or maintained by a physician, psychiatrist, psychologist, or other recognized professional or paraprofessional acting in his professional or paraprofessional capacity, or assisting in that capacity, and which are made, maintained, or used only in connection with the provision of treatment to the student, and are not available to anyone other than persons providing such treatment, except that such records can be personally reviewed by a physician or other appropriate professional of the student's choice.

(5) (A) For the purposes of this section the term "directory information" relating to a student includes the following: the student's name, address, telephone listing, date and place of birth, major field of study, participation in officially recognized activities and sports, weight and height of members of athletic teams, dates of attendance, degrees and awards received, and the most recent previous educational agency or institution attended by the student.

(B) Any educational agency or institution making public directory information shall give public notice of the categories of information which it has designated as such information with respect to each student attending the institution or agency and shall allow a reasonable period of time after such notice has been given for a parent to inform the institution or agency that any or all of the information designated should not be released without the parent's prior consent.

(6) For the purposes of this section, the term "student" includes any person with respect to whom an educational agency or institution maintains education records or personally identifiable information, but does not include a person who has not been in attendance at such agency or institution.

(b) **Release of education records; parental consent requirement; exceptions; compliance with judicial orders and subpoenas; audit and evaluation of federally-supported education programs; recordkeeping.—**

(1) No funds shall be made available under any applicable program to any educational agency or institution which has a policy or practice of permitting the release of education records (or personally identifiable information contained therein other than directory information, as defined in paragraph (5) of subsection (a) of this section) of students without the written consent of their parents to any individual, agency, or organization, other than to the following—

(A) other school officials, including teachers within the educational institution or local educational agency, who have been determined by such agency or institution to have legitimate educational interests, including the educational interests of the child for whom consent would otherwise be required;

(B) officials of other schools or school systems in which the student seeks or intends to enroll, upon condition that the student's parents be notified of the transfer, receive a copy of the record if desired, and have an opportunity for a hearing to challenge the content of the record;

(C) (i) authorized representatives of (I) the Comptroller General of the United States, (II) the Secretary, or (III) State educational authorities, under the conditions set forth in paragraph (3), or (ii) authorized representatives of the Attorney General for law enforcement purposes under the same conditions as apply to the Secretary under paragraph (3);

(D) in connection with a student's application for, or receipt of, financial aid;

(E) State and local officials or authorities to whom such information is specifically allowed to be reported or disclosed pursuant to State statute adopted—

(i) before November 19, 1974, if the allowed reporting or disclosure concerns the juvenile justice system and such system's ability to effectively serve the student whose records are released, or

(ii) after November 19, 1974, if—

(I) the allowed reporting or disclosure concerns the juvenile justice system and such system's ability to effectively serve, prior to adjudication, the student whose records are released; and

(II) the officials and authorities to whom such information is disclosed certify in writing to the educational agency or institution that the information will not be disclosed to any other party except as provided under State law without the prior written consent of the parent of the student.(!1)

(F) organizations conducting studies for, or on behalf of, educational agencies or institutions for the purpose of developing, validating, or administering predictive tests, administering student aid programs, and improving instruction, if such studies are conducted in such a manner as will not permit the personal identification of students and their parents by persons other than representatives of such organizations and such information will be destroyed when no longer needed for the purpose for which it is conducted;

(G) accrediting organizations in order to carry out their accrediting functions;

(H) parents of a dependent student of such parents, as defined in section 152 of title 26;

(I) subject to regulations of the Secretary, in connection with an emergency, appropriate persons if the knowledge of such information is necessary to protect the health or safety of the student or other persons; and

(J) (i) the entity or persons designated in a Federal grand jury subpoena, in which case the court shall order, for good cause shown, the educational agency or institution (and any officer, director, employee, agent, or attorney for such agency or institution) on which the subpoena is served, to not disclose to any person the existence or contents of the subpoena or any information furnished to the grand jury in response to the subpoena; and

(ii) the entity or persons designated in any other subpoena issued for a law enforcement purpose, in which case the court or other issuing agency may order, for good cause shown, the educational agency or institution (and any officer, director, employee, agent, or attorney for such agency or institution) on which the subpoena is served, to not disclose to any person the existence or contents of the subpoena or any information furnished in response to the subpoena Nothing in subparagraph (E) of this paragraph shall prevent a State from further limiting the number or type of State or local officials who will continue to have access thereunder.

(2) No funds shall be made available under any applicable program to any educational agency or institution which has a policy or practice of releasing, or providing access to, any personally identifiable information in education records other than directory information, or as is permitted under paragraph (1) of this subsection, unless—

(A) there is written consent from the student's parents specifying records to be released, the reasons for such release, and to whom, and with a copy of the records to be released to the student's parents and the student if desired by the parents, or

(B) except as provided in paragraph (1)(J), such information is furnished in compliance with judicial order, or pursuant to any lawfully issued subpoena, upon condition that parents and the students are notified of all such orders or subpoenas in advance of the compliance therewith by the educational institution or agency.

(3) Nothing contained in this section shall preclude authorized representatives of (A) the Comptroller General of the United States, (B) the Secretary, or (C) State educational authorities from having access to student or other records which may be necessary in connection with the audit and evaluation of Federally-supported education programs, or in connection with the enforcement of the Federal legal requirements which relate to such programs: Provided, That except when collection of personally identifiable information is specifically authorized by Federal law, any data collected by such officials shall be protected in a manner which will not permit the personal identification of students and their parents by other than those officials, and such personally identifiable data shall be destroyed when no longer needed for such audit, evaluation, and enforcement of Federal legal requirements.

(4) (A) Each educational agency or institution shall maintain a record, kept with the education records of each student, which will indicate all individuals (other than those specified in paragraph (1)(A) of this subsection), agencies, or organizations which have requested or obtained access to a student's education records maintained by such educational agency or institution, and which will indicate specifically the legitimate interest that each such person, agency, or organization has in obtaining this information. Such record of access shall be available only to parents, to the school official and his assistants who are responsible for the custody of such records, and to persons or organizations authorized in, and under the conditions of, clauses (A) and (C) of paragraph (1) as a means of auditing the operation of the system.

(B) With respect to this subsection, personal information shall only be transferred to a third party on the condition that such party will not permit any other party to have access to such information without the written consent of the parents of the student. If a third party outside the educational agency or institution permits access to information in violation of paragraph (2)(A), or fails to destroy information in violation of paragraph (1)(F), the educational agency or institution shall be prohibited from permitting access to information from education records to that third party for a period of not less than five years.

(5) Nothing in this section shall be construed to prohibit State and local educational officials from having access to student or other records which may be necessary in connection with the audit and evaluation of any federally or State supported education program or in connection with the enforcement of the Federal legal requirements which relate to any such program, subject to the conditions specified in the proviso in paragraph (3).

(6) (A) Nothing in this section shall be construed to prohibit an institution of postsecondary education from disclosing, to an alleged victim of any crime of violence (as that term is defined in section 16 of title 18), or a nonforcible sex offense, the results of any disciplinary proceeding conducted by such institution against the alleged perpetrator of such crime or offense with respect to such crime or offense.

(B) Nothing in this section shall be construed to prohibit an institution of postsecondary education from disclosing the final results of any disciplinary proceeding conducted by such institution against a student who is an alleged perpetrator of any crime of violence (as that term is defined in section 16 of title18), or a nonforcible sex offense, if the institution determines as a result of that disciplinary proceeding that the student committed a violation of the institution's rules or policies with respect to such crime or offense.

(C) For the purpose of this paragraph, the final results of any disciplinary proceeding—

(i) shall include only the name of the student, the violation committed, and any sanction imposed by the institution on that student; and

(ii) may include the name of any other student, such as a victim or witness, only with the written consent of that other student.

(7) (A) Nothing in this section may be construed to prohibit an educational institution from disclosing information provided to the institution under section 14071 of title 42 concerning registered sex offenders who are required to register under such section.

(B) The Secretary shall take appropriate steps to notify educational institutions that disclosure of information described in subparagraph (A) is permitted.

(c) **Surveys or data-gathering activities; regulations.—** Not later than 240 days after October 20, 1994, the Secretary shall adopt appropriate regulations or procedures, or identify existing regulations or procedures, which protect the rights of privacy of students and their families in connection with any surveys or data-gathering activities conducted, assisted, or authorized by the Secretary or an administrative head of an education agency. Regulations established under this subsection shall include provisions controlling the use, dissemination, and protection of such data. No survey or data-gathering activities shall be conducted by the Secretary, or an administrative head of an education agency under an applicable program, unless such activities are authorized by law.

(d) **Students' rather than parents' permission or consent.—** For the purposes of this section, whenever a student has attained eighteen years of age, or is attending an institution of postsecondary education, the permission or consent required of and the rights accorded to the parents of the student shall thereafter only be required of and accorded to the student.

(e) **Informing parents or students of rights under this section.—** No funds shall be made available under any applicable program to any educational agency or institution unless such agency or institution effectively informs the parents of students, or the students, if they are eighteen years of age or older, or are attending an institution of postsecondary education, of the rights accorded them by this section.

(f) **Enforcement; termination of assistance.—** The Secretary shall take appropriate actions to enforce this section and to deal with violations of this section, in accordance with this chapter, except that action to terminate assistance may be taken only if the Secretary finds there has been a failure to comply with this section, and he has determined that compliance cannot be secured by voluntary means.

(g) **Office and review board; creation; functions.—** The Secretary shall establish or designate an office and review board within the Department for the purpose of investigating, processing, reviewing, and adjudicating violations of this section and complaints which may be filed concerning alleged violations of this section. Except for the conduct of hearings, none of the functions of the Secretary under this section shall be carried out in any of the regional offices of such Department.

(h) **Disciplinary records; disclosure.—** Nothing in this section shall prohibit an educational agency or institution from—

(1) including appropriate information in the education record of any student concerning disciplinary action taken against such student for conduct that posed a significant risk to the safety or well-being of that student, other students, or other members of the school community; or

(2) disclosing such information to teachers and school officials, including teachers and school officials in other schools, who have legitimate educational interests in the behavior of the student.

(i) **Drug and alcohol violation disclosures.—**

(1) **In General.—**Nothing in this Act or the Higher Education Act of 1965 [20 U.S.C. 1001 et seq.] shall be construed to prohibit an institution of higher education from disclosing, to a parent or legal guardian of a student, information regarding any violation of any Federal, State, or local law, or of any rule or policy of the institution, governing the use or possession of alcohol or a controlled substance, regardless of whether that information is contained in the student's education records, if—

(A) the student is under the age of 21; and

(B) the institution determines that the student has committed a disciplinary violation with respect to such use or possession.

(2) State law regarding disclosure Nothing in paragraph (1) shall be construed to supersede any provision of State law that prohibits an institution of higher education from making the disclosure described in subsection (a) of this section.

(j) **Investigation and prosecution of terrorism.—**

(1) **In General.—**Notwithstanding subsections (a) through (i) of this section or any provision of State law, the Attorney General (or any Federal officer or employee, in a position not lower than an Assistant Attorney General, designated by the Attorney General) may submit a written application to a court of competent jurisdiction for an ex parte order requiring an educational agency or institution to permit the Attorney General (or his designee) to—

(A) collect education records in the possession of the educational agency or institution that are relevant to an authorized investigation or prosecution of an offense listed in section 2332b(g)(5)(B) of title 18, or an act of domestic or international terrorism as defined in section 2331 of that title; and

(B) for official purposes related to the investigation or prosecution of an offense described in paragraph (1)(A), retain, disseminate, and use (including as evidence at trial or in other administrative or judicial proceedings) such records, consistent with such guidelines as the Attorney General, after consultation with the Secretary, shall issue to protect confidentiality.

(2) **Application and approval.—**

(A) **In General.—**An application under paragraph (1) shall certify that there are specific and articulable facts giving reason to believe that the education records are likely to contain information described in paragraph (1)(A).

(B) The court shall issue an order described in paragraph (1) if the court finds that the application for the order includes the certification described in subparagraph (A).

(3) **Protection of Educational Agency or Institution.—**An educational agency or institution that, in good faith, produces education records in accordance with an order issued under this subsection shall not be liable to any person for that production.

(4) **Record-keeping.—**Subsection (b)(4) of this section does not apply to education records subject to a court order under this subsection.

Title II of the Higher Education Act of 1965
[Perkins Sections 122(C)(2) & 124(b)(3)(E)]

Title II refers to **"Teacher Quality Enhancement"**

Section 101 of the Higher Education Act of 1965
[Perkins Sections 3(18) & 3(34)]

(a) **Institution of Higher Education.—**For purposes of this Act, other than title IV, the term "institution of higher education" means an educational institution in any State that—

(1) admits as regular students only persons having a certificate of graduation from a school providing secondary education, or the recognized equivalent of such a certificate;

(2) is legally authorized within such State to provide a program of education beyond secondary education;

(3) provides an educational program for which the institution awards a bachelor's degree or provides not less than a 2-year program that is acceptable for full credit toward such a degree;

(4) is a public or other nonprofit institution; and

(5) is accredited by a nationally recognized accrediting agency or association, or if not so accredited, is an institution that has been granted preaccreditation status by such an agency or association that has been recognized by the Secretary for the granting of preaccreditation status, and the Secretary has determined that there is satisfactory assurance that the institution will meet the accreditation standards of such an agency or association within a reasonable time.

Section 102 of the Higher Education Act of 1965
[Perkins Section 203(a)(1)]

(a) **Definition of Institution of Higher Education for Purposes of Title IV programs.**—

(1) **Inclusion of Additional Institutions.**—Subject to paragraphs (2) through (4) of this subsection, the term "institution of higher education" for purposes of title IV includes, in addition to the institutions covered by the definition in section 101—

(A) a proprietary institution of higher education (as defined in subsection (b) of this section);

(B) a postsecondary vocational institution (as defined in subsection (c) of this section); and

(C) only for the purposes of part B of title IV, an institution outside the United States that is comparable to an institution of higher education as defined in section 101 and that has been approved by the Secretary for the purpose of part B of title IV.

(2) **Institutions Outside the United States.**—

(A) **In General.**—For the purpose of qualifying as an institution under paragraph (1)(C), the Secretary shall establish criteria by regulation for the approval of institutions outside the United States and for the determination that such institutions are comparable to an institution of higher education as defined in section 101. In the case of a graduate medical or veterinary school outside the United States, such criteria shall include a requirement that a student attending such school outside the United States is ineligible for loans made, insured, or guaranteed under part B unless—

(i) (I) at least 60 percent of those enrolled in, and at least 60 percent of the graduates of, the graduate medical school outside the United States were not persons described in section 484(a)(5) in the year preceding the year for which a student is seeking a loan under part B of title IV; and

(II) at least 60 percent of the individuals who were students or graduates of the graduate medical school outside the United States (both nationals of the United States and others) taking the examinations administered by the Educational Commission for Foreign Medical Graduates received a passing score in the year preceding the year for which a student is seeking a loan under part B of title IV; or

(ii) the institution has a clinical training program that was approved by a State as of January 1, 1992, or the institution's students complete their clinical training at an approved veterinary school located in the United States.

(B) **Advisory Panel.**—

(i) **In General.**—For the purpose of qualifying as an institution under paragraph (1)(C) of this subsection, the Secretary shall establish an advisory panel of medical experts that shall—

(I) evaluate the standards of accreditation applied to applicant foreign medical schools; and

(II) determine the comparability of those standards to standards for accreditation applied to United States medical schools.

(ii) **Special Rule.**—If the accreditation standards described in clause (i) are determined not to be comparable, the foreign medical school shall be required to meet the requirements of section 101.

(C) **Failure to Release Information.**—The failure of an institution outside the United States to provide, release, or authorize release to the Secretary of such information as may be required by subparagraph (A) shall render such institution ineligible for the purpose of part B of title IV.

(D) **Special Rule.**—If, pursuant to this paragraph, an institution loses eligibility to participate in the programs under title IV, then a student enrolled at such institution may, notwithstanding such loss of eligibility, continue to be eligible to receive a loan under part B 1 while attending such institution for the academic year succeeding the academic year in which such loss of eligibility occurred.

Section 435(a)(2) of the Higher Education Act of 1965
[Perkins Section 203(a)(1)]

(2) **Ineligibility Based on High Default Rates.**—

(A) An institution whose cohort default rate is equal to or greater than the threshold percentage specified in subparagraph (B) for each of the three most recent fiscal years for which data are available shall not be eligible to participate in a program under this part for the fiscal year for which the determination is made and for the two succeeding fiscal years, unless, within 30 days of receiving notification from the Secretary of the loss of eligibility under this paragraph, the institution appeals the loss of its eligibility to the Secretary. The Secretary shall issue a decision on any such appeal within 45 days after its submission. Such decision may permit the institution to continue to participate in a program under this part if—

(i) the institution demonstrates to the satisfaction of the Secretary that the Secretary's calculation of its cohort default rate is not accurate, and that recalculation would reduce its cohort default rate for any of the three fiscal years below the threshold percentage specified in subparagraph (B);

(ii) there are exceptional mitigating circumstances within the meaning of paragraph (4); or

(iii) there are, in the judgment of the Secretary, other exceptional mitigating circumstances that would make the application of this paragraph inequitable. If an institution continues to participate in a program under this part, and the institution's appeal of the loss of eligibility is unsuccessful, the institution shall be required to pay to the Secretary an amount equal to the amount of interest, special allowance, reinsurance, and any related payments made by the Secretary (or which the Secretary is obligated to make) with respect to loans made under this part to students attending, or planning to attend, that institution during the pendency of such appeal. During such appeal, the Secretary may permit the institution to continue to participate in a program under this part.

(B) For purposes of determinations under subparagraph (A), the threshold percentage is—

(i) 35 percent for fiscal year 1991 and 1992;

(ii) 30 percent for fiscal year 1993; and

(iii) 25 percent for any succeeding fiscal year.

(C) Until July 1, 1999, this paragraph shall not apply to any institution that is—

(i) a part B institution within the meaning of section 322(2) of this Act;

(ii) a tribally controlled community college within the meaning of section 2(a)(4) of the Tribally Controlled Community College Assistance Act of 1978; or

(iii) a Navajo Community College under the Navajo Community College Act.

(D) Notwithstanding the first sentence of subparagraph (A), the Secretary shall restore the eligibility to participate in a program under subpart 1 of part A, part B, or part D of an institution that did not appeal its loss of eligibility within 30 days of receiving notification if the Secretary determines, on a case-by-case basis, that the institution's failure to appeal was substantially justified under the circumstances, and that—

(i) the institution made a timely request that the appropriate guaranty agency correct errors in the draft data used to calculate the institution's cohort default rate;

(ii) the guaranty agency did not correct the erroneous data in a timely fashion; and

(iii) the institution would have been eligible if the erroneous data had been corrected by the guaranty agency.

Section 614(d) of the Individuals with Disabilities Education Act
[Perkins Section 324(c)]

(d) **Individualized Education Programs.—**

(1) **Definitions.—**As used in this title:

(A) **Individualized Education Program.—**The term "individualized education program" or "IEP" means a written statement for each child with a disability that is developed, reviewed, and revised in accordance with this section and that includes—

(i) a statement of the child's present levels of educational performance, including—

(I) how the child's disability affects the child's involvement and progress in the general curriculum; or

(II) for preschool children, as appropriate, how the disability affects the child's participation in appropriate activities;

(ii) a statement of measurable annual goals, including benchmarks or short-term objectives, related to—

(I) meeting the child's needs that result from the child's disability to enable the child to be involved in and progress in the general curriculum; and

(II) meeting each of the child's other educational needs that result from the child's disability;

(iii) a statement of the special education and related services and supplementary aids and services to be provided to the child, or on behalf of the child, and a statement of the program modifications or supports for school personnel that will be provided for the child—

(I) to advance appropriately toward attaining the annual goals;

(II) to be involved and progress in the general curriculum in accordance with clause (i) and to participate in extracurricular and other nonacademic activities; and

(III) to be educated and participate with other children with disabilities and nondisabled children in the activities described in this paragraph;

(iv) an explanation of the extent, if any, to which the child will not participate with nondisabled children in the regular class and in the activities described in clause (iii);

(v) (I) a statement of any individual modifications in the administration of State or districtwide assessments of student achievement that are needed in order for the child to participate in such assessment; and

(II) if the IEP Team determines that the child will not participate in a particular State or districtwide assessment of student achievement (or part of such an assessment), a statement of—

(aa) why that assessment is not appropriate for the child; and

(bb) how the child will be assessed;

(vi) the projected date for the beginning of the services and modifications described in clause (iii), and the anticipated frequency, location, and duration of those services and modifications;

(vii) (I) beginning at age 14, and updated annually, a statement of the transition service needs of the child under the applicable components of the child's IEP that focuses on the child's courses of study (such as participation in advanced-placement courses or a vocational education program);

(II) beginning at age 16 (or younger, if determined appropriate by the IEP Team), a statement of needed transition services for the child, including, when appropriate, a statement of the interagency responsibilities or any needed linkages; and

(III) beginning at least one year before the child reaches the age of majority under State law, a statement that the child has been informed of his or her rights under this title, if any, that will transfer to the child on reaching the age of majority under section 615(m); and

(viii) a statement of—

(I) how the child's progress toward the annual goals described in clause (ii) will be measured; and

(II) how the child's parents will be regularly informed (by such means as periodic report cards), at least as often as parents are informed of their nondisabled children's progress, of—

(aa) their child's progress toward the annual goals described in clause (ii); and

(bb) the extent to which that progress is sufficient to enable the child to achieve the goals by the end of the year.

(B) **Individualized Education Program Team.**—The term "individualized education program team" or "IEP Team" means a group of individuals composed of—

(i) the parents of a child with a disability;

(ii) at least one regular education teacher of such child (if the child is, or may be, participating in the regular education environment);

(iii) at least one special education teacher, or where appropriate, at least one special education provider of such child;

(iv) a representative of the local educational agency who—

(I) is qualified to provide, or supervise the provision of, specially designed instruction to meet the unique needs of children with disabilities;

(II) is knowledgeable about the general curriculum; and

(III) is knowledgeable about the availability of resources of the local educational agency;

(v) an individual who can interpret the instructional implications of evaluation results, who may be a member of the team described in clauses (ii) through (vi);

(vi) at the discretion of the parent or the agency, other individuals who have knowledge or special exper-

tise regarding the child, including related services personnel as appropriate; and

(vii) whenever appropriate, the child with a disability.

(2) **Requirement that Program Be in Effect.**—

(A) **In General.**—At the beginning of each school year, each local educational agency, State educational agency, or other State agency, as the case may be, shall have in effect, for each child with a disability in its jurisdiction, an individualized education program, as defined in paragraph (1)(A).

(B) **Program for Child Aged 3 through 5.**—In the case of a child with a disability aged 3 through 5 (or, at the discretion of the State educational agency, a 2 year old 1 child with a disability who will turn age 3 during the school year), an individualized family service plan that contains the material described in section 636, and that is developed in accordance with this section, may serve as the IEP of the child if using that plan as the IEP is—

(i) consistent with State policy; and

(ii) agreed to by the agency and the child's parents.

(3) **Development of IEP.**—

(A) **In General.**—In developing each child's IEP, the IEP Team, subject to subparagraph (C), shall consider—

(i) the strengths of the child and the concerns of the parents for enhancing the education of their child; and

(ii) the results of the initial evaluation or most recent evaluation of the child.

(B) **Consideration of Special Factors.**—The IEP Team shall—

(i) in the case of a child whose behavior impedes his or her learning or that of others, consider, when appropriate, strategies, including positive behavioral interventions, strategies, and supports to address that behavior;

(ii) in the case of a child with limited English proficiency, consider the language needs of the child as such needs relate to the child's IEP;

(iii) in the case of a child who is blind or visually impaired, provide for instruction in Braille and the use of Braille unless the IEP Team determines, after an evaluation of the child's reading and writing skills, needs, and appropriate reading and writing media (including an evaluation of the child's future needs for instruction in Braille or the use of Braille), that instruction in Braille or the use of Braille is not appropriate for the child;

(iv) consider the communication needs of the child, and in the case of a child who is deaf or hard of hearing, consider the child's language and communication needs, opportunities for direct communications with peers and professional personnel in the child's language and communication mode, academic level, and full range of needs, including opportunities for direct instruction in the child's language and communication mode; and

(v) consider whether the child requires assistive technology devices and services.

(C) **Requirement with Respect to Regular Education Teacher.**—The regular education teacher of the child, as a member of the IEP Team, shall, to the extent appropriate, participate in the development of the IEP of the child, including the determination of appropriate positive behavioral interventions and strategies and the determination of supplementary aids and services, program modifications, and support for school personnel consistent with paragraph (1)(A)(iii).

(4) **Review and Revision of IEP.—**

    (A) **In General.—**The local educational agency shall ensure that, subject to subparagraph (B), the IEP Team—

        (i) reviews the child's IEP periodically, but not less than annually to determine whether the annual goals for the child are being achieved; and

        (ii) revises the IEP as appropriate to address—

            (I) any lack of expected progress toward the annual goals and in the general curriculum, where appropriate;

            (II) the results of any reevaluation conducted under this section;

            (III) information about the child provided to, or by, the parents, as described in subsection (c)(1)(B);

            (IV) the child's anticipated needs; or

            (V) other matters.

    (B) **Requirement with Respect to Regular education Teacher.—**The regular education teacher of the child, as a member of the IEP Team, shall, to the extent appropriate, participate in the review and revision of the IEP of the child.

(5) **Failure to Meet Transition Objectives.—**If a participating agency, other than the local educational agency, fails to provide the transition services described in the IEP in accordance with paragraph (1)(A)(vii), the local educational agency shall reconvene the IEP Team to identify alternative strategies to meet the transition objectives for the child set out in that program.

(6) **Children with Disabilities in Adult Prisons.—**

    (A) **In General.—**The following requirements do not apply to children with disabilities who are convicted as adults under State law and incarcerated in adult prisons:

        (i) The requirements contained in section 612(a)(17) and paragraph (1)(A)(v) of this subsection (relating to participation of children with disabilities in general assessments).

        (ii) The requirements of subclauses (I) and (II) of paragraph (1)(A)(vii) of this subsection (relating to transition planning and transition services), do not apply with respect to such children whose eligibility under this part will end, because of their age, before they will be released from prison.

    (B) **Additional Requirement.—**If a child with a disability is convicted as an adult under State law and incarcerated in an adult prison, the child's IEP Team may modify the child's IEP or placement notwithstanding the requirements of sections 612(a)(5)(A) and 614(d)(1)(A) if the State has demonstrated a bona fide security or compelling penological interest that cannot otherwise be accommodated.

Section 7207 of the Native Hawaiian Education Act
20 U.S.C. 7517
[Perkins Section 116(a)(5)]

(5) The term "Native Hawaiian organization" means a private nonprofit organization that—

    (A) serves the interests of Native Hawaiians;

    (B) has Native Hawaiians in substantive and policymaking positions within the organization; and

    (C) is recognized by the Governor of Hawaii for the purpose of planning, conducting, or administering programs (or portions of programs) for the benefit of Native Hawaiians.

Section 504 of the Rehabilitation Act of 1973
[Perkins Section 324 (c)]

This reference refers to **"Nondiscrimination Under Federal Grants and Programs"**

Part A of Title IV Social Security Act
42 U.S.C. 601 et seq.
[Perkins Section 3(10)(A)(iii)]

This reference refers to **"Block Grants to States for Temporary Assistance for Needy Families"**

Section 2 of the Tribally Controlled College or University Assistance Act of 1978
25 U.S.C. 1801(a)
[Perkins Section 3(33), Section 117(h)(1) & Section 203(a)(1)(B)(i)(I)(bb)(AA)]

(a) For purposes of this chapter, the term—

    (1) "Indian" means a person who is a member of an Indian tribe;

    (2) "Indian tribe" means any Indian tribe, band, nation, or other organized group or community, including any Alaskan Native village or regional or village corporation as defined in or established pursuant to the Alaskan Native Claims Settlement Act [43 U.S.C. 1601 et seq.], which is recognized as eligible for the special programs and services provided by the United States to Indians because of their status as Indians.

    (4) "tribally controlled college or university" means an institution of higher education which is formally controlled, or has been formally sanctioned, or chartered, by the governing body of an Indian tribe or tribes, except that no more than one such institution shall be recognized with respect to any such tribe;

Section 15(f) of the Wagner-Peyser Act

[Perkins Section 118(b)(2), Section 118(c)(5), Section 118(c)(7)(C), Section 118(d)(1), Section 118(f)(3), & Section 321(b)(2)]

SEC. 15. EMPLOYMENT STATISTICS

(a) **System Content.—**

    (1) **In General.—**The Secretary, in accordance with the provisions of this section, shall oversee the development, maintenance, and continuous improvement of a nationwide employment statistics system of employment statistics that includes—

        (A) statistical data from cooperative statistical survey and projection programs and data from administrative reporting systems that, taken together, enumerate, estimate, and project employment opportunities and conditions at national, State, and local levels in a timely manner, including statistics on—

            (i) employment and unemployment status of national, State, and local populations, including self-employed, part-time, and seasonal workers;

            (ii) industrial distribution of occupations, as well as current and projected employment opportunities, wages, benefits (where data is available), and skill trends by occupation and industry, with particular attention paid to State and local conditions;

            (iii) the incidence of, industrial and geographical location of, and number of workers displaced by, permanent layoffs and plant closings; and

            (iv) employment and earnings information maintained in a longitudinal manner to be used for research and program evaluation;

        (B) information on State and local employment opportunities, and other appropriate statistical data related to labor market dynamics, which—

            (i) shall be current and comprehensive;

            (ii) shall meet the needs identified through the consultations described in subparagraphs (A) and (B) of subsection (e)(2) of this section; and

            (iii) shall meet the needs for the information identified in section 134(d);

        (C) technical standards (which the Secretary shall publish annually) for data and information described in subparagraphs (A) and (B) that, at a minimum, meet the criteria of chapter 35 of title 44, United States Code;

        (D) procedures to ensure compatibility and additivity of the data and information described in subparagraphs (A) and (B) from national, State, and local levels;

        (E) procedures to support standardization and aggregation of data from administrative reporting systems described in subparagraph (A) of employment-related programs;

        (F) analysis of data and information described in subparagraphs (A) and (B) for uses such as—

            (i) national, State, and local policymaking;

            (ii) implementation of Federal policies (including allocation formulas);

            (iii) program planning and evaluation; and

            (iv) researching labor market dynamics;

        (G) wide dissemination of such data, information, and analysis in a user-friendly manner and voluntary technical standards for dissemination mechanisms; and

        (H) programs of—

            (i) training for effective data dissemination;

            (ii) research and demonstration; and

            (iii) programs and technical assistance.

    (2) **Information to be Confidential.—**

        (A) **In General.—**No officer or employee of the Federal Government or agent of the Federal Government may—

            (i) use any submission that is furnished for exclusively statistical purposes under the provisions of this section for any purpose other than the statistical purposes for which the submission is furnished;

            (ii) make any publication or media transmittal of the data contained in the submission described in clause (i) that permits information concerning individual subjects to be reasonably inferred by either direct or indirect means; or

            (iii) permit anyone other than a sworn officer, employee, or agent of any Federal department or agency, or a contractor (including an employee of a contractor) of such department or agency, to examine an individual submission described in clause (i); without the consent of the individual, agency, or other person who is the subject of the submission or provides that submission.

        (B) **Immunity from Legal Process.—**Any submission (including any data derived from the submission) that is collected and retained by a Federal department or agency, or an officer, employee, agent, or contractor of such a department or agency, for exclusively statistical purposes under this section shall be immune from the legal process and shall not, without the consent of the individual, agency, or other person who is the subject of the submission or provides that submission, be admitted as evidence or used for any purpose in any action, suit, or other judicial or administrative proceeding.

        (C) **Rule of Construction.—**Nothing in this section shall be construed to provide immunity from the legal process for such submission (including any data derived from the submission) if the submission is in the possession of any person, agency, or entity other than the Federal Government or an officer, employee, agent, or contractor of the Federal Government, or if the submission is independently collected, retained, or produced for purposes other than the purposes of this chapter.

(b) **System Responsibilities.—**

    (1) **In General.—**The employment statistics system described in subsection (a) of this section shall be planned, administered, overseen, and evaluated through a cooperative governance structure involving the Federal Government and States.

    (2) **Duties.—**The Secretary, with respect to data collection,

analysis, and dissemination of labor employment statistics for the system, shall carry out the following duties:

(A) Assign responsibilities within the Department of Labor for elements of the employment statistics system described in subsection (a) of this section to ensure that all statistical and administrative data collected is consistent with appropriate Bureau of Labor Statistics standards and definitions.

(B) Actively seek the cooperation of other Federal agencies to establish and maintain mechanisms for ensuring complementarity and nonduplication in the development and operation of statistical and administrative data collection activities.

(C) Eliminate gaps and duplication in statistical undertakings, with the systemization of wage surveys as an early priority.

(D) In collaboration with the Bureau of Labor Statistics and States, develop and maintain the elements of the employment statistics system described in subsection (a) of this section, including the development of consistent procedures and definitions for use by the States in collecting the data and information described in subparagraphs (A) and (B) of subsection (a)(1) of this section.

(E) Establish procedures for the system to ensure that—

  (i) such data and information are timely;

  (ii) paperwork and reporting for the system are reduced to a minimum; and

  (iii) States and localities are fully involved in the development and continuous improvement of the system at all levels, including ensuring the provision, to such States and localities, of budget information necessary for carrying out their responsibilities under subsection (e) of this section.

(c) **Annual Plan.**—The Secretary, working through the Bureau of Labor Statistics, and in cooperation with the States, and with the assistance of other appropriate Federal agencies, shall prepare an annual plan which shall be the mechanism for achieving cooperative management of the nationwide employment statistics system described in subsection (a) of this section and the statewide employment statistics systems that comprise the nationwide system. The plan shall—

(1) describe the steps the Secretary has taken in the preceding year and will take in the following 5 years to carry out the duties described in subsection (b)(2) of this section;

(2) include a report on the results of an annual consumer satisfaction review concerning the performance of the system, including the performance of the system in addressing the needs of Congress, States, localities, employers, jobseekers, and other consumers;

(3) evaluate the performance of the system and recommend needed improvements, taking into consideration the results of the consumer satisfaction review, with particular attention to the improvements needed at the State and local levels;

(4) justify the budget request for annual appropriations by describing priorities for the fiscal year succeeding the fiscal year in which the plan is developed and priorities for the 5 subsequent fiscal years for the system;

(5) describe current (as of the date of the submission of the plan) spending and spending needs to carry out activities under this

section, including the costs to States and localities of meeting the requirements of subsection (e)(2) of this section; and

(6) describe the involvement of States in the development of the plan, through formal consultations conducted by the Secretary in cooperation with representatives of the Governors of every State, and with representatives of local workforce investment boards, pursuant to a process established by the Secretary in cooperation with the States.

(d) **Coordination with the States.**—The Secretary, working through the Bureau of Labor Statistics, and in cooperation with the States, shall—

(1) develop the annual plan described in subsection (c) of this section and address other employment statistics issues by holding formal consultations, at least once each quarter (beginning with the calendar quarter in which the Workforce Investment Act of 1998 is enacted) on the products and administration of the nationwide employment statistics system; and

(2) hold the consultations with representatives from each of the 10 Federal regions of the Department of Labor, elected (pursuant to a process established by the Secretary) by and from the State employment statistics directors affiliated with the State agencies that perform the duties described in subsection (e)(2) of this section.

(e) **State Responsibilities.**—

(1) **Designation of State Agency.**—In order to receive Federal financial assistance under this section, the Governor of a State shall—

  (A) designate a single State agency to be responsible for the management of the portions of the employment statistics system described in subsection (a) of this section that comprise a statewide employment statistics system and for the State's participation in the development of the annual plan; and

  (B) establish a process for the oversight of such system.

(2) **Duties.**—In order to receive Federal financial assistance under this section, the State agency shall—

  (A) consult with State and local employers, participants, and local workforce investment boards about the labor market relevance of the data to be collected and disseminated through the statewide employment statistics system;

  (B) consult with State educational agencies and local educational agencies concerning the provision of employment statistics in order to meet the needs of secondary school and postsecondary school students who seek such information;

  (C) collect and disseminate for the system, on behalf of the State and localities in the State, the information and data described in subparagraphs (A) and (B) of subsection (a)(1) of this section;

  (D) maintain and continuously improve the statewide employment statistics system in accordance with this section;

  (E) perform contract and grant responsibilities for data collection, analysis, and dissemination for such system;

  (F) conduct such other data collection, analysis, and dissemination activities as will ensure an effective statewide employment statistics system;

  (G) actively seek the participation of other State and local agencies in data collection, analysis, and dissemination activities in order to ensure complementarity, compatibility, and usefulness of data;

(H) participate in the development of the annual plan described in subsection (c) of this section; and

(I) utilize the quarterly records described in section 136(f)(2) of the Workforce Investment Act of 1998 [29 U.S.C. 2871(f)(2)] to assist the State and other States in measuring State progress on State performance measures.

(3) **Rule of Construction.**—Nothing in this section shall be construed as limiting the ability of a State agency to conduct additional data collection, analysis, and dissemination activities with State funds or with Federal funds from sources other than this section.

(f) **Nonduplication Requirement.**—None of the functions and activities carried out pursuant to this section shall duplicate the functions and activities carried out under the Carl D. Perkins Vocational and Applied Technology Education Act (20 U.S.C. 2301 et seq.).

(g) **Authorization of Appropriations.**—There are authorized to be appropriated to carry out this section such sums as may be necessary for each of the fiscal years 1999 through 2004.

(h) **"Local area" Defined.**—In this section, the term "local area" means the smallest geographical area for which data can be produced with statistical reliability.

INDEX

U

Unified plan requirement. *See* **State plans**
Uses of funds
   local 56–61, 58–63, 86–87, 136–140
   state 47–53, 48–54, 83–84, 127–130

V

Valid and reliable
   congressional statements 7
   coordination with NCLB 152, 156
   performance indicators 20, 76, 103, 104
   state uses of funds 52, 84, 130
Virgin Islands 14, 74, 97, 101, 102
Voluntary selection and participation 90, 145

W

Wagner-Peyser Act 36, 37, 80, 91, 118, 119, 146, 161,
      162, 163
   technical amendments to 149
   text of relevant sections 175
Waivers
   of consortium requirements 85, 133
   of distribution formula 53, 54, 84, 85, 131, 133
   of maintenance of effort requirement 70, 90, 145
   of minimum allocation 53, 85, 131
   of sanctions 45, 46, 82, 83, 125, 126
Work-based learning
   local uses of funds 57, 59, 86, 87, 136, 137
   Tech Prep 15, 65, 66, 88, 89, 141
Workforce Investment Act
   coordination with 44, 81, 120, 121, 124, 135
   joint funding 91, 146
   non-duplication 37, 80, 119
   referral to system 51, 60, 129, 139
   technical amendments to 149
   unified plan option 44, 82, 124
Workforce investment board/entity
   local coordination with 55, 135, 159
   national assessment advisory panel 25, 78, 109
   purpose of law 13, 72, 93
   relevant text of Wagner-Peyser 176
   relevant text of WIA 160, 162
   state coordination with 37, 38, 80, 82, 120, 121, 159
   themes of law 10